The POETICS *of* GARDENS

The MIT Press

Cambridge, Massachusetts

London, England

CHARLES W. MOORE

WILLIAM J. MITCHELL

The POETICS of GARDENS

WILLIAM TURNBULL, JR.

CONTENTS

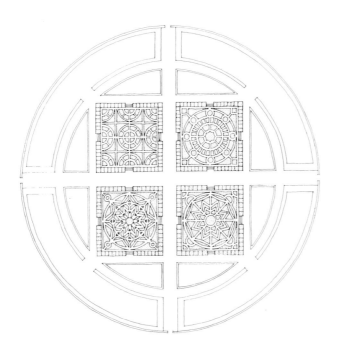

4

OUR OWN PLACES

PREFACE

The basic needs of living creatures—to breathe, to eat, to reproduce themselves—are joined, for most members of most species, including the human one, by the need to dwell, to inhabit some piece of our world. Birds claim space acoustically; the sound of their call marks the limits of their territory. Wolves employ a system of scented boundary markers. Human beings, since our appearance on this planet, have fought and died to define, defend, and sometimes extend our domains. The occupation has been celebrated and perfected with words and shelters and monuments, and, in some specially favored times and places, with gardens, where the streams and trees and flowers of the fields, and the rocks of the mountains, have been collected, or remembered, and ordered into an extension of ourselves onto the face of the earth. This book is written for people who mean to do that themselves.

At some time during the eleventh century, toward the end of the Heian period in Japan, an anonymous court noble set down the rules and cautions of garden art in a book called *Sakuteiki*. His advice was simple: Begin by considering the lay of the land and water. Study the works of past masters, and recall the places of beauty that you know. Then, on your chosen site, let memory speak, and make into your own that which moves you most. In the same spirit, we claim that there is a universality about the creation of gardens which makes it directly useful to examine great gardens, made in other places, with other climates, at other times, by people quite different from ourselves; to learn their devices and remember their images, scents, and sounds; to collect and remake and transform, composing into orders that make sense to us, and often squeezing in, miniaturizing to fit on the site at hand (likely to be smaller as the world grows more full of people).

We begin by exploring those qualities of a place that create the promise of a garden: the pattern of land and water, the established plants and the possibilities for further cultivation, the relation to the surrounding fabric of human settlement and the forms of its architecture, the orientation to the sun and wind and stars, the local cycles of the days and seasons, and the connections made by memory to vanished moments and distant places.

Nature's places, no matter how beautiful and moving we may find them to be, are not yet gardens; they become gardens only when shaped by our actions and engaged with our dreams. So we go on to consider the acts that make a garden: molding the earth, defining and connecting spaces with walls and ceilings and paths and monuments, irrigating, planting and tending, weaving patterns of recollection with names and images and souvenirs, and possessing the place by rituals of habitation. (We have no practical horticultural tips to offer, we hasten to add. Our concern is with the ways that places are given special meaning through these actions and rituals.)

Next, we present a score of landscapes and gardens, not just as a bouquet of pleasures but as sources, lodes to be mined for materials, shapes, relationships, and ideas. This is the heart of the book; we draw each place carefully (mostly in large axonometrics), guide you through it, tell something of its history, and examine the most important patterns and ideas that it contributes to the lore of gardens. In different cultures, times, and corners of the world, different possibilities for gardens have been revealed, so our examples range from ancient Rome to modern England, from the court of Ch'ien Lung to the Magic Kingdom of Walt Disney, from monasteries high in the Himalayas to convict settlements on the shores of Botany Bay.

Finally, we examine the transplantation and adaptation of the great garden traditions of the past to North American soil. We ask what these traditions might mean to us today, and we imagine Lucian, the Greek author of satirical dialogues, calling together the makers of great gardens to discuss proposals for some typical modern American sites. We eavesdrop for hints and suggestions about how the garden patterns and ideas of the past can be appropriated, reinterpreted, and transformed for our own time and in our own places. As T. S. Eliot remarked, in *The Sacred Wood*, "Immature poets imitate; mature poets steal; bad poets deface what they take, and good poets make it into something better, or at least something different."

ACKNOWLEDGMENTS

Maya Reiner made a major contribution to this book by producing most of the large axonometric drawings. Additional drawings were produced by Julie Eizenberg, Leon J. N. Glodt, Hank Koning, Regina Maria Pizzinini, and Barbara Russell. J. M. W. Turner's *Petworth Park: Tillington Church in the Distance* (page 63) is reproduced by permission of the Tate Gallery, London. Scenes from the Yuan Ming Yuan (pages 87–89) are reproduced by permission of the Bibliothèque Nationale, Paris. William Kent's planting plan for Rousham (page 131) is reproduced by permission of *Country Life*. Claude Lorrain's *Coast View of Delos with Aeneas* (page 142) is reproduced by permission of the National Gallery, London. G. M. Butt's guest house at Nasim Bagh, Kashmir, provided the necessary ambience for writing the first draft; Debra Edelstein of The MIT Press sympathetically edited the final draft; and Rebecca Daw found elegant ways to integrate text and graphics.

The POETICS *of* GARDENS

1

The GENIUS of the PLACE

The Romans read places like faces, as outward revelations of living inner spirit. Each place (like each person) had its individual Genius—which might manifest itself, on occasion, as a snake.

According to the ancient Chinese science of the winds (*feng*) and the waters (*shui*), the earth is traversed by the flowing breath of nature. The forms of the ground will reveal the presence of azure dragons (the male principle) and white tigers (the female), and propitious sites for buildings or gardens will be found where the different currents they represent happen to cross each other. The art of *feng-shui,* like that of the acupuncturist, is to choose precisely the right spot.

In eighteenth-century England, Alexander Pope advised his patron, Lord Burlington, and other enthusiastic gardeners of the day to

Consult the Genius *of the* Place *in all,*
That tells the Waters or to rise, or fall. . . .

But by this time the snakes and dragons and tigers of old lived only in metaphor and allusion; classically educated, Whiggishly confident Englishmen now saw Nature as an immanent force striving toward perfection but prone to diversion from this course by unfortunate accidents. To "consult the Genius of the Place" was to seek an understanding of the potential natural perfection of a site and to assist its emergence, where necessary, by discreet intervention.

By the latter half of the eighteenth century, references to the inherent qualities of sites were acquiring a subtly different, more exploitative tone. The great landscape garden designer of this era, Lancelot Brown, spoke so often of taking advantage of the "capabilities" of his clients' estates that he acquired the nickname "Capability" Brown.

Today we survey and inventory a site's assets, then speak even more aggressively of "environmental impacts." Mother Nature is to be mugged, it seems, and we cold-bloodedly analyze the old lady's chances of surviving the blows.

Underlying all these metaphors and mythic constructions is the simple fact that each site has its own special qualities of stone and earth and water, of leaf and blossom, of architectural context, of sun and shade, and of sounds and scents and breezes. Seek these out, and you will discover promises of formal order or of artful naturalism—the beginnings of your garden.

SHAN AND SHUI

The Chinese word for "landscape" is written with two characters that identify both an elementary opposition and a complementarity: *shan* ("mountains") and *shui* ("water"). The rigid, erect forms of mountains are *yang* to water's yielding, submissive *yin*. Each shapes the other; water is contained and molded into streams and cascades and lakes and seas by the surrounding mountains, while the mountains themselves are eroded and carved by the flow of water. The character of a site develops from the balance of *shan* and *shui* found there—at least for a moment of geological time.

Taos, New Mexico

Impressions of the Moon, Hangzhou

The West Lake, Hangzhou

Taughannock, New York

The Southern Ocean

From the *yang* side may come ridges and peaks or even ranges. These may be flattened on top to yield plateaus, mesas, or buttes. The sides can become slopes or cliffs or terraces. At edges and crests of rises we sometimes find places of special magic, celebrated by the construction of parapets and outlooks. Mountains may diminish into hills, hillocks, swells, mounds, and bumps, sharpen into crags, or be smoothed into dunes. Very small pieces, broken off, may become boulders, rocks, stones, pebbles, and gravel. Valleys, the opposite of ridges, may go down into the earth. Of different proportions, and more or less rugged, they may become ravines, arroyos, canyons, gulches, swales, hollows, dells, and dingles. Deeper into the ground may go holes, caverns, caves, and grottoes. The more or less level parts (which are never dead level if water is to run off them) may extend into plains, prairies, and steppes.

From the water on a site (formless in itself) *yin* forms emerge to complement those of the land and complete the whole (*yin-yang*). Valleys may shape rills, creeks, brooks, and rivers. Changes in elevation may form

The *yang* forms of land

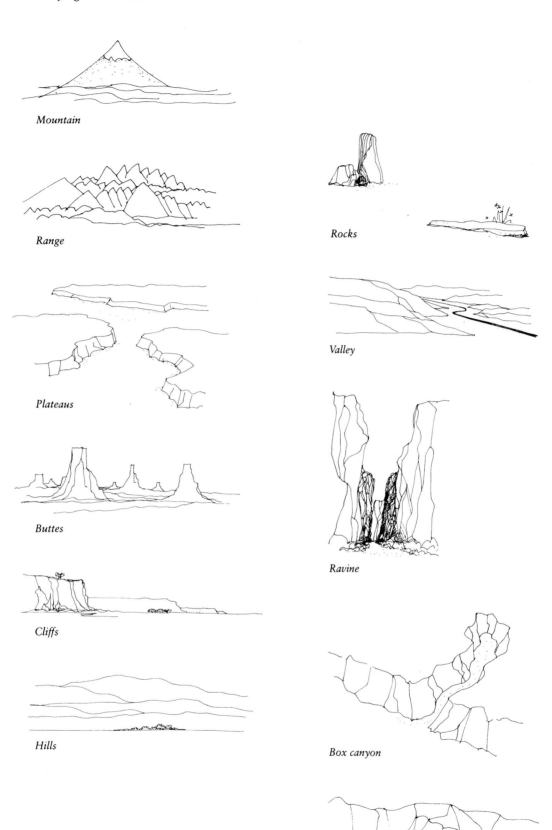

Mountain

Range

Rocks

Plateaus

Valley

Buttes

Ravine

Cliffs

Hills

Box canyon

Cavern

The *yin* forms of water

Brook

River

Lake

Marsh

Ocean

chutes, rapids, cascades, or waterfalls. Depressions may collect puddles, pools, ponds, bayous, billabongs, and lakes. Edges may become banks, shores, or beaches, with indentations (bays, bights, coves) and protuberances (headlands, isthmuses, peninsulas, points) or man-made bridges, bunds, breakwaters, piers, dikes, and barges. Earth and water may mingle to produce marshes, swamps, fens, bogs, and playas. Surrounded fragments of land may become islands, shoals, and archipelagoes.

If the surface of water is still it reflects the sky, and so breaks open the plane of the ground; most of us remember childhood fascinations with mud puddles, reflecting the clouds above and therefore immeasurably deep. On a tiny island in the West Lake at Hangzhou this becomes the theme for a garden. The roughened surface of the surrounding lake destroys reflections and stretches wide to the distant shores, but within the island are small pools whose still surfaces reflect the moon, infinitely far below.

Some sites derive special qualities from the invisible presence of underground water. Thistles, wire grass, and, more dramatically, stands of oak, concentrate above water in California; this surface detail commemorates an underlying structure, much like the carved ornament of a medieval cathedral. The ancient Nabateans of the Negev constructed long, low walls of stone (little more than raised lines on the ground) to direct runoff from occasional rains to their fields and gardens. These remained patches of green, nourished from beneath, long after the surrounding land had become parched once again. The modern inhabitants of the Negev have also learned to concentrate the runoff at particular points, so that tiny groves of eucalyptus may survive there among the barren hills. And beneath the arid Iranian plateau lies a vast system of man-made canals (*kanats*) which carry water down from the mountains in the north. These reveal themselves (especially from the air) as lines of wells—the beginning of settlements, fields, and gardens.

For most of history the appearance of life-giving water, from beneath the earth or falling from the sky, seemed to be a miracle. It was easy to see how water always eventually flowed down to the ocean, but it was hard to imagine where it came from. It was not until the eighteenth-century discovery of the cycle of evaporation and precipitation (to be exuberantly depicted in the Trevi Fountain in Rome) that the puzzle was solved. So sources of water—springs, wells, mountain peaks that precipitate the rain—have gathered about them an air of power and mystery; they have not only provided the practical possibility of cultivation, but have always seemed appropriate symbolic beginnings for gardens. Desert springs and wells are concentrated sources, so gardens that depend on them (such as the formal walled ones of Persia) naturally radiate from a cool, shady center to become dense, symmetrical, inward-looking oases. Gardens that celebrate mountainside sources (the Mughul gardens of Kashmir, for instance) tend to become linear—narrow strips of green with paths along cascading streams. Falling rains and mountain mists provide diffuse sources of water, so in damp places like England wide, green expanses— lawns, meadows, and woods—become basic elements of garden composi-

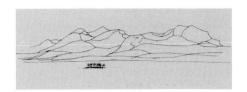

A desert spring

A concentrated desert garden

Surrounded fragments of land

Island

Archipelago

A mountain stream

A linear mountain garden

Water breaks open the plane of the ground

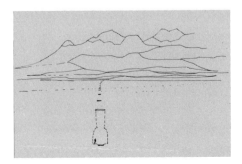

Underground water: kanats

tions. (Where a modern garden is served by concealed sources of piped water, such evident clarity of connection to the Genius of the Place can easily be lost.)

The forms of *shan shui* that we find at a site may carry resonances of myth and intimations of distant wonders that can be woven into a garden. Mountains have traditionally played the role of cosmic axes—connectors between the lands of men and the heavenly abodes of the gods. (And the painted concrete Matterhorn at the center of Disneyland still vibrates with this ancient power, even in Anaheim, and even if there's nothing above but Cessnas from John Wayne Airport.) Valleys can seem Shangri-las, and grottoes can become portals to the underworld. In *Moby Dick* Herman Melville described how the flow of a stream can point to the far-off mystery of ocean depths. At water's edge the land of humankind meets the uninhabitable and therefore magic deep—peopled in the imagination by Poseidon and Neptune, Nereus and the fifty Nereides, Proteus herding his seals beneath the waves, mermaids, water sprites, the crocodile who lurked beneath the waters of the great grey-green greasy Limpopo River, and the Great White Whale. And whatever we place on an island, in a bounded special world, takes on extra significance. Rousseau's tomb at

A green landscape garden in a damp climate

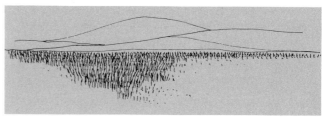

Ground cover makes a carpet

Ermenonville, near Paris, is made unforgettable by its placement on a tiny isle of poplars in a lake; you must cross the water to read, "Ici repose l'homme de la nature et de la *vérité*." (Actually he isn't there; he's been moved to the Panthéon, as you would expect, but the lack of *vérité* doesn't vitiate the carefully contrived effect.)

GOD AND CAIN

"God the first garden made," wrote Abraham Cowley, "and the first city, Cain." A garden is partly an extension of architecture—a fragment of a city—and partly natural paradise. So garden possibilities are further shaped and suggested by the balance (or tension) found at a site between natural growth and the artifices of man.

At sites within wild, unmanaged landscapes, all the plant material will be reaching out for a state of balance. In such a state, which biogeographers call a climax landscape, the various members of the plant community have reached an equilibrium where each contributes and each takes an acceptable portion of light and air and water, and the processes of germination and growth, death and decay, balance each other. In man-made gardens the plants are trying to do the same thing but are held in another balance through pruning, weeding, and watering.

Groupings of trees

Grove

Thicket

Jungle

A site may offer existing plants, which can be retained in a garden, plus a palette of natives that flourish in the area (the flamethrower foliage of New England, perhaps, or the anorexic palm trees of Beverly Hills, poking at a smog-bruised sky) and whose introduction onto the site will weave the garden into its natural context. There will be exotics, too, that you can get from nurseries or from other gardens—some that will grow without difficulty, and others from alien shores and climates, which must be nurtured with the greatest of care. These can become poignant reminders of distant places; oaks and elms in Australia recall the early colonists' home half a world away, while palm trees in Scotland conjure up warm Mediterranean breezes.

Like Robinson Crusoe, the gardener creates a habitation from whatever nature offers at a particular site. Trees can be used to shape the space with their trunks and crowns and to provide shade and evaporative cooling; they may be grouped into clusters, groves, thickets, woods, or jungles, eliminated to produce clearings, or strung into windbreaks, hedgerows, and lanes. A carpet of ground cover can be provided by grasses, herbs, mosses, lichens, reeds, and other small plants, which may extend into beds, parterres, lawns, savannahs, and tundras. If trees and ground cover

Trees shape space with their trunks and crowns

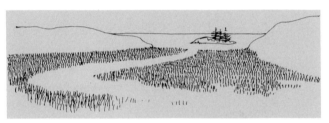

Landforms, trees, and ground cover create the architecture of outdoor space

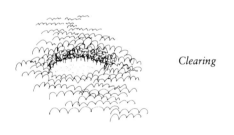

Clearing

Windbreak

Lane

create the architecture of outdoor spaces—the walls and floors and canopies—then bushes and shrubs, with a scale closer to that of the human body, can become the furniture. They may stand alone, like sculpture, or they may cluster densely into hedges, thickets, patches, and borders. Surfaces may be smoothly contoured and patterned to recall overstuffed Victorian armchairs and couches or clipped into topiary shapes. Creepers and vines can provide wall and floor coverings and may hang in screens and scrims.

The natural landscape may form the ground on which the figure of a building is presented, as when a Greek temple asserts its existence upon a wild acropolis; it is *in* nature, but not *part* of nature. At a smaller scale, pavilions, follies, and gazebos may punctuate gardens with marks of human habitation. Sometimes (particularly in urban settings) the architectural fabric becomes continuous, capturing and framing fragments of nature in courtyards, terraces, planters, and window boxes. On other occasions architecture flows through nature, and nature through architecture; the Indian architect Charles Correa notes that in warm climates you need no more protection during the day than what is afforded by an open-sided canopy (*chhatri*)—which creates no barriers to breezes and scents

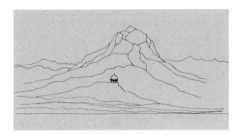

Nature and culture: a temple on an acropolis

Nature and culture: a guru under a banyan tree

and views—and that in the early morning and at night the best place to be is under the open sky. "Thus in Asia," he writes, "the symbol of enlightenment has never been the school building but rather the *guru* sitting under a banyan tree; and the monumental buildings of south India are experienced not just as *gopurams* and shrines, but as a movement through the great open-to-sky spaces that lie between them." Other cultures, with different climates, have invented their own devices for relating architectural and garden space. In Spain shaded arcades open onto garden patios. In China and Japan there is often no more than a light screen, which slides or swings open, between dwelling space and garden; the intimate connection that this establishes is more important than summer heat or winter cold. Twentieth-century architects in Europe and North America have shown us how to have it both ways (if we're prepared to pay the fuel bills) with glass walls.

SUNLIGHT AND SHADOW

Gardens exist in sunlight. Without it the plants would not grow, the water would not sparkle, and the shadows would not fall. So the qualities of the sunlight that a site receives—its intensity, color, movement, and angles, its filtering by atmosphere and foliage, its reflections off ground and water—create cadenced patterns that may sometimes recall but will never be quite like those of any other place.

In northern lands the sun moves low across the sky, and there are long summer evenings. But near the equator the sun arcs high, and the transition from light to dark is sudden. So different latitudes cast gardens in different lights. English gardens are characteristically seen in horizontal light, almost parallel to the ground, which produces long shadows, gives a silvery sparkle to water, and accentuates the green of foliage and grass by back-lighting. But we usually see tropical gardens in vertical light, which leaves deep pools of shade beneath trees and emphasizes the detailing of walls and other surfaces perpendicular to the ground.

Qualities of atmosphere may diffuse, color, and obscure the light of the sun in subtle ways. The moisture-laden atmosphere of England, for instance, creates an exaggerated aerial perspective that causes receding hills to fade into the distance like layers of watercolor wash. (So it is not surprising that the English traditions of watercolor painting and landscape gardening are intimately connected: the watercolorists painted ideal landscapes, the gardeners then built them, and the watercolorists painted these in turn.) In dry, desert atmospheres, though, the clarity of the light makes distant mountains seem eerily sharp and close by. In Australia the filtering of sunlight through atmospheric haze turns distant eucalyptus forests to a surprising powdery blue. In damp, tropical places the skies are often brilliant white, so objects against the sky are seen only in contrasting silhouette (like shadow puppets); while the less intense overcast skies of the north provide a delicate, diffuse light that reveals the most intricate details of surface. And when the low afternoon sun emerges through a break in the clouds, it infuses scenes with the tranquil, golden luminosity of Giorgione and Titian.

As the sun moves through its daily arc, some places on a site may remain always in the shade, cool (or cold) and refreshing (or dank). Other parts may be in the sun all day long, warm (or hot) and cheerful (or withering). Some may greet the morning sun and be in afternoon shade; others may be shady in the morning and catch the sun of afternoon. A sheltered, sunny corner may be a pleasant place to spend the afternoon when chill winds or drifted snow lie just around the corner. And a screened gazebo or porch in the shade may be a comfortable place to spend a summer afternoon, almost in the garden but protected from the blazing sun.

Nineteenth-century imaginations were captivated by visions of a natural paradise in which the qualities of sun and breeze would be so perfectly adjusted that we could inhabit it in naked freedom, like Adam and Eve in Eden. The young Herman Melville dramatized this fantasy in the tale of Fayaway, the beautiful Polynesian heroine of *Typee*, who, in her South Pacific paradise, "disengaged from her person the ample robe of tappa which knotted over her shoulder (for the purpose of shielding her from the sun), and spreading it out like a sail, stood erect with upraised arms in the head of the canoe." In less benign settings, though, gardens must often transform the microclimates of their sites to make them comfortable for habitation or to allow exotic plants to flourish; the harsher the natural climate, the greater the required modification. So we find that the Koran, for example, contrasts the hot, dry desert of its prophet with a cool and shady paradise of flowing waters and gentle breezes; while the gardens of Islam deploy protective walls against sun and sand and suggest paradise on earth with green foliage, pavilions to catch cool breezes, and the sound of splashing water. Conversely, the iron and glass of the Industrial Revolution allowed Europeans to create bright tropical paradises of palms and orchids in the gray, cold north.

Inside our buildings, at least before the energy crisis, we were heading for a dreary monotony, advocated by mechanical engineers, in which we were to be immersed in light of optimum intensity and air of constant temperature and humidity. The outdoors, thank Heaven, is immune from this, and the promise of deep shade beneath a leafy canopy, of blossoms brilliant in the full light of noon, of the warm sun on a nippy afternoon, or of the delicious feel of a breeze on a warm day can still draw us to the garden.

Proust remarked on a paradox of experience—that beauty, in reality, is often disappointing, since the imagination can only engage that which is absent. Sometimes the most poignant qualities of a site come not from what is actually there, but from what is connected to it, through time and space, by our recollections and hopes. The vision, and even more powerfully the scent, of a blossom may remind us of a moment in our past and let us store up future memories or form links with poems or paintings that hold meaning for us. It is touching to see in the Australian outback, or a Caribbean or Malaysian plantation, places that reconstruct the colonists' home turf thousands of miles away; and touching, too, to see the home turf brightened with souvenirs of travel—or perhaps with the signs of a longing otherwise unfulfilled for exotic places.

Old trees and ruins make visible the depth of time and carry our imaginations back into history. In a Cambridge college garden a decrepit but still-surviving tree reminds us of the heroic intellect of Sir Isaac Newton. In Sri Lanka a still more ancient bo-tree thrillingly seems about to invoke the luminous presence of the Buddha. And in Yorkshire the medieval ruins of Fountains Abbey stand among eighteenth-century trees—bringing two widely separated moments of the past into unexpected and moving juxtaposition.

Planting a new tree is one of the noblest acts of optimism. The civilized, self-confident makers of eighteenth-century English landscape gardens readily accepted that they would never see their incipient elm groves grow to maturity. On Johannesburg's barren plateau the first settlers (a much rougher lot who came in search of gold, but no less optimistic) planted thousands of slow-maturing trees—oak, sycamore, cypress, eucalyptus—to adorn the city of their children and grandchildren. But German friends tell us that during the dark days of National Socialism nursery sales of oak trees, for instance, dropped to almost nothing—people brought, instead, locusts and other "weed trees" that would provide shade soon, with nothing for generations not yet born. In our own fragmented and desperately ambiguous time the rhythms of season, and the cycles of growth and decay that we engage with a gardener's care still allow us the sense of participating in a greater pattern.

The two basic garden ideas

The formal garden: Black Pavilion,
Shalamar Bagh, Kashmir

The natural garden: view of the lake,
Stourhead, England

The DESIGNER'S PLACE

In *The Poetics of Music* Stravinsky pointed out that natural sounds such as the calls of birds and the whispering of breezes, though they may delight us, are materials for music rather than music itself. To become music, sounds must be chosen and arranged. So it is with gardens. Natural landscapes are not yet gardens; it is only through the selection and composition of their elements and materials that gardens are made. To compose is to adjust the balances and tensions of *yin* and *yang*—water and mountains, human order and the Tao of nature, sun and shadow, breeze and stillness, sound and silence—to create new relations that carry meaning for us.

We're not sure whether it comes as a disappointment or as a great relief to note that in all of human history there seem to have emerged just two basic notions of how to do this. There are just two *Ur*-gardens. Each represents not only an idea of what is pleasurable, but also an ideal of felicitous equilibrium between humankind and nature.

The first is a model of orderly paradise, devised in the flat desert of Persia. It has a wall around it to exclude the messy world. In its center is a water source, from which channels carrying the water go north, east, south, and west, dividing the garden into quarters. Each quarter is similarly divided into quarters, and, if the garden is large enough, each of these sixteen squares is divided again ("recursively" is the mathematicians' word) into another four squares, little paradises nestled inside the bigger ones. Groves of trees or pavilions provide shade from the blazing sun; spouting of falling water cools the summer air; flowers are chosen for their colors and scents and to attract the birds whose plumage will vie with the flowers and whose songs will counterpoint the splash of water.

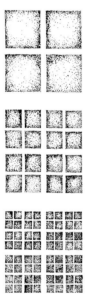

The fourfold paradise and its ramification

The foursquare garden pattern (*chahar bagh*) was painted onto miniatures and woven into carpets even as the garden builders modified it to adjust to the sites they had chosen. In Persia itself the symmetry of the square was often reduced to the lesser symmetry of the rectangle, and the canal was often widened into a reflecting pool. The Mughul emperor Babur carried the idea of the Persian garden to India, the "charmless and disorderly" place (as he called it) that he had been so unfortunate as to conquer. On the dusty plains he made cool, walled, symmetrical havens, built around wells, amid the surrounding heat and chaos. When Babur's successors built their summer residences in the Vale of Kashmir, they encountered

Persian variations on the theme of the
fourfold paradise

a. Bagh-i-Takht, Shiraz
b. Narenjestan-i-Qavam, Shiraz
c. Bagh-i-Fin, Kashan
d. Haft-Tan, Shiraz
e. Chehel-Sutun, Ishfahan
f. Shah Goli, Tabriz
g. Bagh-i-Eram, Shiraz
h. Hesht-i-Behest, Isfahan
i. Bagh-i-Gulistan, Tehran

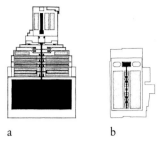

a

b

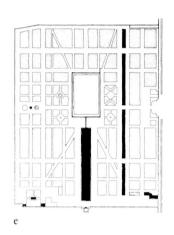

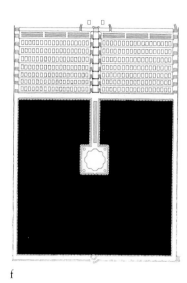

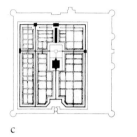

c

d

e

f

sloping mountainside sites, with the water coming from above, not up
from the center; so the central axis, from high to low, became wider and
wetter, and the cross axes became many and small.

In the south of Spain, to which the Arabs had earlier carried the Persian
vision of a garden, there were hillsides and hilltops (with better breezes) to
choose as garden sites, so the paradise model was modified to emphasize
terraced slopes and belvederes. The Italian garden designers also used the
paradise model, though modified again to make it an extension of a palace
or great house instead of a separate place centered about itself. But by the
mid-sixteenth century, at the Villa Lante, the palace had been split in half,
becoming a pair of casinos flanking the sloping garden on its two sides,
which allowed the garden itself to get back into the central position, to
become again the *pièce de résistance*.

All these gardens, though, are simply versions of the fourfold walled paradise, adapted with great skill to a variety of places. It was André Le Nôtre,
in the confident seventeenth century, who broke down the very walls of
Eden. At first he did it tentatively, at Vaux-le-Vicomte, where he turned his
water channels at right angles to the axis and let the water (and the eye
and the imagination) out of the garden into the countryside. Then he did it
with bombast at Versailles, where his *allées* fan out from the château into
the infinite and bring the whole countryside, wrested from the "charmless
and disorderly," into the frame of the expanding garden.

This brings us to the second garden idea, which has flourished in countries
where individuals have felt less pressure to protect themselves from, or to

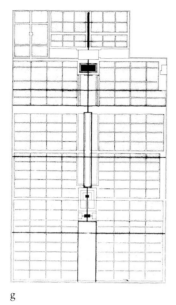

g

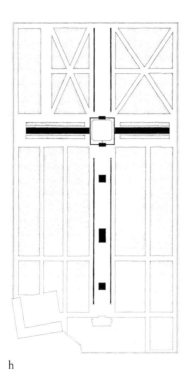

h

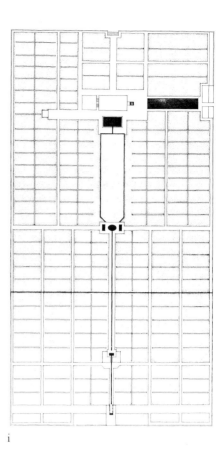

i

overpower, nature and have felt easy about entering into a close partnership with it. A diagram that has appeared repeatedly in Japanese garden
books since the fifteenth century illustrates how to compose a "natural"
world in an apparently casual but in fact precisely contrived way. There
are sixteen pieces of land and water arranged around a central "guardian
stone." These are not similar squares in symmetrical disposition, but di-
verse elements in asymmetrical balance. Not all are required in any particular garden, and many variations of relationship and emphasis are implicit
in the diagram, but each piece has a distinct identity and importance. They
require individual introduction, like the characters of a play.

1. The *guardian stone* (called also the *host* stone, the *main* or *face* rock),
is the central point in the garden. Much of it may be buried to enhance the
sense of its "naturalness," of the stone's belonging to that place, though it
probably has come from somewhere else, perhaps at enormous expense
from a great distance.

2. A *small hill* or rock (*guest* rock or *side* rock) snuggled close to the
guardian stone creates a crevice that provides natural lodging for a cascade of water, or perhaps for an abstracted cascade made by a plant—the
bough of a white azalea, for instance, whose blossoms might recall a froth
of water, or the more delicate white starry splashes of jasmine.

3. A *side mountain* (which might be no more than a few feet high) suggests a plane in front of the guardian stone, like a flat flanking a stage set
might, and makes the central piece seem farther away, hence bigger.

4. A *sand-blown beach* on the right balances the side mountain on the left
and recalls real beaches in the big landscape. The sand is fine in texture, so

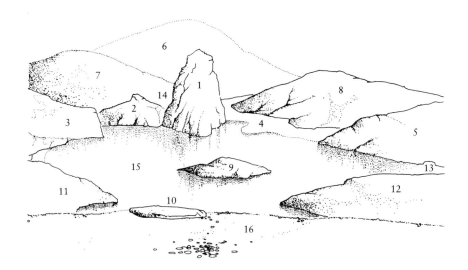

Diagram of a Japanese garden composed around a guardian stone

even quite a small beach can seem to have the form and qualities of a full-sized one.

5. At the right edge of the sand-blown beach is a *near mountain,* asymmetrically balancing the side mountain and creating a stage-flat plane that gives additional depth to the landscape.

6. Behind everything, and perhaps contributing most to the definition of the setting, is the *distant mountain.* It has to be high enough to close the view (perhaps seven or eight feet will do) and must be planted, if it is planted, with material that does not disclose, by eccentricity of shape or coarseness of texture, its true size, but rather enhances the illusion that the distant mountain is just that and not a nearby knob.

7. Yet another element in the composition of balanced rows of receding ranges is, on the left, the *middle mountain,* which frames and pushes back the distant mountain. It is distinguished by a soft but unmistakable summit.

8. On the right a *mountain spur,* balancing the middle mountain, suggests by its summitless contour that it is the edge of a mountain range that extends out of the picture and into the infinite, rather than part of an isolated set piece in someone's backyard.

9. Perhaps the most highly charged element is the *central island,* considered as the sole survivor of the mysterious Islands of the Blessed, where the immortals of ancient Chinese tradition are said to have found eternal happiness.

10. The *worshipping stone* on the near shore is big enough and near enough to invite the presence of the human body as well as the human imagination. This is where one inhabits the garden, participates in and feels its spirit.

11. On the left, extending out of the picture, is the *master's island,* which is large and suggests by its incompleteness greater size still. It is especially important because of its position, near enough to accept, for instance, interesting planting without damaging the scale of the whole. If the garden is to be allowed expressive quirks or eccentricities then here, in the realm of the master, the host, would be the place.

12. On the right, flanking the master's island, but smaller and fitting completely within the picture, is the *guest's island*. It complements but does not seek to outshine or even entirely to balance the dominant master's island.

13. The *lake outlet* lies beyond the guest's island and leads the eye out of the picture, which makes the lake seem of indeterminate extent and therefore far larger than it is.

14. The *cascade mouth* serves as source for the lake, introducing it into a continuous organization so the water at the heart of the garden is not trapped, still and dead, but part of a living system that by implication includes all the water on the planet.

15. The *lake* is the heart of the garden, encompassing it all, extending past its boundaries, and vanishing both to the right and to the left. In gardens more miniature still, the lake might be suggested without water, with a surface of pebbles or raked sand that accepts the dry cascade of white blossoms.

16. The *broad beach* lies on the near shore, and this proximity makes its detail especially important. If the broad beach is of pebbles, they might well be individually selected, so that no jarring shapes or colors are introduced unless they are intended.

The gardens of China had long anticipated this mode of composing miniature worlds of mountains and water. It baffles Westerners how free-form garden design and free-thought Taoism manage to coexist with bureaucratic Confucianism, which found its formal expression in the rigid rectangular hierarchies of Chinese urban design. But so it is with the coexisting opposites, *yin* and *yang*. Therefore lines in a Chinese garden are never straight if they can be crooked, never symmetrical if they can be asymmetrical, never evident all at once if they can allow for layers of discovery. In the ancient walled city of Suzhou, for instance, the grid of sycamore-lined streets and canals is as rigorously ordered as that of any fourfold paradise. But behind the whitewashed facades, in dozens of hidden gardens, arrangements of stones and ponds twist and tease, intimate and delude—shattering the Confucian clarity into mirages and allowing the breath of nature to flow through.

Far to the west, the British Isles exhibit striking parallels with the Japanese archipelago; like Japan, they lie far enough off the Eurasian land mass to achieve a degree of security. British scenery is less dramatic than Japan's but beautiful still, and the beauty and the security have allowed some of the inhabitants over the centuries to form a close attachment to their land. (It is helpful to contemplation, one can see, to be located in peripheral islands, where the Mongolian hordes aren't always thundering through, breaking up whatever intimacies between people and landscape the elements have spared.) In spite of that, though, the British garden through the seventeenth century had been an enclosed pattern garden like those on the Continent. It was at Rousham in the eighteenth century that the painter and architect William Kent "leaped the fence and saw that all nature was a garden" (as Horace Walpole, the great chronicler of English

Layout principles of a typical Suzhou
garden: Zhuo Zheng Yuan (Garden of
the Humble Administrator)

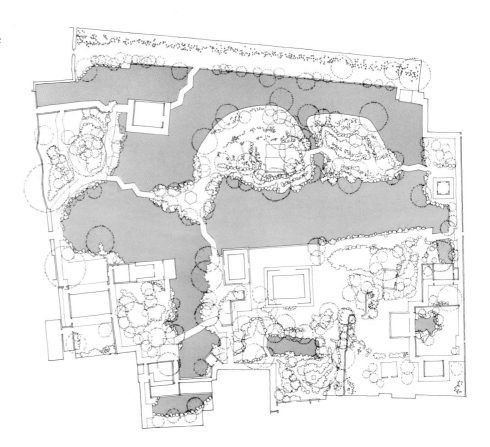

Plan

Rocks and water

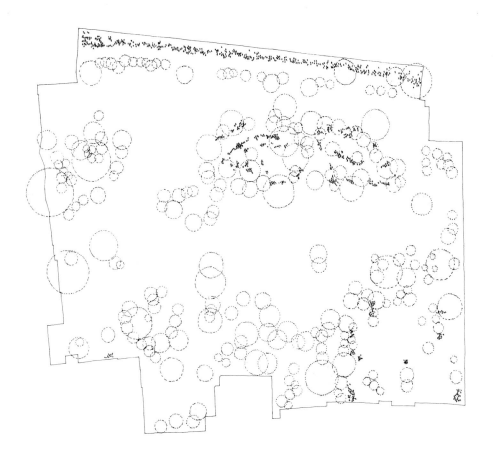

Planting

Pavilions and covered walkways

Variations on the theme of the
Suzhou garden

Yi Yuan

He Yuan

Chang Yuan

Hu Yuan

Shi Zi Lin

Liu Yuan

Wang Shi Yuan

landscape gardening, put it). Like Le Nôtre in France the century before, Kent saw no further need to exclude a hostile nature. In his leap, though, he ran to embrace a congenial new partner, not, as in Le Nôtre's case, to celebrate victory over a vanquished foe. After Kent, English gardens would become attempts (different from, but curiously parallel with the Japanese) to simulate nature, embrace it, and perfect it.

It can be argued that, in these Chinese and Japanese and English gardens, an order understandable to human philosophers is still being imposed, but it is an order not far removed from the harmonies discoverable in the natural world. Edgar Allan Poe vividly evoked its character in his descriptions of the Domain of Arnheim and Landor's Cottage—places brought by some eerie intervention to absolute perfection (no weeds, no fallen leaves, no pebble blemished or out of place).

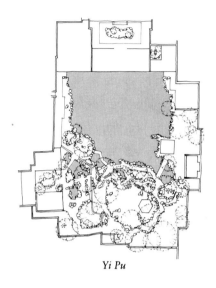

Yi Pu

"The Domain of Arnheim" pivots on a paradox constructed by Poe:

No such paradises are to be found in reality as have glowed on the canvas of Claude. In the most enchanting of natural landscapes, there will always be found a defect or an excess—many excesses and defects. While the component parts may defy, individually, the highest skill of the artist, the arrangement of these parts will always be susceptible to improvement. In short, no position can be attained on the wide surface of the natural *earth, from which an artistic eye, looking steadily, will not find matter of offense in what is termed the "composition" of the landscape. And yet how unintelligible is this! In all other matters we are justly instructed to regard nature as supreme. With her details we shrink from competition. Who shall presume to imitate the colors of the tulip, or to improve the proportions of the lily of the valley?*

Poe's protagonist, the landscape gardener Ellison, replies, "The slightest exhibition of art is an evidence of care and human interest. . . . A mixture of pure art in a garden scene adds to it a great beauty." Yet there may be something beyond; the materials of nature, "brought into something like harmony or consistency with the sense of human art," may convey "the sentiment of spiritual interference." So Ellison devotes his wealth to making

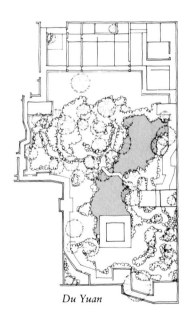

Du Yuan

a landscape whose combined vastness and definitiveness—whose united beauty, magnificence, and strangeness, *shall convey the idea of care, or culture, or superintendence, on the part of beings superior, yet akin to humanity. . . . The sentiment of* interest *is preserved, while the art intervolved is made to assume the air of an intermediate or secondary nature—a nature which is not God, nor an emanation from God, but which still is nature in the sense of the handiwork of the angels that hover between man and God.*

What we offer below is a catalogue of compositional strategies and moves—incomplete, but we hope suggestive of the ways in which a site can be transformed either into the paradise of a prophet whose rigorous laws bring order and clarity to a chaotic world, or into that of angels who inflect the immanence of nature toward greater perfection.

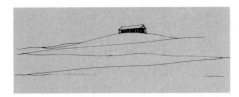

A building stakes a claim

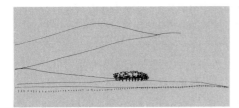

A circle of trees appropriates its surroundings

OCCUPYING THE SITE

Gardens, like buildings, can engage a site in several different ways. One way is for the garden to stake a claim over the site, just as a perfectly formed, symmetrical Greek temple takes spiritual control of the whole landscape that it surveys. Circles of trees on hilltops, found in the English landscape since the days of King Arthur and Merlin, similarly appropriate their surroundings.

Classical Chinese gardeners asserted gentler claims; they spoke of "borrowing" distant scenery by inserting a pagoda or pavilion into it, then making places to view this distant eye-catcher from within the confines of the garden. In Japan the principle of borrowing is called *shakkei;* the scenery of adjacent fields and mountains and the strength of the pastoral ordinary (from which so much of the power of the Japanese aristocratic aesthetic comes) are made a visible part of the garden. The Katsura Imperial Villa employs a bit of this, at its edge, but the most celebrated borrowing is at the Shugakuin Imperial Villa above Kyoto, where the adjacent rice field becomes an important part of the garden design.

Sometimes the act of claiming becomes an imperial gesture; the great *allées* that André Le Nôtre made for Louis XIV at Versailles are memorable perhaps even more as claims than as compositions. And many of us were surprised indeed by the poignant power developed by Christo's 1976

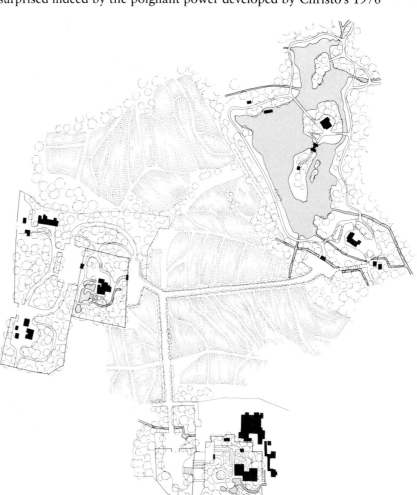

Shugakuin Imperial Villa borrows the scenery of adjacent rice fields

Merging

Enfronting

Enclosing

Running Fence, an eighteen-foot-high fabric wall extending twenty-six miles through California grassland. The symbolic force of a great wall seems as strong today as it was long ago when the Chinese built theirs.

On the other hand, buildings or gardens can be made to *merge* into the landscape, making a part of it special without setting themselves off from it. The English "natural" gardens we shall later look at depend upon being a heightened part of their surroundings, which fits easily into what lies beyond. And the Japanese gardens that we shall also examine, though often tiny, seem from within to be fragments of larger worlds that extend indefinitely in all directions.

The third mode of engagement is *enfronting,* facing forward to present a display. False-fronted buildings do it, on a western American street, as can a row of trees, a floral clock greeting the passerby, or perhaps even a waterfall, like the one along a whole side of Paley Park in New York.

Finally, *enclosing* (the opposite of merging), surrounding a piece of the landscape, encapsulating a bit of nature or a formal symmetrical patio, is a way to fit to the land and to take over a piece of it. The Garden of Eden was enclosed. So, too were the paradise gardens of Islam and the cloistered gardens of medieval Europe, built on their model.

Each of these strategies, when followed on a particular site, expresses a disposition toward the spirit of the place—to collude with or control it, accept or oppose, temper or intensify. And each, as well, becomes a social act—of welcome or exclusion, ostentation or modest discretion.

ESTABLISHING THE GAME

Many of the pleasures of gardens come from sharing a point of view, from playing a game with agreed-upon pieces and rules and procedures. There is a collector's game, a painter's, a cinematographer's, a storyteller's, and a philosopher's, and of course there are many others, too. To call them games is to suggest no lack of seriousness. On the contrary, it supposes the supremely serious existence of conventions, which give a garden special significance for people who share its concerns. It is always fascinating in English flower gardens, for instance, to see little groups of devotees avidly concerned over whether some tiny shrub is the same as one they have in their gardens or have seen somewhere. It is a game, an absorbing one, and no fair if you break the rules.

The collector's game can become an obsession. People for centuries have been fascinated by exotic plant material and the skills required to make it grow in unlikely conditions. They fuss over palm trees in greenhouses, in sheltered coves on the Irish and Scottish coasts, or in the lee of south-facing walls in southern Utah. Others breed and collect new species of plants. The Chinese collect weirdly eroded rocks, and the Japanese bring from great distances rocks that look particularly "natural." The Roman emperor Hadrian collected souvenirs from all of his empire (which included most of the known world) at his villa at Tivoli, and sixteen centuries later the Chinese emperor Ch'ien Lung recalled, in a collection of gardens at the Yuan Ming Yuan near Beijing, the varied splendors of his own enormous kingdom. In our time, Walt Disney extrapolated from his childhood electric train, and the tunnels and towns it went through, to the bigger and more varied collection of miniatures at his Magic Kingdom. People collect and display fuchsias, irises, alpine plants, cacti, and flowers that blossom blue or white or in the fall.

This brings us to the edge of another game, the painter's. Many European gardens of the seventeenth century consisted of formal geometric shapes (squares, triangles, circles, and more elaborate ones) laid out to contrast the seasonal colors of flowers against the constancy of green borders of privet or yew—colors from a painter's palette in patterns that might have come from a set of stencils. In Brazil for the last forty years the great landscape architect Roberto Burle-Marx has been making vast paintings out of flowers; the shapes are his own (with a strong kinship to such contemporaries as Matisse, Miro, and Arp), the colors the flamboyant ones of the Brazilian tropics. In France Monet derived the colors for his palette from his garden at Giverny, especially his water garden, vibrant with the water lilies he cultivated. And in England Gertrude Jekyll made garden plans like painter's cartoons, showing precisely how masses of blossoms were to be shaped and placed to form, as she wrote, "beautiful pictures." Her herbaceous borders reflect knowledge of the sophisticated color theories of Michel Chevreul and admiration for the effects achieved by the Impressionists.

For centuries painters have explored ways to create the illusion of space on a two-dimensional surface. Gardeners have struggled to suggest larger worlds within the bounded confines available to them, and they have learned the painters' tricks. Once Renaissance painters discovered (or, rather, rediscovered) perspective, which allows the flat plane of a picture to seem three-dimensional through lines leading back to one, two, or three vanishing points, it wasn't long before gardens were being made to be seen in perspective, with parallels to converge and clear geometric shapes to foreshorten. This became an architect's game. The use of convergence to create spatial illusion soon rebounded back into three dimensions, as Renaissance architects angled lines and planes that had been parallel and exaggerated the depth (or shallowness) of a space to titillate and defy our expectations.

Chinese and Japanese painters have other rules to help them amplify distance in their landscapes, which involve distinguishing the near, middle, and far distance; pulling the near closer with heightened detail while pushing the distant back by making it smaller; softening the contrasts; and eliminating detail. Japanese gardeners use the same pictorial principles, say on a pond, to make the near shore seem nearer, the far shore much farther away than it really is.

The cinematographer's game transfers these painterly concerns to time. In the Cypress Gardens in South Carolina, for instance, a boat slowly plies through a cypress swamp, and the visitor observes the softly changing green and black shapes of water and tree trunks, punctuated in the spring

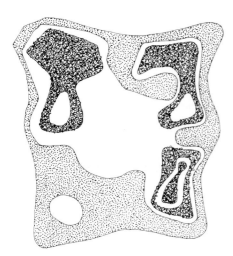

Roberto Burle-Marx plays the painter's game in his garden plans

Converging parallels

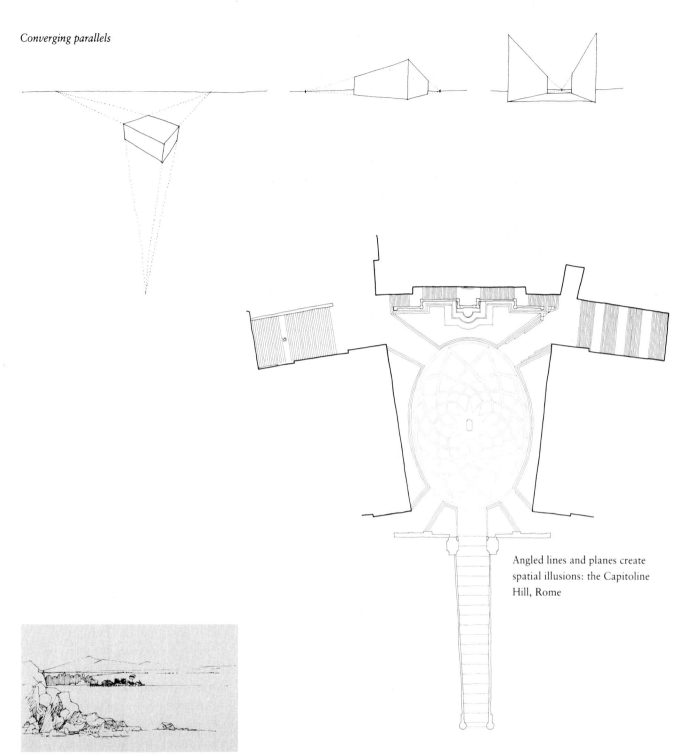

Angled lines and planes create
spatial illusions: the Capitoline
Hill, Rome

Near, middle, and far distance

The gradient of detail

by bright azaleas. At Hidcote, in the English Cotswolds, the effect in room after outdoor room is of a sequence of shapes and colors. The focus close at hand is on individual plants and beds, while the choreography encourages you to wander in any number of directions. And a garden can become a moving picture thanks to its inhabitants—skaters on the pond or hummingbirds at the flowers or aspens quivering and palm fronds swaying.

Some gardens tell a story so evocative or so complex that they invite comparison with the storyteller's art. Later we will see how Sir Henry Hoare at Stourhead, in England, evoked Virgil, and Disneyland is a garden woven out of tales of pirates and ghosts and American heroes. Many of us carry recollections of secret gardens, magic glades, and private eyries from children's stories, or have images we received as adults which tell us a tale.

And some gardens, especially in Japan, can only be described as philosophers' works—systems for understanding the world, made immanent in a garden. Philosophers' gardens seem generally to be made of few and simple materials, so that the smallest nuance of arrangement can seem important, as at the Zen garden of Ryoan-ji, in Kyoto, which is just fifteen rocks in a rectangle of raked sand, with a wall at its back and trees, and at Saihoji, which is a wood around a lake, with all the ground covered with moss.

A garden designer can play by any of these rules, and a garden (like a poem or a painting) can be about anything you find interesting or moving. There may be multiple games, and different layers of meaning. But it is worth keeping in mind a maxim of Sir Edwin Lutyens (who made many fine gardens in collaboration with Gertrude Jekyll): a garden should have one clear, central idea.

SHAPING SPACES

Garden-making has often been closely identified with horticulture, but to make a garden is, first of all, to shape a space. The objects in a garden and the space between form necessary complements (*yin-yang,* again) that can change character to work with each other. An object, which can be a building, tree, bush, or birdbath, can stand alone in space, visible from all sides, or it can merge into the boundary of the space (like a hedge, a floral border, a carpet of flowers, or the filigree of branches overhead). The space between (whose nature philosophers have discussed through the ages, for it is, after all, nothing) is for the designer (much to the philosopher's annoyance) a palpable something, which can be shaped precisely by walls and floors and ceilings or can erode and fade away, around a corner and out of sight, in picturesque ambiguity.

In this respect, the art of the garden designer is much like that of the architect. The ground plane is the natural starting point, and vertical elements can be raised from it to bound and focus spaces. Roofs and canopies can be added where shelter is needed. Connections can be made by forming openings, and sequences of movement through the spaces can be composed.

Yin *and* yang

Object alone in space

Object merging into the boundary

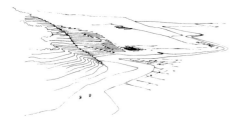

Terraced hillsides

Cutting and filling

Molding the Earth

There are, however, differences between designing a building and designing a garden; one of the most fundamental is that building floors are planes (generally horizontal, occasionally slightly tilted) and the earthen floor of a garden site usually isn't. One of the garden designer's first tasks, then, is to consider the lay of the land and decide how to modify its surface to receive construction, water, and plants.

Undulations of the earth can be accommodated in just two ways. You can sculpt the earth into smooth, continuous slopes, or you can form flat terraces with abrupt transitions. Where the surface must remain flooded, you *have* to segment hillsides into terraces; this gives characteristic form to the landscape of the rice-growing areas of Asia.

A terrace is usually most efficiently made by cutting out a bit of the hillside above and filling in a bit below the chosen level. The filled part tends to be unstable, so you have to be careful about placing heavy objects there—particularly swimming pools. Unless there is sufficient room to slope the earth at a stable angle, retaining walls will be needed to hold it back at the edges. These become much more difficult and expensive to construct as they get taller. The problems with retaining walls and the cost of shifting earth usually impose very strict limitations on the widths of terraces. The steeper the slope, the narrower they get.

Traditional rice terraces are laboriously cut by hand, and their simple earthen retaining walls can't be made very tall, so they fit closely to the original form of the land. Walls follow the contours, and where slopes become steep, the terraces become very narrow. The terraced lemon groves of Amalfi, with their stone retaining walls, can climb more dramatically. Modern earth-moving equipment and concrete retaining walls give still greater freedom to reshape the land, but also allow us to violate its character with alarming casualness.

Different natural landforms provide opportunities for a variety of terraced compositions. You can run retaining walls across the floor of a valley to form terraces stepping up a stream, with the chance to make cascades at each level change. Or you can segment a hillside into a giant staircase. A concave slope can be formed into an amphitheater. Very rarely, as at the Altar of Heaven in Beijing or the *stupa* at Borobudur in Java, isolated hills have been formalized into concentric circular terraces. And by cutting terraces into the ground, you can create a sunken garden.

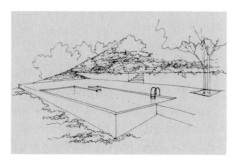

A swimming pool fitted to a slope

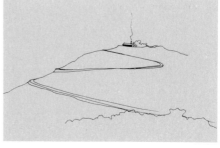

A path fitted to a slope

Garden steps

If you have the means, you can pile up earth and stone to make wholly artificial terraced gardens. The illustrious ancestor of all such structures is the famous Hanging Gardens of Babylon. Not much of them is now left among the mud and archaeologists' trenches of Babylon's ruins, but Diodorus Siculus recorded that "several parts of the structure rose from one another tier on tier" and that it "resembled a theater."

Garden steps are simply terraces shrunken to the scale of a stride. Often (as Italian and French baroque gardeners, in particular, delightedly realized) there is more room to make a magnificent stairway outside in the open air than there is within the confines of building walls. And a garden stairway can evoke the mysteries of the infinite. It can ascend toward a patch of open sky, or it can disappear into earth or water—suggesting hidden ruins extending who-knows how far beneath the surface.

Smoothed earth can replicate the forms of the natural landscape at a smaller scale. Rounded hills can become banks, berms, and little mounds, and vales can become hollows. Even the sweep of rolling grasslands toward the horizon can be suggested by an undulating lawn.

Covering the Ground

You can divide the ground surface of your garden site into parts that are almost flat or steeply sloped, planted or paved, one material or many, earth or plants or masonry or wood, but you must temper your fancy with strict common sense. The surface cannot be absolutely flat or water will stand on it after a rain, probably with injurious effect. And if it is earth, it cannot slope more steeply than the kind of earth allows (generally about one foot up for every two sideways) lest falling water erode and disperse it. If it is masonry or wood, of course, it can be any steepness you choose. Hard surfaces, of wood or masonry, have the advantage of durability and all-weather use. Soft surfaces, of earth or gravel or grass, can be soggy in wet weather, but they let the water through, which may be essential for the roots of trees or shrubs. Masonry surfaces can be laid in sand with open joints to let water through and provide a hard surface to walk on.

Masonry floor materials include brick, which comes generally in 2⅜-by-8-inch blocks (minus a little for the joints), though it also comes thinner (called pavers) and longer (Roman) and bigger. It is sometimes very hard, with sharp corners, sometimes softer with slightly rounded corners. Its colors, determined by the clay from which it is made, range from white to yellow to red to brown to almost black, from beautiful to nasty depending, as beauty does, on our associations and our memories.

Then there is stone, which comes in a far greater variety of sizes and colors (blues and reds and tans and browns) and is usually more irregular than brick, therefore involving much greater cost in laying. And there are very small stones—pebbles and gravel. In the United States smooth "river-washed" gravels are generally favored; they crunch nicely underfoot, stay fairly dry after a rain but let water penetrate to tree roots, and have for most of us pleasant associations with, for instance, the courtyards of elegant houses. Their drawback becomes apparent, though, when a child or vandal starts hurling them in handfuls through windows. In other countries, especially France, little stones of about the same size, but sharp, are often used; they hook onto each other better and can be rolled to a fairly tight mass, which does get a bit slick in the rain but makes in many French gardens (most notably the Tuileries) an admirable surface underfoot. Concrete and asphalt are relatively inexpensive surfaces with attributes of masonry. They can be beautiful or (more often) they can be hidden, by exposing aggregate on the surface of the concrete or rolling it into the surface of asphalt.

And there are tiles, square or rectangular or shaped baked-clay plaques, usually terra cotta but able to be glazed in a spectrum of colors almost as wondrous as that of the flowers themselves. The glaze can be dull or shiny, able to sparkle and shimmer as though it were wet, the better to seem moist and cool on a hot sunny day.

Wooden boards or blocks can make the surface underfoot as well. Wood feels warmer than masonry when the weather is cool, and so may seem more congenial to sit on or just above. Wooden decks have another advantage: they are lightweight, so they can easily be located high above the ground, even in the treetops.

Earth itself is a combination of sand, clay, and organic matter. It too comes in a variety of hues and a variety of consistencies, from porous (dry after a rain) to impervious (a muddy, gooey mess), from alkaline to acid, from poor to rich. Underfoot in the garden it can be bare or covered with lawn, ground cover, or higher shrubs or grasses. Many of these surfaces invite our footsteps (indeed some, like chamomile, even oblige with a pleasant odor when they are crushed underfoot). Others are to look at only, and die under the heel.

The soil and climate and the resources of the nurseries to which you have access will determine a palette of plant material for clothing the ground. Plants can be selected for the color and texture of their foliage, for their fragrances, and for the colors of their flowers. In the English tradition of gardening, since the nineteenth century, floral color has been a central preoccupation (as traditional Chinese and Japanese gardeners have been preoccupied with stones, and Islamic gardeners with the display of water). The zeal of plant collectors and breeders and the development of commercial nurseries have opened up a vast range of possibilities (just as the development of synthetic dyes and pigments has enabled us to clothe our

A hard surface to walk on (Death Valley)

A soft surface to look at only (Saihoji)

bodies in fabrics of just about any color). And sophisticated gardeners have developed elaborate theories, comparable to those of painters, of how to mass blossoms, combine different kinds, and produce subtle harmonies or striking contrasts.

Mughul emperors, and the Persians before them, favored wool or silk carpets in their gardens, often woven with the patterns of the gardens themselves. The thought of such exposure to the elements scandalizes many contemporary gardeners, but for them indoor-outdoor carpeting has been devised, if they require it.

Raising Landmarks

One of the most universal of human instincts is to raise a landmark from the surface of the earth. This gives a center to a fragment of the world—a particularly poignant gesture when the surrounding landscape provides few orienting features. The aboriginals of the Australian desert have woven a beautiful myth around this act. There was, the story goes, a group of ancestors who wandered in the desert, carrying with them a long pole. Every evening they would carefully plant the pole upright in the ground to create the place for making camp. In doing so one evening, they accidentally broke it. Now, lacking the means of making a special place in which to dwell, they became tired and sad, and eventually they lay down and died.

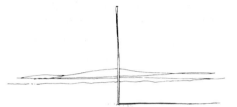

A simple landmark creates a place

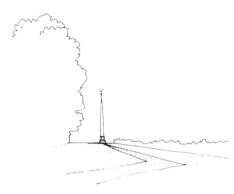

A landmark becomes the starting point for a garden

Landmarks may serve to announce a destination, to create the promise of arrival in a place of human habitation. Proust's recollections of how he was beckoned by the church steeple at Combray describe this suggestive power:

There was a spot where the narrow road emerged suddenly on to an immense plain, closed at the horizon by strips of forest over which rose the fine point of Saint-Hilaire's steeple, but so sharpened and so pink that it seemed to be no more than sketched on the sky by the fingernail of a painter anxious to give to such a landscape, to so pure a piece of "nature," this little sign of art, this single indication of human existence.

In a garden, at a smaller scale, the "little sign of art" might be a statue or obelisk or summer house, revealed at the end of a vista, or an "eye-catcher" forming the focus of a distant prospect.

Instead of marking a center, a landmark may also be used to define a boundary. The Romans employed statues of the god Terminus (term figures) in this way to protect the edges of properties. And in the rectangular walled gardens of Islam we often find towers guarding the corners.

You can begin to compose a garden, then, by taking a landmark as your starting point. It might be a tree or stone or ruin found on the site, or even something visible from the site—a distant mountain peak, perhaps. Or it might be a prized object brought from somewhere else. Modern gardeners, unlike those of past centuries, have the chance to purchase and bring in large trees, so that they don't have to wait for the imagined key element of a composition to establish itself.

Edging and Walling

Forming edges with walls, hedges, and earth

A wooden fence overgrown with vines

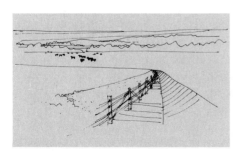

A fence in a ditch makes a concealed boundary: the ha-ha

Perhaps the most important determinants of what we see in a place and how we feel about it are the walls that surround it. That is not surprising, given our own configuration, which includes an upright stance and eyes so placed as to look out horizontally, right at the walls. In a building the enclosing walls are usually planar and vertical, though layers of arcades and colonnades sometimes give depth to the boundary. In a garden the possibilities expand, and to solid walls we can add hedges, vines, shrubbery, and groves of trees.

Garden walls can be of wood (vertical, horizontal, or diagonal boards, shingles, or board and batten), of brick, of stone "dressed" (that is, made rectangular) or natural, of tile, of stucco, or of sheets of fiber or metal; they can be constituted as fences, of grape stakes or reeds or board louvers (to allow air circulation), even of wire mesh and vines. A sudden change in grade can end the view, in a bank or berm or cliff or even a waterfall; or the terminus can be planted—with a hedge, which can make a stop almost as solid as a wall, or with a looser border of shrubbery, or even with a grove or forest, in which the space gradually comes to an end among the tree trunks.

A garden wall, unlike the wall of a room, stands out in the sun and the rain where it rapidly weathers and perhaps becomes a place for things to grow, so that an encrustation of surface layers becomes part of the garden. The courtyard gardens of Mexico and of the California missions are given a special character by the surrounding walls of worn, stained, patched adobe, peeling to reveal ancient layers of stucco and whitewash. Mosses and lichen will grow on damp surfaces, and you can let a wall be overtaken by vines and creepers—well-groomed ivy, perhaps, bountiful grape or passion-fruit, or exuberantly flowering bougainvillea.

Hedges have two possible kinds of surfaces, clipped or unclipped, which will modulate the light in different ways. Clipped hedges may be sculpted into regular curves or shaped into irregular masses—like huge, worn boulders.

Another game is to treat a wall as a blank sheet of paper, to be painted upon by silhouettes and shadows of objects placed in front. Chinese gardens often relate blank white wall and sparsely planted bamboo in this way, quite explicitly recalling the watercolorist's brush strokes (which may then complete the circle by depicting the bamboo).

In gardens, more often than in buildings, where walls usually need to be high enough to hold up roofs, we have the opportunity to look out over low walls that don't need to hold up anything. This creates places that, poignantly, invite our gaze but forbid our step: the ocean beyond the sea wall, the hazy distance beyond a rampart, the parterre of flowers surrounded by a low, clipped hedge.

You can make a wall disappear completely, by placing it in a ditch, so that you have the illusion of looking out over an unbounded sweep of countryside. This device became known in eighteenth-century England, apparently

Natural edges

Edges forming axes in the landscape

Ambiguous spaces

Enclosures formed by walls

Enclosure formed by columns

in recognition of its surprising effect, as a *ha-ha*. It provided a way to let the fields seem to come right up to the walls of a country house, without the attendant nuisances of sheep in the shrubbery and cowpats on the lawn.

You can even make edges that are little more than marks upon the ground: changes of surface material; curbs and gutters; low terraces; transitions from mown to unmown grass; boundaries of watered areas, where green gives way to brown; even boundaries between sunny and shady areas, marked by changes in vegetation. These can be deployed as hints and cautions to guide the garden visitor's steps and to inflect patterns of occupation.

An artificial edge, such as a stone wall, usually forms a fairly permanent and stable boundary. But natural edges are often ecotones—zones, like shorelines and the boundaries of forests, at which natural processes come together in a balance that may be precarious and temporary. So the natural edges in a garden tend to shift, or even to disappear; and their forms contrast with those of walls and buildings, as was pointed out long ago by Sir Henry Wotton in his *Elements of Architecture*:

I must note a certain contrariety between building and gardening: For as Fabriques should be regular, so Gardens should be irregular, or at least cast into a very wilde Regularitie.

Enclosing

A single edge or wall introduced into a landscape can form an axis around which a composition may be organized, much as a single landmark can form a center. Or you can deploy walls to create more-or-less ambiguous boundaries. For centuries Chinese painting has included the concept of "dragon's veins," linear fingers of clouds or space which permeate objects and landscapes, ventilate them, and vanish around the objects and out of sight to suggest vast distances beyond the flat surface of a painting. The gardens of China and Japan, and picturesque gardens in the West (especially in England) are full of such ambiguous spaces, which slide around edges and suggest that the garden goes on indefinitely.

When walls are arranged to form definite enclosures, the space within can be given clarity of shape, proportion, and extent, like a fine Georgian room (though the ceiling of the room is constructed, and in the garden may just be suggested). But an enclosure need not necessarily be formed by walls; it may be implied by columns defining corners. The Kashmiri device of the *char-chenar* (four trees arranged in a square) does this, and indeed, a tetrastyle of trees has often been seen as an incipient building. The Abbé Laugier's celebrated "primitive hut," which played such an important role in neoclassical architectural theory, was formed in this way. And Viollet-le-Duc observed that you might bend the trees to form pointed arches, rather than letting them stand upright, so that a "gothic" primitive hut emerged instead.

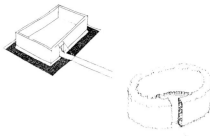

Single bounded realms

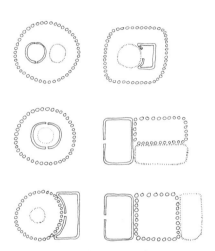

Fitting two enclosures together

Fitting three enclosures together

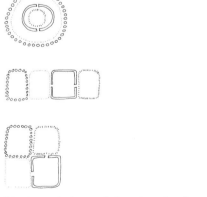

Nesting, stringing, and clustering of enclosures

The most elementary pattern of enclosure is, of course, a single bounded realm. The boundary divides the world into two parts; everything is either inside or outside. The act of drawing a boundary, to distinguish an inner, privileged place from the outer world, carries a special significance. Among the earliest of man-made gardens were the green hunting preserves that the Assyrian kings divided off from the surrounding desert. The name they gave to them has become, via the Persian and Greek, the English word "paradise." Medieval painters sometimes signified the biblical paradise merely by showing the simplest of enclosures around the figures of Adam and Eve. And some actual gardens are nothing more than enclosures formed by walls, or circles of trees, but potently evocative in their reduction to essentials. Among those that haunt our memories are tiny groves of poplars surrounded by mud-brick walls in Himalayan valleys, carefully cultivated clearings in the New Guinea jungle, and the formal, grassy courtyard of Clare College, Cambridge.

Surprisingly, there are only a few basic ways to fit several enclosures together. There are just two ways to add a second enclosure to a first, for example. The second enclosure may either be made inside (with intimations of hierarchy) or alongside (with intimations of equivalence). It isn't hard to see how we can add a new enclosure, inside or alongside either of the spaces in either of these patterns to produce a three-enclosure garden. A little experimentation with pencil and paper should convince you that there are no more than six possibilities. If you sketch out four-enclosure and five-enclosure patterns, you will find, of course, that the possibilities begin to multiply rapidly. But you will also discover that only three fundamental principles are manifested in the multiplicity. The first is *nesting* one enclosure within another. The second is *stringing* enclosures together, like beads, in a line. And the third is *clustering*.

Any one of the enclosure patterns that you can construct has an endless variety of particular geometric realizations. It might be materialized in straight lines or arcs of circles or free-form curves. There might be smooth corners or sharp angles, and the angles might vary or be disciplined to ninety degrees. There might be a strong order of repetition and symmetry, or there might be none.

Roofing

Ceilings in buildings are relatively free of the functional restrictions that are the natural lot of floors and walls, so they are able to assume a large part of the mythical and symbolic freight of the building, and the wise architect invests much of his energy in them. The ceiling of the garden does not so readily fall within the designer's grasp, since its basic element is the sky.

Of course there are skies and skies. The low, rain-bearing skies of England create an entirely different, closer ceiling than the skies of the American prairie, across which march vast cumulus clouds. And the sky changes, from the blues or grays of midday to the magenta and orange of sunrise or sunset. At night there are the stars, if urban illuminations are far enough

A gazebo

A trellis

Openings in Chinese garden walls

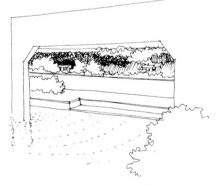

A view is framed by a low wall and a giant arch at the Burns house, Los Angeles

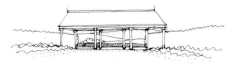

An open loggia to look under

away; we know an Australian garden that suddenly enchants as the Southern Cross rises above the eucalyptus fronds and the night birds begin to call.

Then there are more intimate ceilings for a part of the garden, generally variations on an umbrella. A single tree provides a canopy rather like a giant beach umbrella, with its support in the center, its shade around. The trees can be planted in bosques or orchards, to form a regular canopy, or irregularly in groves, to change the depth and quality of shade and enclosure. Trees of different sizes and types can multiply the layers of shelter overhead (low and higher and very high) and the kinds of shade they make (dense or delicate).

Even outdoors it sometimes seems desirable to construct ceilings of wood or cloth, even occasionally of masonry. They can be built around a single point, like a gazebo or a pavilion, or along a line, like an arbor or a trellis, or even over larger spaces, perhaps in a continuous canopy. They can be built to shed rain or just to filter sunshine and perhaps provide a heightened sense of enclosure.

Opening

One of the most interesting aspects of walls and roofs and enclosures is the way their continuity is broken, as openings are thrust through them. In buildings these openings are classed as doors, windows, and arcades; over the centuries they have been honored and elaborated with special shapes and moldings and borders and caps. In gardens the celebration of the act of piercing the walls tends to be more relaxed, except maybe in China, where moon gates are only one shape among many traditionally used. The circle of the moon gate finds favor, it is often said, because this shape does least to disrupt the continuity of the wall—especially if its perimeter does not quite touch the ground and if the wall smoothly humps over the top. But there are other attitudes toward walls and openings. In courtyard walls of Balinese temples there are split gates, at which the wall is thickened, heightened, celebrated by elaborate carving, then brutally divided by stark parallel planes, the better to emphasize the violation of the boundary.

In the West, when there is something to see beyond the garden, the wall might almost vanish and be replaced by a low terrace wall to look over or an open loggia to look under, or both. A garden we know in Los Angeles has a pleasant but confusing view across a little canyon. A low terrace wall, full walls at the sides, and an overhead wall (an irregular, giant single arch) together frame the view, making it seem to recede, which adds dimension to the garden without disturbing its aura of privacy.

Landscape painters have their own devices. Claude Lorrain invariably framed a scene with foreground trees, and he was much imitated in this by eighteenth-century English landscape gardeners. Later, the practitioners of the picturesque explored ways to occlude and fragment and vignette scenes by arranging stones, foliage, and fragments of ruins like stage flats.

Connecting

The traditions of the Australian aboriginal people suggest (more vividly than those of any other culture we have encountered) a close interrelation of landscape, music, and narrative. The land of these nomadic people is criss-crossed by the invisible tracks of mythic ancestors who traveled across the country, dreaming its features into being as they went. The rhythms of traditional songs recall the footsteps of the Dreamtime creators, and the words narrate sequences of creation along the way—of mountains and water holes, animals and men. Songs become maps, performances become magical regenerations of the world, and the land itself is read as score and text. Similarly, in the miniature, artificially created world of a garden, paths create sequences of *shan* and *shui*—able to be shaped into rhythms and to tell tales.

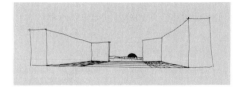

Wings of walls to look between

The paths of Islam are straight and narrow, leading directly into the heart of paradise. Those of Versailles are equally single-minded, but climax in the bedchamber of the Sun King. The goose-foot patterns of seventeenth- and eighteenth-century French hunting parks tell of the headlong flight of the stag, while English parks may be patterned on the winding tracks of the devious fox. Rococo gardens cut paths into the curlicued rhythms of courtly frivolity, and Japanese gardeners have, for centuries, deployed precarious stepping stones with such artful irregularity that the placement of each *geta*-constrained foot must become a conscious, exquisitely shaped act.

A frame of foliage to look through

A garden path can become the thread of a plot, connecting moments and incidents into a narrative. The narrative structure might be a simple chain of events with a beginning, middle, and end. It might be embellished with diversions, digressions, and picaresque twists, be accompanied by parallel ways (subplots), or deceptively fork into blind alleys like the alternative scenarios explored in a detective novel. (Borges saw the analogy, and in his murder mystery "The Garden of Forking Paths," the bifurcations are not in space, but actually in time—to alternative futures.) If a path is connected back to its starting point there is a loop of events—potentially repeating endlessly, like those concocted by Samuel Becket.

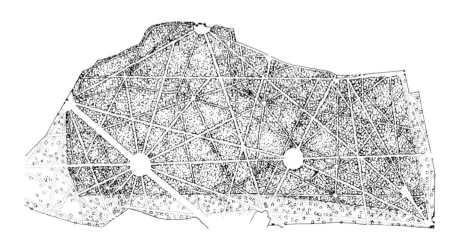

Goose-foot patterns in the Bois de Boulogne

Rococo curlicues: a path layout by Batty Langley

CREATING CLIMATES

Just as an architect must create appropriate climates in the spaces of a building, a garden designer must do so in the spaces of a garden. Water must be introduced to keep the plants alive (and perhaps to provide cooling), and it is equally vital to drain it out, so that it won't drown or rot the plants or make the ground smelly and treacherous underfoot. Sunlight and shadow must be deployed appropriately, and the air itself may be warmed or cooled, scented, and filled with sound.

Irrigating and Draining

As the water does its essential, practical work, there will be occasions for play and celebration—of glittering surface or drifting mist, of foaming cascade or silent depth.

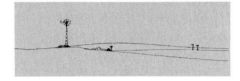

Windmills mark the source of water

Water flows from a hidden source

A well can become a reflective pool, as at the center of many Persian gardens, while a spring bubbling up from beneath the ground can be dramatized as a fountain. A hillside source can become a grotto or a cascade. In many places springs have been enshrined within pavilions or personified with statues of gods or spirits. In the drought-ridden Australian outback, tall windmills that pump the artesian water from far below become exclamation points over life-giving pools and attract laconically poetic names—Broken Bucket Bore, Moonlight Tank. But in traditional Japanese gardens, as specified by the *Sakuteiki*, the source of water is, even more dramatically, never allowed to be visible; its presence in the miniature mountains is merely implied by the emergence of a cascade from behind a stone.

There is pleasure in seeing the water on display—by itself in ponds, lakes, channels, swimming pools, and basins; filled with plants (water lilies, lotus, water hyacinths, iris, various reeds and grasses); and moving and falling or just moistening a tile basin. If it is still, its surface is perfectly flat, which may nicely contrast with roughened or undulating surfaces. Very few soils are sufficiently impermeable for water to stand on them without leaking away, so masonry, usually concrete, is used to line the basin. Clay or a layer of plastic (or even both, the plastic protected and hidden by the clay) is sometimes employed, and now more frequently a porous rock (also sold for kitty litter) is rolled on. The water needs, of course, to circulate and be mixed with oxygen if it is to stay fresh and not harbor slimy invaders.

Water is very exactly governed by the laws of hydraulics, so the choreography of its movement must take close account of these. Witness the careful advice of the *Sakuteiki:*

After setting the elevations for the course of the running stream, if you make the ratio of the drop of the elevation to the distance of the running stream to be three to one hundred (3%), the stream will flow smoothly with a murmuring sound. If it is difficult to dig the channel and flush it with water at the time of construction, in order to set the elevation, lay pieces of split bamboo on the ground with the hollow sides up, run water through them and determine the elevations.

It suggests a way to change direction:

The placing of stones for the garden stream should start at a place where it makes a turn and flows along. This turn is supposed to have been caused by the presence of the rock which the stream could not demolish.

And it warns of the dangers of stagnation in a pond:

The water will smell bad after one or two nights and insects will come out of it, therefore the fountain must flow regularly and the bottom of stones should be washed.

At changes of level you can let the water fall, in imitation of natural cascades, or create formal chutes and spouts. Where the necessary pressure is available, you can also install nozzles to send up a solid column of water, to distribute a fine feathery spray, or to produce a multitude of tiny spurts. You can make the water bubble, gurgle, dribble, and slop around, or you can hurl it high to be caught by the breeze. You can arrange the relation between the water, the viewer, and the sun to produce glittering reflections from falling droplets, drifting rainbows, or incandescent back-lit spray (especially effective against a background of dark foliage). The nozzle can be elaborated into a formal fountain, which then becomes the center of a garden composition. A more pragmatic approach is to lay out a hidden spray irrigation system or to ad-hoc it with garden hoses and sprinklers.

In the natural landscape a complex system of catchments and aquifers, ponds and lakes, streams and rivers evolves to drain the water. If you're lucky, the natural drainage of a garden site will suffice. But it is more likely that you will have to build a system to carry the water away. This can be done invisibly, by laying agricultural drains beneath the earth. Or it can be done by imitating nature—carefully sloping the surfaces of the ground and making miniature streams and ponds. Or, in a more formal garden, you can deploy architectural elements: basins and gutters and gargoyles.

Lighting

The sunlight (and the moonlight and starlight) that reaches a garden is never static and never flat; it changes direction minute by minute, hour by hour, and changes quality from bright days to cloudy, from the blue brilliance of noon to the warm glow of sunset. Artificial light can be animated, too. Great candles in containers might flicker on a lawn or float on the surface of a pool. Oil lamps might flash from niches behind a waterfall. Fireworks might even extend the garden's display. Only electrical lighting is even and constant.

By filling your garden with light-colored, reflective surfaces and opening it up to the sky, you can create a bright (or even brilliant) atmosphere. Or, by darkening surfaces, closing off the sky with foliage or canopies, and turning the garden's back to the sun, you can make a shady place (or a gloomy one). You might want the drama of a sudden contrast: a shady cloister beside a sunny courtyard, perhaps, or a dazzling clearing in the depths of a grove. Or you might want to play a game of nuances, gradations, and transitions, leading the visitor into the gathering gloom of a thicket or grotto, then, slowly, out again into the full light of day.

The glitter of droplets in sunlight

A soft wash of English light

Brilliant planes and deep shadows in Aegean light

The colors of the garden will change with its brightness. In medium light the hues of foliage and of blossoms will be at their purest, but in soft moonlight most of the hue will wash away. Japanese gardens have often included moon-viewing platforms for contemplation of the silvers and grays that remain, moon shadows on white sand, and cherry blossoms against the dark sky. The brilliance of tropical sunlight will fade colors to a pastel residue; the scarlet bougainvillea can seem a shy pink.

The brightness of flat surfaces, of walls and floors, depends upon the angle of incident light—greatest when the light is perpendicular, least when the light washes almost parallel to the surface, and constantly changing as the sun moves. But textured surfaces will seem flattest in perpendicular light and are at their most dramatic in glancing light. The shadows cast by clouded sunlight on a red-brick English garden wall create gentle variations, but the shadows cast by the Aegean sun on a whitewashed wall produce glaring contrast. Carefully plot the daily arc of the sun across your site, and study its variation between the summer and winter solstice, then angle your wall and floor surfaces to produce a composition of shade, shadow, texture, and contrast that unfolds through the day like a melody and varies the theme as the seasons progress.

Another beautiful quality of light is the glow that appears when a luminous source stands against a dark ground. At night we have the moon and stars, and perhaps the flicker of flame. Stage designers employ the glow of back-lit, translucent scrims, and architects may use stained glass. In the garden, most often, it is foliage or blossom seen against the light that glows. Grass will glow against the low morning sun, especially if there is dew or frost, and canopies of leaves will filter the light later in the day.

Finally, there will be glitter and sparkle from shiny surfaces—especially water, though glass, glazed titles, and metal may shimmer too. To get this effect, you must arrange for the angle of light incident to the shiny surface to be equal to the angle of reflection to the viewer's eye. When water is still and flat (or far away) and the sun is low (or you're at a particularly high vantage point) and in front of you, for example, the whole surface can become like molten metal. And when the surface is rippled, even the higher sun of the middle part of the day will reflect momentarily from the changing angles, so that the surface shimmers with tiny sparks and flashes.

Warming and Cooling

The gardener's devices for creating cool places are shade and water. Physically they work in different ways; shade reduces the radiant heat from the sun, while the evaporation of water from pools, from foliage, or (best of all) from fountain sprays reduces the temperature of the air. A shady oasis may seem cool even though the air is warm, and water can cool the air even in the full glare of the sun.

If you want to create warm places, on the other hand, you must deploy devices to capture the sun's energy. A sheltered east-facing corner will be warm in the chilly morning air, and a west-facing corner will catch the

The warmth of the sun

The cool of the cave

golden rays of afternoon. You can retain more of the warmth by building glass enclosures—greenhouses that readily let the radiant energy in but inhibit its transmission back out again. Orangeries, sunny rooms where delicate shrubs in pots could be wheeled in to spend the winter, were early attempts to exploit this principle. But they didn't always work very well, since it was hard to make windows in masonry walls big enough. William Chambers's beautiful white stucco orangery at Kew Gardens in London, for example, has never effectively served its intended purpose. When the Industrial Revolution had created the means, the idea of light, metal-framed glasshouses emerged—Decimus Burton's great Palm House at Kew, for instance. These can maintain the climate of a tropical jungle, even in the depths of a northern winter (with a little help, where necessary, from artificial heating).

Insulating materials, like wood, will normally seem pleasantly warm to the touch. Conductors, like metal, will usually make the warmth flow away from your skin, and so seem cold, but can become burning hot in full sunlight. Some other materials, particularly stone and brick and concrete, are slow to heat up but will store the heat for a very long time. A masonry wall that has been in sunlight all day may radiate a genial warmth through the chilly evening, and a shaded wall may retain the cool of the night long after the sun has risen high in the sky. A stone grotto retains a surprisingly even temperature throughout the year, seeming cool in summer and warm in winter. (Boswell reports that a Lincolnshire lady showed Dr. Johnson a grotto she had been making. "Would it not be a pretty cool habitation in summer, Mr. Johnson?" she said. "I think it would, Madam," replied he, "for a toad.")

In cool and windy climates you may want to create sunny, sheltered corners in the lee of the wind. Where it is warmer, and particularly where the air is clammy and humid, you can create shaded, open-sided, elevated places—pavilions, gazebos, summer houses, and eyries—to capture the breezes. You may need to provide shelter from the rain too. Eighteenth-century English gardens are full of temples and follies not just to delight the eye, but also to offer strollers refuge from sudden showers. And tropical gardens would be uninhabitable without pavilions to provide shelter from the inexorable monsoons.

The suggestion of warmth or coolness or shelter can be as important as the physical presence. The tinkle of a fountain in a courtyard promises cool refuge on a sunny day, and a belvedere at the crest of a hill suggests warm evening breezes.

Scenting

The delight of garden air is its fragrance. The Persian poet Hafiz wrote:

Oh! bring thy couch where countless roses
The garden's gay retreat discloses;
There in the shade of waving boughs recline
Breathing rich odors, quaffing ruby wine!

The scents of flowers

And, in his essay "Of Gardens," Francis Bacon suggested that knowledge of the qualities of scent provided by plants is essential to those who would make gardens:

And because, the Breath of Flowers, is far Sweeter in the Air (where it comes and Goes, like the Warbling of Musick) than in the hand, therefore nothing is more fit for that delight, than to know, what be the Flowers, and Plants, that do best perfume the Air.

He then classified flowers and trees according to the strengths of their perfumes, the times when these perfumes are produced, and whether the scent is experienced as they are "passed by" or as they are "trodon upon and Crushed."

But the fragrances of flowers and foliage are not the only ones at the gardener's disposal. English landscape gardens are often permeated by the smell of moist summer earth, hay, and the farmyard. Australian gardens become especially poignant at those moments when the unmistakable smell of drought-breaking rain falling onto warm dust is added to the sharp tang of eucalyptus. We know a Greek garden redolent of ouzo and onions, and a Turkish garden that reeks of raki and roses. Recollections of Indian gardens are evoked, for us, by the scents of incense, coconut oil, teapots, or smoke from picnic fires. And there are Balinese courtyard gardens of such layered olfactory complexity that they seem to have been concocted by a talented but crazed winemaker: salt breezes, rice-field mud, clove cigarettes, and frangipani.

Filling with Sound

Sound in a garden comes from many sources, each of which can be attenuated or intensified. The wind in the trees can stir our thought: Thomas Hardy noted that "almost every species of tree has a voice." In his *Writer's Notebook* Somerset Maugham described how the breeze stirring the lace-like foliage of casuarinas made a sound "as of people talking" and how the natives say that "if you stand under them at midnight you will hear voices of unknown people telling you the secrets of the earth."

The song of birds

You can fill the air with song if you cultivate plants that attract birds and lure them with food and shelter. If you choose to house birds, though, remember that many species are as finicky as if they were paying very high rents. Some prefer apartments, some are single-family occupants. The entry hole has to be the right size, the compartments have to be the right dimensions and clean, etc. Apparently architectural style is not a factor in their choice of a home, but just about everything else is.

A more constant source of sound in a garden is water, splashing in a fountain, running, falling, dripping, coming sometimes from the sky. Both the sound of water and its shape can be manipulated, as it is in the formal cascades of Mughul gardens. We've even found that a serrated copper edge at a miniature weir can be tuned with pliers to simulate the babble of a brook, which seems innocent enough in an age when, to help them fall asleep, people plug in by their beds little boxes with an electronic simulation of surf.

LENDING LIFE

In his "Essay on Man" Alexander Pope challenged his readers with the suggestion that the sin of pride, which caused man's fall from paradise, was that pride which led him to separate himself from the animals and to dwell in houses and towns. Before the fall,

Pride then was not, nor arts that pride to aid;
Man walked with beast, joint tenant of the shade.

A garden can recall this vision of Eden by creating a place of human habitation among living plants, animals, and birds.

Cultivating

You can plant a garden for foliage—for shade, privacy, and muted light. You can plant it for seasonal color, so that your garden changes from summer green to bright fall to chiaroscuro winter to the delicate pastels of spring. Or, if it is in the Sun Belt, you can have blue jacaranda blossoms in June, lavender silk floss in October, red and purple bougainvillea in November, and the yellow acacia in February. You can plant for scent—of roses, perhaps, or boxwood, of pine trees or herbs. Gardens for the blind pay special attention to juxtaposing fragrances, but the rest of us should not forget their pleasures, either.

One of the most affecting characteristics of a garden is the vulnerability of its green fabric. If you don't tend it the signs of neglect will soon appear, and eventually it will die. But a gardener's rituals of care are rewarded, and their performance cements a bond between person and place. Trees and shrubs must be pruned and shaped; lawns must be mown; edges must be trimmed; hedges must be clipped; the ground must be fertilized and renewed; flower beds must be sown; and flower pots, perhaps, must be moved as the seasons change. In a natural garden the game is to conceal the signs of care, so that a scene appears to have evolved naturally to perfection. In a formal garden, by contrast, the grooming is conspicuous, and dominion over nature rather than complicity with it is suggested. We see the perfect lawn, that shaven hedge—perhaps even topiary—and the precisely controlled parterre.

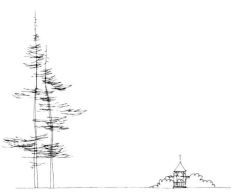

Living compositions change over time

Growth and change over time brings its compositional problems as well as its optimistic boons: we all know sunny gardens that have gone gradually to shade and beyond. While man-made objects like buildings, though they deteriorate or grow a patina, generally maintain their initial size and shape, trees don't. That tree on the left might seem to balance a greensward on the right, perhaps with a gazebo on it, or maybe a drift of bushes. But watch out! The gazebo won't grow, and the bushes won't grow much, but the tree may have it in mind to become a forest giant, in which case the balance will most surely be upset.

Populating

Peacocks strut through the great parks of Europe, sacred giant carp inhabit many Japanese garden ponds, and the Mughul gardens of Kashmir are filled with the song of the bul-bul. In a few very grand gardens, human inhabitants have been made part of the scene. The emperor Ch'ien Lung peopled an island in the Yuan Ming Yuan with industrious peasants, and eighteenth-century English gentlemen occasionally employed suitably unkempt hermits to dwell in rustic huts or grottoes set up in their picturesque gardens. Merlin's Cave in Queen Caroline's park at Richmond was inhabited for a while by one Stephen Duck, who produced great quantities of awful verse. The marquis René-Louis de Girardin had a higher-class act in mind for his "English" park at Ermenonville. In 1778 he invited Rousseau, by then down on his luck, to live out his days on the estate. Girardin prepared a suitably rustic rock-and-thatch one-room cottage, to be known as the "Maison du Philosophe," but Rosseau died before it was ready (or perhaps before he was ready for it).

Very practical alternatives to live guests are statues, which have been a traditional part of European gardens since Roman times. They are much less common in Chinese and Japanese gardens, though, and religious tradition bans them from Islamic gardens. Disneyland is peopled by hundreds of realistically animated, even talking, statues; Donald Duck replaces Stephen Duck.

When Washington Irving visited the palace and gardens of the Alhambra in 1829, he found them ruinous and largely uninhabited, so he populated them in his imagination. He wrote of brigands and beggars and princes, of Alhamar, Yusef Abdul Hagig, and Boabdil. He retold or just made up legends—of the philosophic Ibrahim Ebn Abu Ayub, who "would fain have a few dancing women" and who eventually disappeared beneath the earth with "a Christian damsel of surpassing beauty"; of Prince Ahmed al Kamel, who spoke of love with the birds visiting his lonely tower in the Generalife; of a Moor from Tangiers and a pimping barber; of three sisters and three gallant cavaliers; and of the Rose of the Alhambra and her vigilant aunt. "It is impossible to contemplate this scene so perfectly Oriental without feeling the early associations of Arabian romance, and almost expecting to see the white arm of some mysterious princess beckoning from the gallery, or some dark eye sparkling through the lattice," he wrote. "The abode of beauty is here, as if it had been inhabited but yesterday."

Furnishing

In the rooms of a house one would expect to discover the treasures and possessions of its inhabitants. The spaces of a garden, too, can be furnished with objects to serve and please.

In Chinese gardens weirdly eroded rocks are displayed on pedestals, and Japanese gardens are furnished with fine stone lanterns. Prize trees with space around for viewing and flowers grouped into floral borders are more usual decorations in European gardens. Another strategy, which has been used around the Mediterranean for millennia, is to make flowers mobile, to grow them in pots which are displayed only when there is bloom.

The furniture in a garden might be of a humble sort, to sit on or put things on. Such furniture in some of the great gardens is massive masonry:

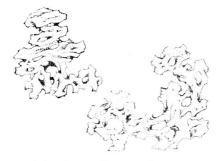

Eroded rocks in a Chinese garden

A prize tree

Mobile flowers in pots

the central stone banqueting table at the Villa Lante, seating dozens, had a channel of water running down its middle, making it a little like the serpentine watercourses that run through garden pavilions in China and Japan, down which cups of wine were floated while the scholarly inhabitants composed poetry. Drinking the contents of the cup was the reward for writing the poem in time or the penalty for not, we have forgotten which. In other gardens, fine stone and wood benches make impressive (but hard) places to sit, though the interests of comfort may be better served by cushioned chairs and chaises that encourage lounging in the midst of a special place.

Other needs can be met by providing pools, hot tubs, barbecues, swings, dog kennels, pigeon houses, devices for electrocuting flying bugs, and lines to hang out the laundry. ("Nothing grows in our garden," complained Polly Garter in *Under Milk Wood,* "only washing. And babies.")

Naming

There is a scene in *The Story of the Stone,* the great eighteenth-century Chinese novel, in which the father, Jia Zheng, remarks of a newly made garden: "Those prospects and pavilions—even the rocks and trees and flowers will seem somehow incomplete without the touch of poetry which only the written word can lend a scene." Then the characters tour the garden, suggest names for each of its many parts, and write commemorative verses, which they quote back and forth. The garden is completed before the reader's eyes.

The undoubted real-life champion of this game was the emperor Ch'ien Lung. His Yuan Ming Yuan garden was not only the biggest and most magnificent one around, it was also the most elaborately completed by naming and description. Indeed the evocative names of its forty scenes, together with calligraphic descriptions and painted views, are all that now remain (apart from a few sad ruins); it was razed by the vengeful English soldiers in the nineteenth century.

Of course the English had a way with garden names themselves: classical, mostly. Rousham has a Vale of Venus and a Praeneste, and, to make sure that you get the point, it is dotted with statues of Apollo, Mercury, and others. Stowe, one of the grandest of the eighteenth-century landscapes, has a Grecian Valley headed by an Ionic Temple of Concord and Victory, Elysian Fields, and a River Styx.

The English also invented a complicated and fascinating game of assigning landscape scenes to aesthetic categories. Edmund Burke began it (or at least established some of the most important rules) by setting out definitions of the *beautiful* and the *sublime* in his *Philosophical Enquiry into the Origin of Our Ideas of the Sublime and Beautiful* (1756). The beautiful was characterized by its smallness, smoothness, and gradual variation, and it was exemplified in the gentle, rolling landscapes designed by Capability Brown.

The beautiful contrasts with the sublime, characterized as the awful, the rugged, and the wild—mountains, chasms, and ferocious beasts. Sir

William Chambers took this cue, in his *Dissertation on Oriental Gardening* (1772), and he conjured up a fantasy vision of Chinese gardens of terror, in which

the buildings are in ruins; or half consumed by fire, or swept away by the fury of the waters: nothing remaining entire but a few miserable huts dispersed in the mountains, which serve at once to indicate the wretchedness of the inhabitants. Bats, owls, vultures, and every bird of prey flutter in the groves; wolves, tigers and jackals howl in the forests; half-famished animals wander upon the plains; gibbets, crosses, wheels, and the whole apparatus of torture, are seen from the roads.

And the visitor had to watch out for "showers of artificial rain," "sudden violent gusts of wind," "instantaneous explosions of fire," and even "repeated shocks of electrical impulse." Nobody was actually to go quite this far, though, until Walt Disney.

More mysteriously, to our modern ears, seventeenth- and eighteenth-century commentators on gardens frequently announced that they had discovered *sharawaggi* in some particularly admirable prospect. The word is probably a corruption of some Chinese phrase, though scholars are not sure which, and it suggests pleasing, apparently casual intricacy, asymmetry, and a touch of things Chinese.

Toward the end of the eighteenth century the term *picturesque* was popularized by William Gilpin and Sir Uvedale Price (in his 1794 *Essay on the Picturesque*). Price suggested that it should be applied to "every kind of scenery, which has been, or might be represented with good effect in painting." He meant romantic landscape painting, with its scenes characterized by roughness, sudden variation, and irregularity. The picturesque tends toward the sublime, but without such strong intimations of the terrible and the infinite, and it avoids the smoothness of the beautiful. Unexpectedness is a part of it, too, as Thomas Love Peacock had "a very profound critic from Edinburgh" solemnly announce in *Headlong Hall,* only to be queried, "Pray sir, by what name do you distinguish this character when a person walks around the grounds for a second time?" The landscape gardener Humphry Repton was a prolific exponent of picturesque composition, and his style was imitated in innumerable nineteenth- and early-twentieth-century parks and gardens.

The Japanese tradition has its own set of categories. There is a traditional thematic typology, distinguishing between hill gardens, flat gardens, and so on. Then there are categories of elaboration and degrees of finish: *shin* (very elaborate and highly finished), *gyo* (intermediate), and *so* (simple, pure, and natural). And there is also a system of aesthetic categories analogous to the English ones of beautiful, picturesque, and sublime. *Shibui,* for example, alludes to unaffected natural beauty. Quiet solitude in natural surroundings is suggested by *wabi.* And *sabi* intimates weathered rustic simplicity.

Flaubert couldn't resist poking fun at all this in *Bouvard et Pecuchet.* He had his two heroes discover that gardens come in "an infinity of styles": melancholy and romantic (everlasting flowers, ruins, tombs, and a votive

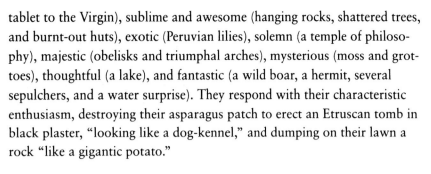

tablet to the Virgin), sublime and awesome (hanging rocks, shattered trees, and burnt-out huts), exotic (Peruvian lilies), solemn (a temple of philosophy), majestic (obelisks and triumphal arches), mysterious (moss and grottoes), thoughtful (a lake), and fantastic (a wild boar, a hermit, several sepulchers, and a water surprise). They respond with their characteristic enthusiasm, destroying their asparagus patch to erect an Etruscan tomb in black plaster, "looking like a dog-kennel," and dumping on their lawn a rock "like a gigantic potato."

Inhabiting

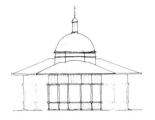

In Chinese landscape paintings you can often see a tiny human figure, or an isolated hermit's hut, almost lost amid a vastness of mountains and mist but still establishing a connection to human life. Similarly, in a Chinese garden pavilions not only invite habitation of a miniature world of stones and water, but also signify and celebrate that habitation.

Pavilions are an essential part of many Persian gardens as well. Two particularly splendid examples remain in the old royal gardens of Isfahan. The teak-columned hall of the Ali Qapu is like a gigantic throne, in scale with the vast open rectangle of the Maidan-i-Shah, which it overlooks. And the Chehel Sutun (Hall of Forty Columns, twenty of which are shimmering reflections in the water) is a Sybaritic center of symmetries within a leafy oasis.

Turkish kiosks

In Turkey the kiosk developed. Kiosks were places to smoke, drink coffee, and listen to music while contemplating the scene outside. Unlike Persian and Mughul gardens, which of course were inland, many of the great Turkish gardens were built along the shores of the Bosphorus and the Golden Horn, so that the kiosks could overlook the sea rather than a closed, walled domain.

Mughul gardeners adapted the Hindu form of the *baradari*. Its role has been described by Mohinder Singh Randhawa in his book *Gardens through the Ages:*

Baradari is a typically Hindu structure evolved by them to meet the requirements of the rainy season. People sit in baradaris *to enjoy fresh breezes, and to watch the black clouds and the rain. In the Kangra paintings, we often see princesses surrounded by slave-girls watching the flights of white egrets, with their snow-white feathers contrasting with slate-blue clouds in the background.*

This puzzled the English, apparently:

In the cold temperate climate of northern Europe, particularly in England, where the rain is usual and the sunshine is rare, people cannot imagine the joy and pleasure which the first monsoon showers bring to the young and old alike in the parched plains of northern India, where the hot sun of June scorches all vegetation. To them, these Indian pictures look funny, as they cannot imagine that anyone can be so balmy as to like rain and clouds, which they always associate with bad weather.

But in India it's different, as anybody who has experienced the monsoon season can surely understand:

Indians love the monsoon rains and clouds. In their baradaris, *they listen to the songs of their dancing-girls, watch the rain and the clouds, and suck mangoes cooled in iced water. It is hardly to be wondered that the Mughuls adopted the* baradari *in their gardens in the plains. They painted the masonry pillars of the* baradari *with their favorite design of bouquets in vases, and furnished them with thick carpets and cushions.*

The English did develop their own version of the garden pavilion, attuned to their climate, sky, and sensibility. In eighteenth-century landscape gardens we find innumerable miniature classical temples, usually sited on a rise or beside a lake to provide a carefully framed prospect. These are places for long, quiet summer afternoons, of low light, elongated shadows, and soft, fading distances. Perhaps the most magnificent of them is the four-sided Palladian temple designed by Sir John Vanbrugh for a hilltop at Castle Howard. Vanbrugh's biographer Kerry Downes has described it as "a place to spend the afternoon with a good book, a bottle and Ciceronian thoughts." And one of the most affecting is Cowper's Seat, built not in a park at all, but amidst the fields near the village of Olney—a memorial to a simple rural spot the poet loved.

European travelers to the Orient have sometimes remarked a bit scornfully on the sedentary habit of resting in kiosks or *baradaris.* This reflects the view, appropriate enough in more temperate northern latitudes, that gardens are places to be inhabited *actively*—to be strolled in (or even ridden through) and explored.

In a garden designed for exploration it is essential, of course, not to reveal everything at once. Alexander Pope advised English gardeners:

He gains all ends who pleasingly confounds,
Surprises, varies, and conceals the bounds.

Later we shall look at two great eighteenth-century English gardens, Rousham and Stourhead, whose makers followed this advice by hiding temples and follies among woods and hillsides and winding carefully contrived paths between them. We shall also see some Japanese gardens made for strolling rather than for contemplation from a house or boat.

A labyrinth

The most extreme form of a garden made for exploration is the *labyrinth* or *maze:* a pattern of paths tightly wound in on themselves, so that a vast distance is compressed into a tiny area. Jesuits made one for Ch'ien Lung at the Yuan Ming Yuan, and Le Nôtre created another at Versailles. At Hampton Court, at Somerleyton in Suffolk, and at Williamsburg, Virginia, there are hedge mazes. There was also a medieval tradition of cutting mazes in the turf outside churches (Shakespeare's "quaint mazes in the wanton green"), so that a miniature religious pilgrimage could be enacted—the trek to the terrestrial Holy Land or the winding spiritual path of the believer toward the Heavenly City.

On a grander scale, the great *stupa* of Borobudur, in Java, is also a highly compressed religious pilgrimage. It is a sequence of concentric terraces, forming an artificial mountain. The pilgrim circles each one before ascending to the next, and in doing so imitates the wanderings of the young Siddhartha in search of Buddhahood. Scenes from the quest of Siddhartha are depicted in panels along the walls of the perambulation galleries, and each level represents a higher state of enlightenment. First the pilgrim is shown the misery caused by the wheel of life, then how the Buddha preached the Law of Salvation, attained Buddhahood, and sought the Highest Wisdom. Finally, on the topmost terrace, the sphere of timeless meditation—the ultimate habitation of the spirit—is reached.

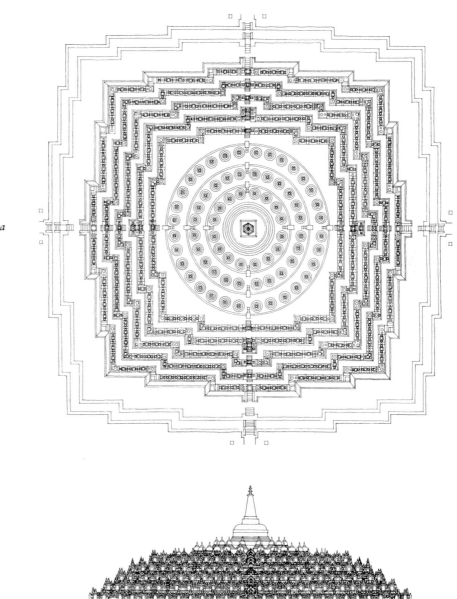

Borobudur, Java

3

The PLACE of the PAST

Gardens are rhetorical landscapes. They are made of the same materials as all the rest, just as the rhetorician's words are those given by the language, but they are composed to instruct and move and delight (Cicero's definition of the rhetorician's duties). We can read gardens for content, and we can analyze the devices of structure and figure and trope by means of which they achieve their effects.

From among the millions of gardens on this planet we have chosen about two dozen great gardens of the past to examine closely in this way. Together they illustrate the full scope of possibilities for the design of a garden—a range capable of being focused and transformed into something of your own.

Clearly, places as rich and complex as great gardens are not going to settle easily into strict categories, and clearly, too, there are many ways of categorizing gardens: by climate, for instance, or terrain, size, shape, soil, or more ephemeral qualities, like mood or atmosphere. We think it most helpful to arrange the gardens we have chosen into four categories: settings, collections, pilgrimages, and patterns. Gardens in all four come in a wide variety of sizes, shapes, and atmospheres, and all seek either the symmetrical patterns of paradise or the encapsulated and perfected asymmetries of nature (and sometimes both).

Our four categories are, really, categories of use, of how we dispose ourselves to interpret and enjoy places. Settings, with some affinities to metaphor in literature, are places where the relationship of things is so moving or so clear that the rest of the world is illuminated for us. T. S. Eliot once defined the function of the playwright as creating an order *in* reality that helped to make clear to the viewer the order *of* reality. The garden designer, creating a setting, seeks to do that as well, and nature herself occasionally crashes through with a clarified landscape that has the compelling qualities of a work of art.

If settings are metaphors, collections might be seen as metonymies, made of fragments and relics that evoke their origins. Nature occasionally collects startling arrays of natural wonders at some special spot, but collection is mostly a human game. Hadrian's vast collection at Tivoli was supposed to recall, by turns, Egypt, Spain, Bithynia, or wherever. Ch'ien Lung entertained his collector's enthusiasm on an even vaster scale, assembling in his garden everything from French fountains to Tibetan lamaseries. In the confident age of natural science, and of European colonization of Asia, Africa, America, and Australia, exotic plants were collected in distant lands and great botanical gardens made. In our own more populist times, the urgent instincts of avid collectors, like Walt Disney at Anaheim (later his successors would clone his collection in Florida, Tokyo, and Paris) or Sir Clough Williams-Ellis at Portmeirion on the coast of Wales, are supported by a fascinated public.

Some great gardens unfold like a narrative or a piece of music as we move through them and view their carefully choreographed wonders. We are calling them pilgrimages. They occur in nature, too, at places where devotees journey to some sacred spot. The journey in a garden is often around a lake or pond, the memory of it sequential, like a movie, rather than simultaneous, like a painting or the kind of garden we are calling a setting.

Still other gardens, which we call patterns, are laid out in geometric shapes and express some vision of order—of symmetry about a center or an axis, perhaps, or of regular, repetitive rhythm. These have affinities with verse, in which meter and rhyme create patterns of sound.

We may read a text for its metaphoric and metonymic content, for rhyme and meter, or for narrative structure. Each way of reading reveals different aspects of the text's form and meaning. So it is with gardens. Collections may be arranged along pilgrimage routes, or symmetrical patterns may be read as metaphors. Our classification, then, represents the way in which we have found it most interesting to approach our examples, but it does not pretend to be objective or exclusive.

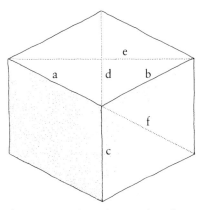

An axonometric projection of a cube

We have made careful axonometric drawings of most of the gardens we describe. These look rather like aerial photographs, but where in a photograph (that is, in perspective) the objects farther from the camera seem smaller, in an axonometric the dimensions along any of the two directions a or b, or the vertical, c, are to scale anywhere in the drawing. Other directions are distorted: the diagonal dimensions, d and e, which are really the same, do not measure the same; and f is longer than it measures. In addition to the view of the entire garden, we have made, when it was germaine, separate drawings for water, plants, and structures in a garden.

Almost any garden of some age has changed greatly over the years, and we have had to decide at what stage to show the gardens we discuss. Others have made, or will make scholarly chronologies of these gardens, so we have elected to show them at whatever phase they seemed to us to be clearest. If we thought the old arrangements more effective or more useful to us and you than present ones, we drew them.

What follows is the heart of this book, the storehouse of images and ideas, the encyclopedia of shapes and relationships, from which our own late-twentieth-century images are bound to come. For while the shapes of buildings may fade into the past, and serve us no more, gardens, though far more ephemeral, are far closer to eternal. Their materials have not changed, the ideas have not changed, and our own gardens, however modest, are going to be made of the same stuff as these.

Some special places have the extraordinary power to serve as a metaphor for the whole world. The power often comes from a concentration, a reduction to essentials, and its effect is altogether to absorb us, to hold us in the spell of the place. Some natural arrangements of great rock monoliths have it, and some artful human arrangers of very much smaller stones have succeeded in capturing it as well. At Ryoan-ji, near Kyoto, the whole world appears before us in a raked rectangle of sand with just a handful of modest stones. The English landscapes of Capability Brown, composed with almost as few pieces—rolling meadows, single trees and clumps and lines of trees, water and cows and English sky—made an entire clarified world as well. Isola Bella, an island garden in Lake Maggiore, shows how metaphoric power can come, as well, from complex overlays of imagery. It is like both a ship and a magic island, and creates a complex, compelling, and complete vision, which stays in the mind and fills it. On the island of Bali the flow of water from the mountain to the sea and the daily arc of the sun from east to west become metaphors of good and evil and of life and death. We have found it useful to call places like these settings. Some settings are big, some small, some can be seen all at once, some must be wandered through, but all achieve, in their disciplined clarity or multi-layered richness, the capacity to fill the mind (and later the memory) with their presence.

Uluru

Scattered across the continents are a few natural rock settings of wide fame. It is not unusual to wonder, on the way to one of these, how the chaotic and untidy stones all around could possibly be combined into a place that would feel like *someplace*. But then, arrival confirms that they can.

Monument Valley, Arizona:
the rock chimneys

Monument Valley, in the northeastern corner of Arizona, is made almost entirely of rock chimneys, which shift gently in color from the ochre sand at their bases to soft reds on their upper shafts. Their bases slope, at about forty-five degrees, and their upper sides are almost vertical. The tops of the tallest ones are flat, marking still the level of the pre-existing plain. Millions of years of water and wind have scoured the soft rock away and left these lofty survivors, which seem from a distance to stand isolated and lonesome, until you find yourself in the place they make, Tsaybegui, the "land between the rocks," surrounded by a council of giants. You know

Tsaybegui: the land between the rocks

The Stone Forest, Yunnan,
China: narrow spaces
between the rocks

you have arrived, that this is the place. There is nothing there but the sand and the rock, some scratchy desert plants, the occasional twisted cedar almost invisible at the feet of the megaliths: it is the space itself that has the power.

Another great gathering of monumental rocks is the Stone Forest in the southwestern Chinese province of Yunnan. The tangle of upright, jagged limestone rocks rests on what had been the floor of a prehistoric sea, whose surging waters scoured chasms between the harder shafts. Ages later, the hand of man has planted trees in the tiny canyons between the rocks and has fashioned stone paths and steps, and even bridges across pools, so that the human presence is a comfortable one.

The most gigantic of all these immense rocks stands alone, among red sandhills, spinifex, and mulga, in the heart of Australia's Western Desert. This monolith, which the aboriginal people of the area call Uluru, marks the center of the continent, hundreds of miles by dusty dirt road from the cities of the coast. When only the dim outlines of *Terra Australis* were known to Europeans, Jonathan Swift had located the kingdoms of Lilliput, Blefuscu, and Houyhnhnm-Land somewhere about here, and early Australian settlers imagined that this vast, unexplored region might contain some fabulous lost land—an antipodean Atlantis, perhaps, or the dominion of an Australian Prester John. But nineteenth-century exploration was to reveal (in the words of Alan Moorehead) only a "ghastly blank."

The rock of Uluru is a thousand feet high, roughly kite-shaped in plan, and about five miles in circumference at ground level. Its flanks are steep, bare, and a startlingly deep terra cotta, which shades off into a delicate pale magenta from a distance (a darker purple on the shady side) and turns fiery on the western face at sunset. Wind and water have shaped its surface into curves that ripple with the changing light like muscles and sinews under the skin. On top there are rock holes that fill with water after the infrequent summer storms, and the water then falls in brief, violent cascades down the sides to create eucalyptus-shaded ponds in the sand at the bottom. All around, but mostly just a few feet above the base, and also high up on the face that is exposed to the blast of the desert westerlies, caves have been scooped out by the wind-borne sand. The same swirling winds have ironed the surrounding desert almost perfectly flat, leaving only a bizarre collection of rock domes called the Olgas on the western horizon and a mesa called Mount Conner far to the east. That, together with the silence, is all.

The Yankunitjatjara and Pitjantjatjara tribes interpret Uluru, like other features of the landscape they have inhabited since long before Europeans knew of it, as a trace left by their mythic ancestors. It is therefore a venerated place—a desert that Borubudur made not by carving stones, but much more subtly, by simply telling tales about them. Uluru first presents itself as a fragment of nature, but as you learn these stories, it reveals itself instead as a monument, the imaginative construction of an ancient culture. Here, if you have eyes to see it, is the great temple of the Australian Atlantis.

You can learn to read, in the boulders and caves around the sunny northern perimeter, the story of the unfortunate Mala people, who had insulted the Wintalka (Mulga Seed) men by refusing an invitation to an initiation ceremony. The Wintalka medicine men fashioned Kurrpanngu, a devil dingo, who surprised the camping Mala at Uluru and drove them off into the desert. Our map shows the locations of some of the stone tableaux depicting scenes from this narrative.

1. *Taputji*, the camp of the Mala women. One of their digging sticks has been transformed into stone.

2. *Fleeing Mala.*

3. *Inintitjara*, where the sleeping Mala men were surprised by Kurrpanngu. Lunpa, the Kingfisher woman who tried to warn them, was turned into a boulder, which surveys Kurrpanngu's paw prints, visible on the face of Uluru.

4. *Cave of the Mala women.*

5. *Tjukutjapinya*, where Kurrpanngu spied on the dancing Mala women. Their clothing, turned to stone, hangs in the cave.

Among the shadows of the south face, the Kuniya (Carpet Snake) men, who had promised to attend the ceremonies of the Wintalka men, met some Lizard women and stayed with them at Mutitjulu rock hole. The Wintalka men, enraged by this slight, dispatched Liru (Poisonous Serpent) warriors to punish the Kuniya; you can read the story of the resulting

The location of Uluru

Plan of Uluru

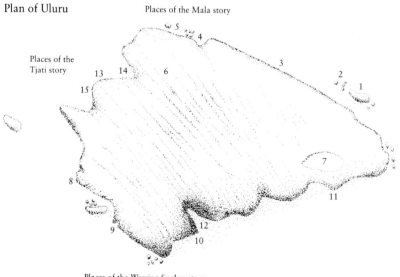

Places of the Mala story

Places of the Tjati story

Places of the Warring Snakes story

The surface of Uluru

Uluru rising from the desert floor

The muscular sides, smoothed by wind and water

The damp, green area at the base

Caves, scooped out by the wind, at the base

A chain of water holes, connected by a dry watercourse, descends the side

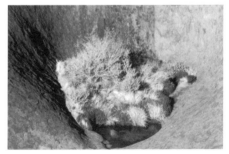

Each water hole becomes a miniature oasis garden

Ridges

Eroded figures

battle in crevices and outcroppings of rock. On top of Uluru deep gutters mark the tracks of Kuniya, and at the southeast end of these is the important Uluru rock hole—said to be inhabited still by a Kuniya who controls the flow of life-giving water to the land below. Our map locates

6. *Tracks of the Kuniya.*

7. *Uluru rock hole*, where a Kuniya dwells.

8. *Alyurungu*, where the Liru warriors left spear marks on the rock face and where the bodies of two warriors can be seen.

9. *Mita Kampantja*, where two Lizard men were burned to death. Their bodies have become boulders, and lichen on the rock face is smoke from the fire.

10. *Kurumpa*, where the Lizard men butchered an emu. The meat is visible as slabs of sandstone.

11. *Kalaiya Tjunta*, where the Lizard men buried the emu's thigh.

12. *Mutijulu rock hole*, where the Kuniya and the Liru battled. An injured Liru warrior, with severed nose, can be seen in the cliff.

At the western end of Uluru there are traces of Marsupial Moles, who sheltered in a cave, and of the frantic digging of Tjati (a little lizard), who was searching for his lost boomerang. We can see

13. *Walaritja*, where Tjati hurled his boomerang at the face of Uluru and scooped out hollows as he searched for it.

14. *Kantju*, the cave where Tjati died in despair.

15. *Itjaritjari cave*, home of the Marsupial Moles.

All this was long, long ago—in the Dreamtime.

In 1872 the explorer Ernest Giles first sighted the silhouette of Uluru on the horizon, but he had to turn his horses and camels around before reaching it. A year later another explorer, William Christie Goss, reached and scaled the monolith, and he gave it a suitable European name, Ayers Rock, after the premier of the colony of South Australia. Now there is a road from Alice Springs and a visit is easy. You can climb the western flank, cross the tracks of the Kuniya, and stand in the wind at the top. And you can suddenly understand just what D. H. Lawrence meant when he wrote, in *Kangaroo*, that the Australian bush "seemed to be hoarily waiting." "It was biding its time," Lawrence thought, "with a terrible ageless watchfulness, waiting for a far-off end, watching the myriad intruding white men."

Ryoan-ji

One of the basic impulses of artists everywhere is to reduce, to erase, to suggest more and more with less and less. The Japanese dry rock garden, where water is suggested with sand only and great mountains are indicated with a few rocks, is perhaps the ultimate ideal landscape, a garden of the mind. In it, as the fifteenth-century Zen priest Tessen Soki wrote, "appears the art of reducing thirty thousand miles to the distance of a single foot." He may have been the designer of the most celebrated of the dry gardens, the stone garden at Ryoan-ji, a monastery near Kyoto.

The summit

Great rocks on a sandy plain:
Uluru with the Olgas in the distance

Humans approach Uluru

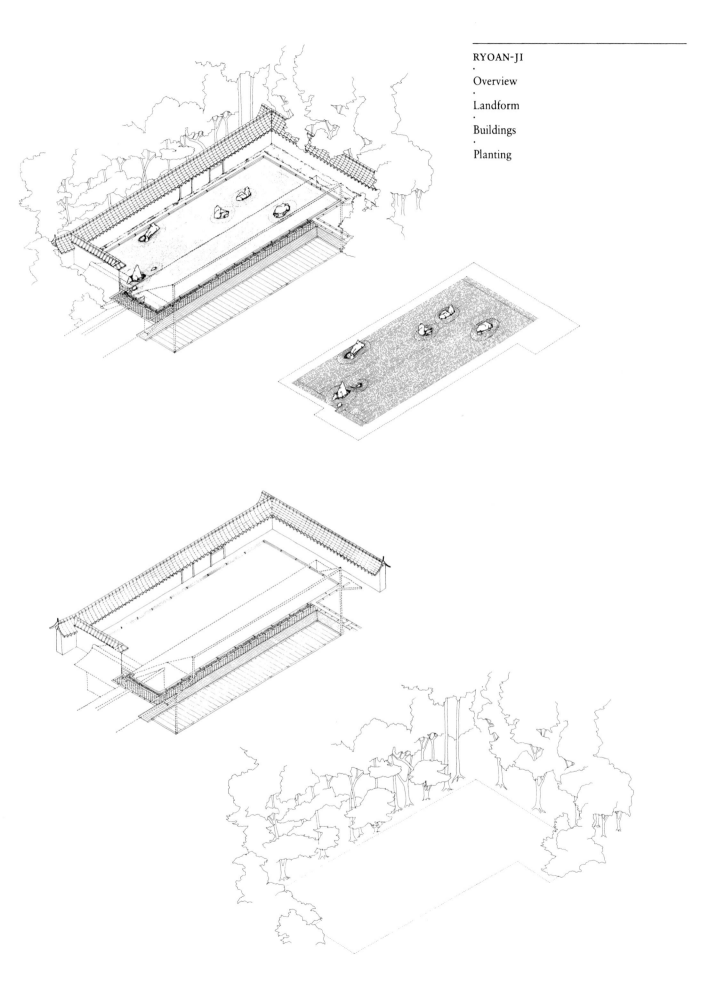

RYOAN-JI
·
Overview
·
Landform
·
Buildings
·
Planting

This garden is about the size of a tennis court, covered in carefully raked luminous quartz, and bounded on the south and west by a low wall, beyond which a lush forest shimmers. Most of the south and east sides are verandahed platforms from which to view the sand garden.

In the sand are fifteen stones, arranged in five groups. No more than fourteen of them are visible from any one place. They have, in their harmonious and satisfying spacing, aroused the wonder of many visitors, who have explained the composition as pictorial, involving a mother tiger and her cubs crossing a stream, or as a seascape, with sand as ocean and rocks as islands, or as a diagram of fixed points in the cosmos, or, in a more fully Zen manner, just as rocks. In his book *The Japanese Garden* Teiji Itoh calls it "the ideal of a garden; it is the living blueprint of the perfect garden."

Contemplating the fifteen stones from our drawing is not the same as being there, but even in the axonometric they have a mesmerizing quality. They are all so perfect, so carefully balanced within each group and the groups with each other, that they induce in the rapt observer a concentrated calm. Precisely why, we don't pretend to know. None of the cosmological interpretations is really convincing to us nonbelievers, but the power that passes understanding is undoubtedly there.

Another Japanese garden authority, Masao Hayakawa, notes that the rocks we admire so much today were not mentioned in any accounts until two centuries after the garden was designed. Before that, he believes, the main attraction of the garden was a group of magnificent cherry trees, one of them the occasion of a visit by the famous dictator Hideyoshi. The remains of his tree are still visible in the corner of the garden: this setting, it seems, has been refined by erasure, the metaphor rendered more delicate, more silent, more pure.

Ryoan-ji speaks to us of miniaturizing, of squeezing the universe into the compass of a few dozen feet, and of simplifying, eliminating, suppressing, erasing everything that doesn't contribute directly to the central idea (and no question that there is a central idea at Ryoan-ji, however it may elude our attempts to pin it down). In the late twentieth century, most of us have to miniaturize more drastically still, to get our whole world into the space we have at hand. Ryoan-ji demonstrates that out of rigorous, relentless reduction can come (as artists have always known) not a reduced and shriveled reality, but rather a vision, purified and freed, as grand as the universe itself.

Capability Brown's Parks

Desert people have often pictured Paradise as a cool oasis, with running streams and fruitful groves. Hunters have imagined well-stocked forests. The Psalms reflect the longings of a pastoral people, with their images of green fields, quiet water, and a protective shepherd. During the latter half of the eighteenth century, the landscape gardener Capability Brown realized this pastoral ideal many times over in the English countryside.

The elements of the parks that Brown made for his aristocratic patrons were simply those he found at hand: rolling hillsides with grassy slopes and stands of trees, cattle, sheep and deer, quiet water, mists and clouds. His procedure was to begin with the existing pattern of these elements, that is, with the "capabilities" of the site, then to "improve" it to more nearly match his conception of natural beauty—Whiggishly confident in the possibility of progress toward perfection by means of incremental reforms and adjustments.

Brown was a practical man, not much given to theoretical analysis, but well-known definitions of "beauty" provided by two of his contemporaries illuminate his intentions. The philosopher Edmund Burke, in his *Philosophical Enquiry into the Origin of Our Ideas of the Sublime and Beautiful,* suggested that beauty consists in smallness, smoothness, regularity, gradual variation, delicacy, and harmony, and he illustrated the notion by reminding his readers of "the sort of sense they have had of being swiftly drawn in an easy coach on a smooth turf, with gradual ascents and declivities. This," he said, "will give a better idea of the beautiful than almost anything else." The painter William Hogarth, in his *Analysis of Beauty,* advocated use of the sinuous "line of beauty." This is a gracefully inflected curve, not the tight, two-dimensional wriggle of the rococo, but a smooth, relaxed, three-dimensional serpentine. Hogarth saw it in the beauties of the human form, and of Chippendale furniture. We find it everywhere in the lines of Brown's compositions.

A typical Brown landscape is an extensive park in which is set a great country house. Sweeping lawns surround the house and are sometimes carried right up to its walls. This first "improvement" was often accomplished by destroying older (usually formal) gardens adjacent to the house.

The "line of beauty," as illustrated in Hogarth's *Analysis of Beauty*

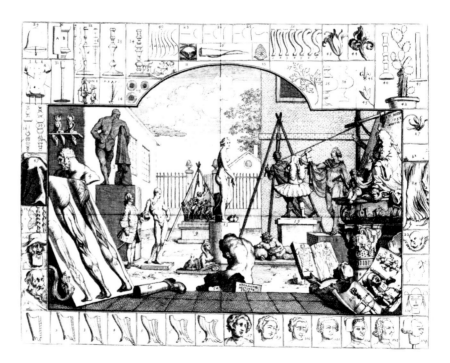

Lines of beauty in Capability Brown's
landscape plan for Bowood, Wiltshire

Capability Brown's landscape plan
for Petworth, Surrey

Critics did not always approve; Payne Knight later complained of the "improver's desolating hand," which left the house

'Midst shaven lawns that far around it creep
In one eternal undulating sweep.

To protect the lawns from the sheep and cows that inhabited the park, while preserving the visual continuity of the foreground with the middle distance, Brown often employed the ha-ha. This device became so characteristic of Brown's style that later commentators were, erroneously, to credit him with its invention.

Usually the lawns slope down to the shores of a broad river or lake, so that the water forms a middle-ground element when viewed either from the house out to the park or from the park back to the house. The existing landform and drainage pattern determined if a body of water could be created, but its character arose from Brown's ideals of natural beauty.

The first of these was that the water should have a noble scale in relation to the house and the surrounding landscape. Usually this meant that dams had to be employed. But all evidence of such artifice was to be concealed; dams were to be disguised, and artificial rivers were to disappear naturally into the distance. This effect might be accomplished by use of hills and planting to hide the ends or by such devices as sham bridges concealing dams. The banks were to take the sinuous form of the line of beauty and were to be kept relatively clear of bushes and trees.

At Bowood, in Wiltshire, for example, Brown made a dam at the confluence of two streams to produce a Y-shaped sheet of water. The dam is concealed in a belt of trees, which forms a backdrop to the water view from the house. It creates the surprise of a cascade in the trees, to be discovered by a walker circling the lake. Set against the trees, and forming the focus for views from the house and its lawns, is a Doric temple. This catches the evening light and casts a brilliant white reflection into the still water.

At Petworth, in Sussex, Brown's lake exploits capabilities of a very different stamp. Here the water is set in a shallow concavity of gently sloping grassland. The shores are mostly bare of trees, so that a serpentine line is clearly defined where turf meets water. Sightlines are established by surrounding rolling hills, together with strategically placed clumps and belts of trees, so that the water is revealed in fragmentary glimpses. It reflects open sky and echoes with the cries of Canadian geese.

Beyond a foreground of lawns and a middle ground of water, Brown sought ways to make a background of undulating grassy hills, interspersed with trees, seem to stretch indefinitely into the distance. To shape this scene into "gradual ascents and declivities," he could not employ large-scale earth movement as we might today (although he did fill ditches). Instead, he made masterly use of trees to modify contours: accentuating rises by planting trees along their crests, smoothing out depressions by filling them with vegetation, and masking out undesirable parts of the scene. We can still see this particularly clearly at Petworth, where the pattern of trees clothes the earth like a figure-flattering garment.

Brown's relation of planting patterns and
buildings to landform

A belt of trees sweeps over a crest

Clumps of trees

Trees dotted on a hillside

Clumping and dotting combined

The grazing line

*A Doric temple, set against foliage and
reflected in the lake, at Bowood*

*A sham gothic ruin by Sanderson Miller
enlivens the belt of trees surrounding
Wimpole, near Cambridge*

Petworth: Tillington Church in the Distance,
by J. M. W. Turner

In the disposition of trees, Brown followed principles that became known as *belting*, *clumping*, and *dotting*. Belts are sinuous ribbons of trees, winding across the contours of the landscape. Clumps are tightly planted, roughly circular stands of trees, sharply distinguished from the surrounding grassland. Dotting entails the scattering of individual trees, or small clusters of trees, across lawn or grassland. Thomas Love Peacock was to poke fun at this in *Headlong Hall,* where his character Sir Patrick O'Prism (an advocate of the picturesque taste) unkindly remarks to a follower of Brown:

Your system of levelling, and trimming, and clipping, and docking, and clumping, and polishing, and cropping and shaving, destroys all the beautiful intricacies of natural luxuriance, and all the graduated harmonies of light and shade, melting into one another, as you see on that rock over yonder. I never saw one of your improved places, as you call them, and which are nothing but big bowling-greens, like sheets of greenpaper, with a parcel of round clumps scattered over them like so many spots of ink, flicked at random out of a pen, and a solitary animal here and there looking as if it were lost, that I did not think it was for all the world like Hounslow Heath, thinly sprinkled over with bushes and highwaymen.

Not only trees, but also animals populate the hillsides. At Petworth, Longleat, or many of the other Brown parks that remain, we can still see long lines of deer and cattle winding between the trees and sheep dotting the hillsides. They give scale to the scene, so that the viewer can easily comprehend the sizes of the trees and the depth of recession of the vista. By their grazing, too, the sheep and cows maintain the smooth surface of the grass and the undersides of trees at a browsing line parallel to the ground.

The boundaries of the park usually are formed by belts of trees, serpentined and broken by clumps so that they appear to be natural. We can see this device clearly in the plans for Bowood and for Wimpole near Cambridge. Where appropriate, breaks were made in the belts to call a view of surrounding countryside into the park. Where a belt seemed too feature-

Blenheim

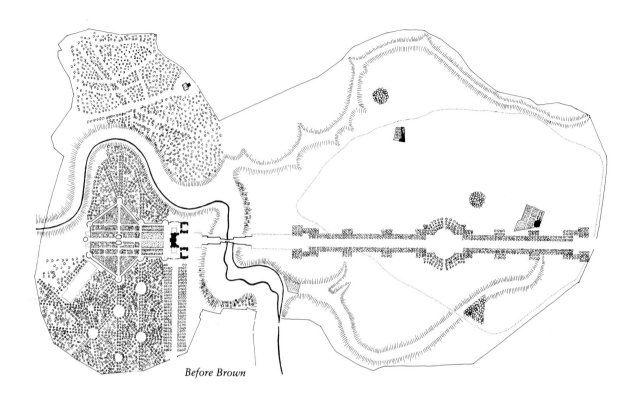

Before Brown

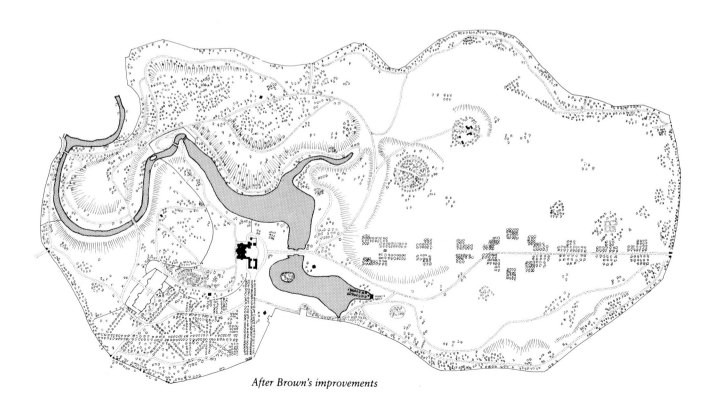

After Brown's improvements

less, it might be relieved by an architectural element placed for pictorial effect, such as the temple at Bowood or Sanderson Miller's sham gothic ruin at Wimpole. Overhead, giving closure to the scene, is the cloudy English sky, its undulating masses of clouds almost a reflection of the landscape forms beneath, casting their shadows down onto the hillsides.

Brown built dozens of great parks, but by far the grandest is at Blenheim, in Oxfordshire. Our drawings show it before and after Brown's improvements.

The bridge and lake at Blenheim

At Blenheim Brown found what must have seemed an intolerable dissonance of scale between the huge stone mass of the famous palace by Sir John Vanbrugh and the modest river Glyme. Furthermore, an axis struck out across the river from the front of the palace, and this was marked by an immense stone bridge and causeway, also by Vanbrugh. Brown altered the drainage pattern of the Glyme valley and built a dam with a grand cascade at a spot to the south of the palace and well concealed from it. This formed a broad, irregular lake, of satisfactory nobility, on the valley floor and also raised the water level under the arches of the bridges so that they are reflected in the tranquil water. He recomposed the background, beyond the lake, into a scene of clumps and belts and misty distances, with flocks of sheep quietly grazing beneath the trees.

Brown's ideal landscapes are not as breathtakingly compressed as that of Ryoan-ji, nor is there such rigorous austerity, but the impulse to reduce to essentials, to clarify relationships and edit out blemishes and imperfections, is the same. It has much in common with the compulsion of his contemporary Sir Joshua Reynolds to improve on the accidents of countenance in his portrait subjects according to a classical vision of nobility. Brown did not seek the uncanny perfection of the Domain of Arnheim, with its suggestions of phantasmal care and interest, but simply tried to eliminate nature's accidental flaws, thereby allowing an immanent beauty to emerge. His masses of trees on the undulating grassy surface of England's green and pleasant land show us the essence of this landscape as understood in eighteenth-century Whiggish, Burkean terms, just as Ryoan-ji's rocks on a gravel plane reveal a Zen conception of the essence of *shan shui*.

Isola Bella

For centuries travelers and writers have agreed that one of the magic places on earth is the lake country of northern Italy. At the very heart of the magic land, in Lake Maggiore, are two islands that have belonged, since they were bare jagged pinnacles rising out of the water, to the Counts of Borromeo. During the Renaissance they planted the largest, Isola Madre, which has gradually come to be a collection, especially favored by the gentle climate of the lakes, of an immense variety of exotic plants. In 1632 Count Carlo III transferred his attention to the remaining rocky outcrop, opposite Stresa, and built a little pleasure casino there. His son, Count Vitaliano IV, completed the work, leveling rocks, bringing soil from the mainland, making what can't escape the label fairyland—half

ISOLA BELLA

Overview

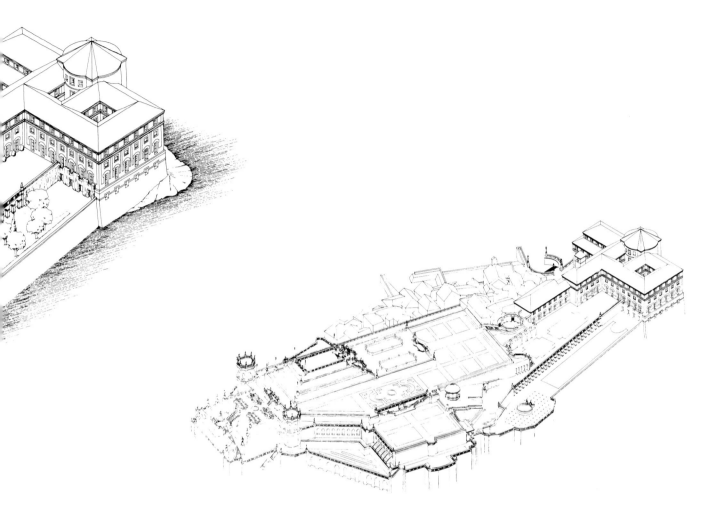

Landform, buildings, and water

Planting

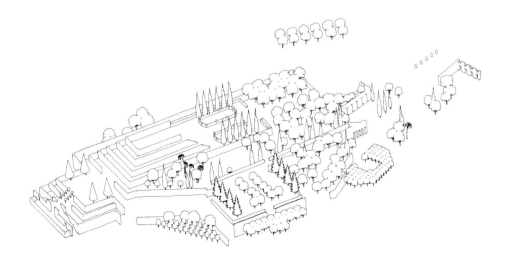

island, half magic-flowered barque. Vitaliano named it after his mother, Isola Isabella, which became before long, for reasons of sound and sense, Isola Bella.

Between 1632 and 1671 a corps of architects and sculptors created the shapes. Castelli and Crivelli raised the terraces, on which Carlo Fontana and a group of Milanese architects built the palace and garden pavilions. The water works, much underdone, were the work of Mora of Rome; the ornamental sculpture resulted from the unbridled zeal of Vismara. The palace at one end of the island is big but mostly undistinguished, and it is difficult to discern any relation between it and the garden, except for a deft courtyard at the end of a long wing heading south, which manages to twist the axis of the building into the axis of the garden (no spiritual overtones in this axis, even though one of the Carlo Borromeos is a saint).

More important than any detail, the hanging gardens (a magic idea since Nebuchadnezzar) rise on ten artificial terraces, the lowest arcaded out past the island. Each terrace, with a wall at the back and a crowd of statues and obelisks and white peacocks, is softened with plantations of roses, jasmine, and camellias and with espaliered oranges and lemons. Toward the top the plants thin out, marble figures gather, and the ascent culminates in a truly awful water theater. On the front edge, which faces across the lake to the misty mountains on the shore, is a marble railing. Statues stand along the top of the railing, and belvederes project forward like nautical flying bridges, so that almost everywhere in the garden you think you are on the deck of an enchanted ship, where the rigging and even the decking underfoot have miraculously turned to greenery and flowers. The image of the fairy galleon is always there. It is all strongly and thrillingly artificial, not always beautiful, not ever real.

Edith Wharton, in *Italian Villas and Their Gardens*, talks about that quality of unreality:

The Isola Bella stills seems to many too complete a negation of nature; nor can it appear otherwise to those who judge of it only from pictures and photographs, who have not seen it in its environment. For the landscape surrounding the Borromean Islands has precisely that quality of artificiality, of exquisitely skilful arrangement and manipulation, which seems to justify, in the garden-architect, almost any excess of the fancy. The Roman landscape, grandiose and ample, seems an unaltered part of nature; so do the subtly modelled hills and valleys of central Italy: all these scenes have the deficiencies, the repetitions, the meannesses and profusions, with which nature grows her great masses on the canvas of the world; but the lake scenery appears to have been designed by a lingering and fastidious hand, bent on eliminating every crudeness and harshness, and on blending all natural forms, from the bare mountain-peak to the melting curve of the shore, in one harmony of ever-varying and ever-beautiful lines.

There is, she continues,

an almost forced gaiety about the landscape of the lakes, a fixed smile of perennial loveliness. And it is as a complement to this attitude that the Borromean gardens justify themselves. Are they real? No; but neither is

A crowd of marble figures gathers

the landscape about them. Are they like any other gardens on earth? No; but neither are the mountains and shores about them like earthly shores and mountains. They are Armida's gardens anchored in a lake of dreams.

This magic island in a mythic sea works its metaphoric sorcery in precisely the opposite way to Ryoan-ji or a Capability Brown park, which are about stripping back to the essence of things—the universe in fifteen bare rocks or in a few trees and clouds. This beflowered galleon, this fantasy-freighted ferry, is a paean to piling it on, layering image onto image over some rocks jutting out of Lake Maggiore to make an altogether improbable garden overladen with frenzied sculptural farragos—a stone vessel of visions too preposterously top-heavy to be sailed by any but Peter Pan's crew, yet held too far aloft on the wings of wonder to be brought down by the likes of us.

For the poignancy of immoderate fantasy has its own power, at the scale of castles, like that of King Ludwig II of Bavaria at Neuschwanstein or his Wagnerian grotto at Linderhof; or at the scale of a successful hostelry like Alex and Phyllis Madonna's Madonna Inn in San Luis Obispo, California, a giant confection of boulders and pink velvet; or at the far humbler scale of reinforcing rods and broken crockery, which Simon Rodia fashioned into his Watts Towers near Los Angeles. All are doxologies praising the power of single-mindedness, elaborated by infinities of energy. And all are able to give us, as well as their creators, enormous pleasure. They have the advantage, too, that they are hard to fake: we can all appreciate fantasies, even ones we cannot easily share, as visible concentrations of human energy. The purified works, like Ryoan-ji, are more susceptible to fakery, in the manner of "The Emperor's New Clothes"; some erasure surely is vandalism, not art at all. It's harder to miss with enthusiastic towers of broken plates, or indeed fairy galleons. Then, as Edith Wharton pointed out, there is the issue of appropriateness: if the landscape around, itself fantastic, unnaturally perfect, demands a fantasy, then of course hurrah!

Bali

There are on the planet very few tiny, clearly ordered, closed worlds that are settings for the customs and rituals of unique cultures. The Indonesian island of Bali, with its idiosyncratic and deeply mystical local version of Hinduism, is one of them.

Today jumbo jets fly into the modern capital of Denpasar, but the traditional approach to Bali has always been from Java. You can begin the journey at Surabaja, the enormous, seedy, port city where Brecht set the ballad of the cold-hearted Surabaja Johnny, who just puffed his sailor's pipe as he abandoned his girl on the waterfront. Take a bus from the station by the municipal zoo (with its baleful Komodo dragons), and travel east through coastal coffee plantations to the sleepy village of Banuwangi. From here you ferry across a short stretch of water, as invading Javanese princes once did, to Gilimanuk in Bali. The bus then continues east along the southern coast of Bali to Denpasar.

A numinous setting: a demon emerges from the Balinese earth at Goa Gajah

The topography of Bali

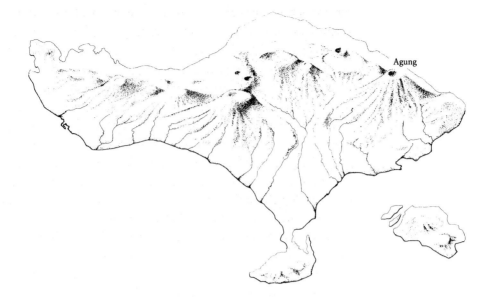

The orientation system

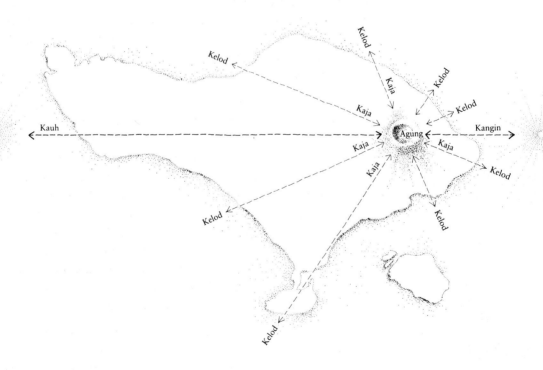

The western half of Bali is a disappointment; there is little but swampy waste filled with mangroves, crocodiles, and malarial mosquitoes. But a transformation takes place as you move east, counter to the arc of the equatorial sun. A range of steep volcanic peaks, forming an east-west backbone to the island, comes into view. The easternmost and highest peak is the smoking cone of Gunung Agung, rising well over ten thousand feet. Deep ravines cut southward, with streams rushing down from the mountains to the sea. The parallel fingers of land between them are elaborately carved into terraces, filled with the brilliant pale green of rice plants. Ravines and uncultivated slopes are overgrown with dark jungle. Roads and paths fit snugly into the rhythmic folds of the land. Some follow contours east-west, and others parallel ravines, so that a rough spiderweb pattern results. Set into the hillsides, among the rice fields, are small villages. On the lower slopes and coastal plains are more substantial market and administrative centers: Tabanan, Denpasar, Gianyar, Klungkung, and Amlapura. To the south the rocky Bukit Peninsula thrusts out into the sea like the prow of a ship, dividing the surf. Elsewhere along the coast are lazy beaches, fringed with coconut and banana trees.

This is an actively volcanic place. Wisps of smoke from craters, beaches of perfectly clean, black volcanic sand, statues carved out of soft tuff, and shrines that are still used though almost buried by ash and lava, are all reminders of the forces beneath the earth. The volcanoes are both creators and destroyers. They have created the mountains, which are the source of water, and the rich volcanic soil, on both of which rice growing depends. But they can suddenly cover fields and habitations with barren layers of dust and stone.

There are places of quiet, innocent, sunlit beauty here. In the early morning you can walk through still rice fields, with the mist rising from the ground and the mountains a gentle blue in the distance. And there are haunted and sinister places, too. At Goa Gajah a pop-eyed toothy demon forces his way out of the living rock, his jaw agape to form the entrance to a cave. Near Kusamba there is a bat-cave temple (Pura Goa Lawah), marked even on a bright afternoon by a dense swarm of circling, chirping bats, where spattered priests and mangy dogs sit desolately among the droppings. In groves and temple courtyards you can be ambushed by malicious troupes of angrily chattering monkeys. On an island in a crater lake high in the mountains there is an unfriendly village that greets you with the dead laid out on platforms to dry in the sun.

If you approach a Balinese village at dawn, you will often meet children herding flocks of ducks out to spend the day in the rice fields. When they reach a chosen spot, the children drive a long bamboo pole into the ground and place a box of feed at its base. This landmark forms the center of the ducks' world; they cluster around it all day until a child comes at evening to uproot it and drive them back to the village.

The cone of Gunung Agung, at the center of the island, has the same significance in the lives of the people. It is visible from almost everywhere, when the clouds part, and it is understood as the source of life, the cosmic axis, and the abode of the gods. Around it, by the traditions of Balinese reli-

Ducks cluster around a bamboo pole

Gunung Agung

gion, there is a magical flow of opposing powers. Powers of fertility and life (called *kaja*) flow downstream from their source in the mountains, while powers of danger, illness, and death (called *kelod*) originate in the sea and surge upstream. Cutting across this flow is a second axis, set up by the direction of sunrise, *kangin*, which is associated with *kaja*, and the direction of sunset, *kauh*, which is associated with *kelod*. Natural cycles of day and night, growth and decay, birth and death are all understood in terms of the opposition and interaction of *kaja* and *kelod*. Life takes place in a world centered on Gunung Agung, bounded by the hostile sea, and ordered by the two powers.

So the mountain, sea, and sun set up fields of force, like the poles of magnets, and everything within is oriented like iron filings. High places and headwaters are pure and safe from the forces of decay and death. Here offerings are made, on elevated altars, to the heavenly forces of fertility and life. Even the heads of beds are pointed toward Gunung Agung, or toward the rising sun, and you try to stand on the uphill side if you want to get the better of a negotiation. Conversely, graveyards and crossroads are impure and dangerous, and here offerings to the netherworldly forces are placed upon the ground.

A *subak* at Bukit Batu: water flows from a source marked by a banyan tree and is distributed to the rice terraces

The land between the mountains and the sea is subdivided into an intricate pattern of descending terrace systems. These systems are developed and operated by cooperative societies, called *subaks*. Usually the land of a *subak* occupies a ridge or a valley. At its head is a dam across one of the many streams flowing down from the mountains to the sea. From here, water is divided and distributed to the terraces. Each terrace is bounded by an earth-walled enclosure, through breaches in which the water flows along the axis from *kaja* to *kelod* and within which earth, water, and sun come together in the rice's cycle of growth, fruition, and decay.

A Balinese house encloses cycles of human life within its mud (or occasionally brick) walls. These form a courtyard and are breached by a gate, which is arranged so that entry is in the propitious direction. Much of daily life takes place in the open air; small pavilions (often open-sided) are scattered about the courtyard for storage, for sleeping, and for shelter from the tropical rain, and there are trees for shade. The locations of pavilions for different uses are determined by the orientation system, and the uphill corner, nearest to the rising sun, is reserved for ancestor shrines.

The source of water is celebrated at a sacred spring (Tirta Empul)

Deities take up residence in temples (of which there are a great many in Bali), so these are planned much like houses. A temple usually consists of three rectangular, brick-walled enclosures, like a sequence of rice terraces stepping up the hillside, making a progression from profane to sacred. The gates into each enclosure are elaborated into tall towers encrusted with decorative carving, protected by bug-eyed, tongue-popping, fangs-bared guardian figures. One type of gate arches over its opening, while the other type, the "split-gate," looks like a Hindu *candi* but is divided down the center and ripped apart—an astonishingly forceful dramatization of the act of penetrating a boundary. Within the enclosures are pavilions for storage and performance and others that serve as houses and thrones for the deities.

Layouts of Balinese houses, based on
a subdivision of the compound into
nine zones

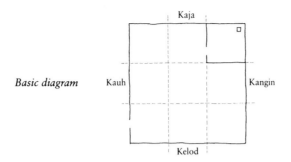

Basic diagram

Kaja

Kauh

Kangin

Kelod

A jero *(modest house)*

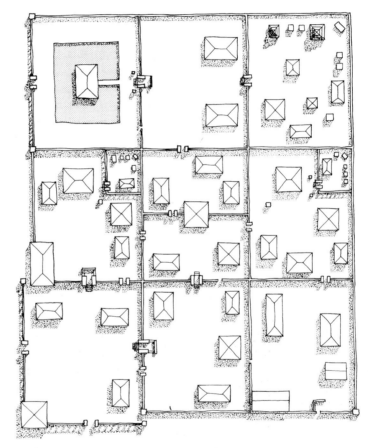

A puri *(large house)*

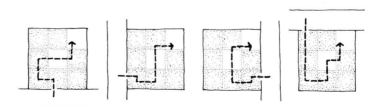

*Four orientations of a house, with
resulting circulation patterns*

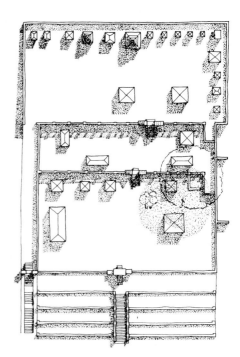

Plan of the Pura Kehen temple, Bangli

Boundaries and their penetration:
Balinese walls and gates

Simple gateway in the mud
wall of a house compound
(Ubud)

Arched gate (Pura Kehen,
Bangli)

Split gate (Gelgel)

Gate in the North Bali style (Sangsit)

Guardian figure (Bangli)

74 · The Place of the Past

Temple plans are inflected in subtle ways to respond to the orientation system. Successive gates are offset slightly to prevent the direct flow through of the netherworldly forces. There are asymmetries in the placing of pavilions and thrones for the deities; usually these form an elbow lining the uphill (in south Bali, northern) and sunrise (eastern) sides of the innermost courtyard, with the most important (often a lotus throne of Shiva) in the northeast corner. Just as the architect of a mosque must solve the problem of how to reconcile an orientation to Mecca with the orientation of a street entrance, the architect of a temple must sometimes organize the plan so as to bring visitors in through a gate opening conveniently to the street, then to turn their steps in the direction of Gunung Agung.

A village is a fabric of house and temple compounds integrated by a simple circulation system, just as the land of a *subak* is a fabric of terraces tied together by a water distribution system. Though not all villages conform to it in every respect, there is a well-defined traditional layout. The main street runs north-south, along the mountain-sea axis, and there is a secondary cross street paralleling the sunrise-sunset axis. Their intersection is the center of the village, and the place of the market, and it is often marked by a huge, ancient banyan tree. There are three essential temples. The *pura puseh,* devoted to the heavenly, creative powers, is sited at the uphill end of the main street. The *pura desa* (or *pura balé agung*), an assembly hall for meetings and ceremonial meals, is located near the center.

Traditional Balinese village layout

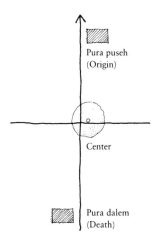

Diagram

A typical example (Tihingan)

Market under the banyan tree at the center of a village (Blankiuh)

Ritual movement through a Balinese village

Procession to a temple festival (Batakaru)

Cremation vessel (Blahbatu)

Cremation procession (Peliatan)

Cremation (Peliatan)

Tripartite vertical division of space

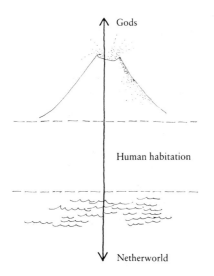

Gods

Human habitation

Netherworld

Balinese cosmological diagram

A meeting hall (Tenganan)

And the *pura dalem,* located at the downhill, seaward end of the main street, is devoted to the powers of death and decay. Adjacent to it is the graveyard. Opening onto the two streets, and sometimes onto a secondary system of back lanes, are the gates of the walled family compounds. So the streets, temples, and central banyan tree diagram the axes, poles, and center of the orientation system, just as the streams, the arc of the sun, the vertical mass of Gunung Agung, and the sea do so on a larger scale.

The streets of the village are a stage for ritual movement. On the days of religious festivals (and these are innumerable), offerings are prepared then carried, in happy, noisy procession, to the accompaniment of a *gamelan* orchestra, through decorated streets to the temple. When the dead are to be cremated, the brightly colored, elaborately decorated cremation vessels are rushed downhill by a shouting, twisting, zigzagging crowd (so that the potentially dangerous souls of the uncremated dead will lose their connections to the axes and become disoriented) to a site adjacent to the *pura dalem,* where great fires are lit.

The villages and rice terraces are generally clustered densely together on the sloping plain of southern Bali, with the revered peaks of the mountains above and the shunned and feared ocean below. This vertical division of space is given further significance by Balinese cosmological tradition, according to which Bali is a rock upon the back of a huge turtle swimming in the ocean, and surmounted by the abode of Shiva. The scheme is explicitly depicted in the Shiva thrones of temples, which rest upon a turtle base and are topped by an empty chair for Shiva's reception. The various forms of pavilions found in houses and temples reflect this pattern as well. There is a base, raising one above the dangers of the ground, then the zone of human habitation, and finally the peak of the roof, recalling the mountains.

Ulu Danu: a mountain on an island within a mountain on an island

One special type of pavilion, found in the more important temples, is called a *meru,* explicitly identifying it with the central, sacred Mount Meru of Hindu tradition. These are tall, narrow, multiroofed towers, with the number of roofs signifying degree of importance. At the ethereally beautiful lake temple of Ulu Danu, each *meru* stands at the center of its own tiny walled island, a miniature of Gunung Agung surrounded by a miniature of Bali itself.

The three themes of the orienting axes passing through a center, the enclosing boundary, with a guarded gate, and the location of human habitation between the netherworld and the heavens are worked out in yet another way—in the vast system of temples that covers the whole island. This begins at the seashore, which is understood as the boundary between the place of habitation and a dangerous outer world. The shore is a place for purification ceremonies and propitiation of netherworldly forces. And at Serangan, Ulu Watu, and Tanah Lot it is protected by spectacularly sited sea temples. Then, within the heartland of Bali, there is a hierarchy of temples, corresponding to a hierarchy of worship groups. There are family temples, village temples, district temples, and finally the great mother temple of Besakih. This is located high upon the slopes of Gunung Agung.

A sea temple guards the boundary of the island at Tanah Lot

Plan of Besakih temple

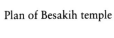

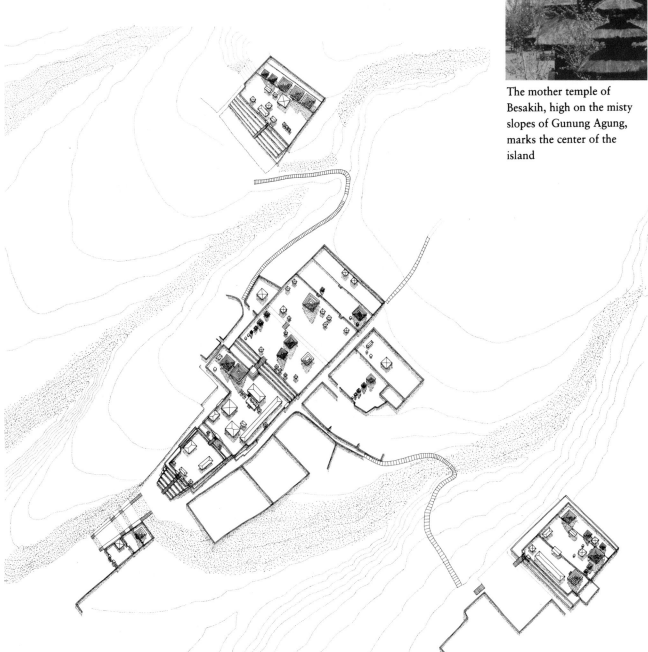

The mother temple of Besakih, high on the misty slopes of Gunung Agung, marks the center of the island

Its terraces and somber black-thatched *merus* step up into the mists, floating above the human world and pointing to the sky. Pilgrims come, ascending from the sea, to this holiest of places at the center of their world.

In Bali, art and nature reflect each other, as in parallel mirrors. Elementary themes are abstracted from the natural landscape, invested with meaning, and replicated in houses and temples and villages. They then rebound to become ways of comprehending and guides to inhabiting the bounded, mountain-centered world itself. We, who do not live in a traditional, closed society on a beautiful tropical island, cannot have a landscape that offers such clarity, certainty, and all-encompassing unity. But we can gather our resources (however meager) onto a site (however small) to construct a clarified fragment, a vision of an ordered world, in a garden.

COLLECTIONS

If Arizona's Monument Valley becomes for us a natural metaphor, somehow managing to sum up complexities in a pithy image, then California's Death Valley speaks to our imaginations metonymically, by collecting together in one place an astonishing array of geological freaks and wonders that evoke their ancient origins in processes of water and wind and sun, landslide and earthquake and volcanic explosion. The human impulse to collect (more purposeful, less accidental) is indulged at a scale from boys' collections of cards with athletes' faces on them to collections of Georgian silver, cactus, or fuchsias, to the gardens of mighty emperors who gathered remembrances of the far-flung regions of their realms.

A collection generates a special kind of meaning through the way in which its spatial ordering suggests similarities, connections, and contrasts among the pieces. It might thus become an instrument of awe at the dazzling diversity of the world—as in the wonder cabinets of Renaissance princes, the overflowing Pitt-Rivers Museum at Oxford, or Sir John Soane's heteromorphic house. In the garden of Linnaeus the formation of a collection became a way of mastering that diversity through systematic classification, and in gardens made by powerful rulers (Hadrian, Ch'ien Lung, and the Dowager Empress, for example) the accumulation of spoils and souvenirs at a single place could serve as reminder of the long reach of imperial power. But perhaps the most touching of the garden collections that we shall examine are autobiographies—records of the moments of individual lives.

Death Valley

Death Valley, in California, really isn't so very different from many other arid depressions in California, Nevada, Arizona, and Utah, but it inevitably became a lot more famous after it got its dramatic name from a group of 49'ers who tried to take a short cut through it, then couldn't get their wagons out. (None of them actually died, but they did find it a particularly desolate and frustrating place.) *Death Valley Days,* a popular radio show of the thirties and then television show of the fifties, helped its reputation too.

Death Valley landscape

Mountains

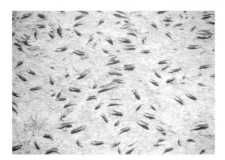

Water

Death Valley's forty-mile salt pan
surrounded by mountains

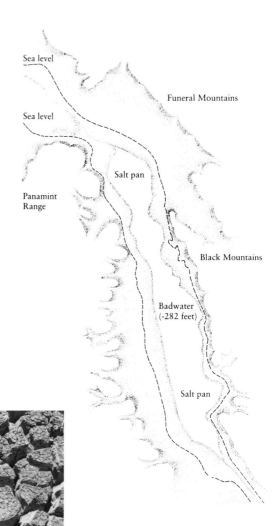

Sea level

Sea level

Funeral Mountains

Salt pan

Panamint
Range

Black Mountains

Badwater
(-282 feet)

Salt pan

Death Valley details

Sand

Stones

Clay

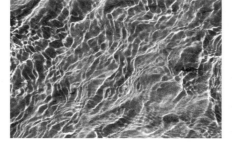

Water

Salt

Most importantly, it contains a magic center—like Uluru at the heart of Australia and Gunung Agung at the spiritual focus of Bali. This is *Badwater*, the lowest (282 feet below sea level) and hottest (134 degrees recorded) point in the United States, the navel of the Wild West. Badwater is surrounded by a salt pan that is about five miles across at its widest and that runs roughly north-south for about forty miles. The white plain of salt is lassoed by the sea-level contour and corralled between the *Panamint Range* to the west, the *Black Mountains* to the east, and the *Funeral Mountains* to the north. The air is clear, the light is vivid: morning sun leaves the valley floor in shadow and picks out the snowy peaks of the Panamints, while evening finds the Panamints purple—sharply contrasting with the orange glow of the opposite slopes. Entry to this anti-Shangri-la is through just a few narrow passes over the surrounding mountains.

Scattered around the salt pan are spots and features that have been picked out and given names, with the result that we can constitute Death Valley in our imaginations not simply as a stretch of desolation but as a collection of places and evocations. There are ghost towns and abandoned mines: Ballarat (named after the fabulous Australian goldfield), Chloride City, Greenwater, Panamint City, Rhyolite, and Skidoo. Leadfield was the site of a famous swindle: a promoter salted the diggings with lead ore and titillated investors with pictures of ships steaming up the (usually dry) Amargosa River to load it. There are spots recalling colorful personalities: Death Valley Scotty, Peter Aguereberry, and Seldom Seen Slim. At a lonely roadside there is a grave inscribed "Here lies Shorty Harris, a single-blanket jackass prospector." There are scenes of earth and air (Zabriskie Point, Dante's View) and of fire and water (Furnace Creek, Stovepipe Wells). And there are scenes of hoked-up dreadfulness: Dry Bone Canyon, the Funeral Mountains, and the Devil's Golf Course.

Death Valley does not work on our imaginations in the same way as Monument Valley or Stone Forest or Uluru: there is no sudden sense of having arrived, of everything falling perfectly and inevitably into place. Its scenes, instead, gradually arrange themselves into a unity in the mind—a process of montage, in the sense illustrated by Eisenstein's films and discussed by him in *Film Sense*. Eisenstein wrote, "The image of a scene, a sequence, of a whole creation, exists not as something fixed and ready-made. It has to arise, to unfold before the senses of the spectator." He added:

The strength of montage resides in this, that it includes in the creative process the emotions and mind of the spectator. . . . In fact, every spectator, in correspondence with his individuality, and in his own way and out of his own experience—out of the wonder of his fantasy, out of the warp and weft of his associations, all conditioned by the premises of his character, habits, and social appurtenances, creates an image.

In the same way, from the scenes of sand and stones and desolation, from the smell of creosote bushes and of wildflowers in spring, from the heat reflected off the surface of the salt, from the sound of the wind among the peaks, from the ghost towns and graves and mining relics, and not least from the names that have been given to things, assembled in our memories, each one of us creates a flickering image of adventure.

Plants

The Roman emperor Hadrian's domain included just about all the world known to him, and he was, it appears, altogether up to the task of ruling it, which he managed in ways that included extensive travel to the far reaches of his realm. His qualities have fascinated historians, as they have noted a Jeffersonian encyclopedic intelligence mixed up with a maudlin memorialization of his favorite, Antinous, who died young. He built an enormous villa, "the graveyard of his travels" (as Marguerite Yourcenar put it) in a hot, dry, and unpreposessing fold in the hills at Tivoli. The location is just a little too low to catch a view of Rome a few miles away across the campagna. The complex architectural geometries of circles and squares must have been startlingly new, though the images, according to Hadrian's biographer Spartianus (a Latin chronicler of a later century), were meant to be familiar—a collection of the places that he had come to know.

"There never was a prince," wrote Spartianus, "who so rapidly visited so many different countries," and after he had given up his travels, he gathered mementoes of them around him. He had the villa inscribed with the names of the most celebrated places he had visited: the Lyceum and the Academy, the Prytaneum, the Canopus, the Poekile, and the Vale of Tempe. Some parts were probably meant as more literal representations (although historians differ on this), and, according to Spartianus, "in order that nothing might be wanting, it occurred to him to make a reproduction of Hell there."

Most of the site is ruinous now, though a few pieces have lately been restored, so it is difficult to identify with much accuracy the distant sites that the parts of the villa may have represented. The clearest, probably, is the

Plan of Hadrian's Villa at Tivoli

1. Canopus
2. Maritime Theater
3. Athenian Poekile
4. Piazza d'Oro
5. Stadium
6. Baths
7. Academy

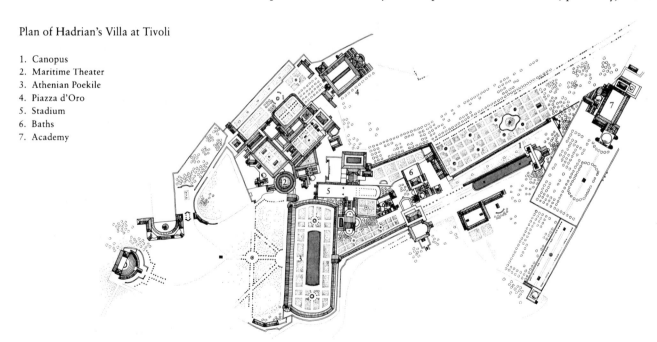

The Canopus

The Maritime Theater

Canopus (identified by the inscription *Delicioe Canopi*), a long pool that dives into a vast domed grotto in the side of the hill. It is meant to recall a place in Egypt visited by Hadrian, where a stirring funerary procession unfolded on still waters at night, in boats ablaze with festival lanterns. At Tivoli the architecture and the sculpture are classical Roman, with no attempt to make them Egyptian: the water, the boats, the lights, the underground terminus of the course were apparently enough to evoke the desired Egyptian memories and the connections with death—specifically Antinous's and Hadrian's own—are part of a recurring theme.

A particularly vivid place is a round island, today called, puzzlingly, the *Maritime Theater*. The island contains ruins of a little palace with apses of varying shapes facing four directions, centered in a courtyard with a fountain. Around the island is a fairly narrow ring of water, and around *that* is another, arcaded ring of space. The ring of water at once affords a full view of the island palace to someone in the outer ring (hence, presumably the Maritime Theater appellation) and achieves for the island a substantial psychic distance from the shore (causing Eleanor Clark, in the beautiful book *Rome and a Villa,* to suppose that the little round palace, with its drawbridge up, was a delicious retreat for Hadrian and Antinous). Especially now, with most of the rest of the villa in ruins, the island (though ruined too) is the quintessential magic island, the most compelling place in Tivoli.

In another part of the grounds, the *Athenian Poekile* (famous for its wall paintings of heroic deeds) is reincarnated as a long, straight wall running east-west, so that one side is in the shade, one side is sunny. Like a medieval cloister it provided a place to walk and perhaps to think. On one side of the wall is a wide field, eerily flat on this hilly site, held aloft on a vast beehive of stone compartments built to house soldiers or slaves.

The *Vale of Tempe* is hard to find. The nineteenth-century French scholar Gaston Boissier thought that it must have been in a small depression between the villa and the hills on which Tivoli rises, although there is little about it to suggest Olympus or Pelion or Ossa or the famous thick woods (but then, Tempe, Arizona, doesn't strikingly suggest them either). "The grandeur is much diminished," wrote Boissier bravely, "but the grace remains."

This was all made long ago, before it seemed to anyone that there was any point in establishing a single composition for such a vast agglomeration. As it is, the Poekile establishes a direction for an orthogonal grid in its part of the villa and the round island seems, in plan, to serve as a pivot to another grid, which collides with a third, of which the Canopus is a highly visible part. Within them all, extraordinarily baroque curved niches and apses whirl in and out to make astonishing figures. Evidently, as Hadrian's biographers have claimed, this "graveyard" of Hadrian's travels held memories of far places, precise and vivid; but evidently, too, these memories were transformed into a fluid and felicitous new style. Much of the opulent surface of marble has been scraped off in the centuries since, but the brick and stone armature is still sufficiently recognizable to evoke the power of the first great collector's vision.

Sixteen centuries later the Chinese emperor Ch'ien Lung was lord over an equally enormous empire, and though his visits to the far corners of it were more ponderous affairs than Hadrian's had been, he too collected mementoes of famous places and had them recreated in a series of incredibly opulent fantasy gardens near Beijing and near the Manchurian frontier at Jehol. The most celebrated of these gardens was the Yuan Ming Yuan, about which many books and scholarly articles have since been written (Hope Danby's *The Garden of Perfect Brightness* is the most readily accessible to English speakers), though it was altogether erased from the landscape by foreign troops in the mid-nineteenth century to punish the reigning Dowager Empress for some unusually heinous duplicities.

The most famous part of the place, for Westerners, was a string of stone pavilions with water works and statues designed by a French Jesuit resident in Ch'ien Lung's court. The pavilions contained baroque systems for lifting and spouting water, the latest thing in France and regarded as fascinating indeed in China, where it had never seemed reasonable to have water do anything but fall, as it does in nature, or lie still. It is even said that in one of the Chinese parts of this garden there was a small mountain peak with a waterfall that was dry until the emperor was on his way, whereupon a cordon of coolies, hidden from his view, formed a bucket brigade to bring water to the summit, from which it might splash and fall, to the passing emperor's delight.

For a twentieth-century eye, however, already familiar with machines for squirting water, the real wonder of the Yuan Ming Yuan is the way it combined "seas" and lakes and "mountains" and habitable islands and bunds and even tiny mountain valleys into a kingdom of remarkable, identifiable places. Ch'ien Lung's father, Yung Cheng, had established twenty-nine favorite scenes in the garden. His son added eleven more, and two painters were commanded to make pictures of the forty scenes, with calligraphic descriptions by the minister of public works. The emperor was so pleased that he had woodcuts made of each picture, with poems and descriptions, and published them in two volumes.

The inspiration for the scenes generally came from elsewhere, for the emperor, according to Hope Danby "had visited some of the most beautiful parts of his empire soon after he came to the throne and he had brought back to Peking many scrolls of the gardens he most admired to guide the architects who copied them faithfully." Memories of West Lake at Hangzhou (mistily beautiful still, though now fringed by an industrial city) seem to have resonated especially powerfully through the recesses of his mind. The names that he bestowed on each place come to the aid of mountains and water and extend the power of the garden to engage the receptive imagination. Here is the list of names, presented in its excruciating entirety to suggest the variety and richness of the imagery.

1. *Central Great Glorious Bright* was the principal audience hall.

2. *Diligent in Government and Friendly with Officials* was a second audience hall.

3. *Nine Continents Clear and Calm,* or the nine islands, contained the apartments of the emperor and empresses.

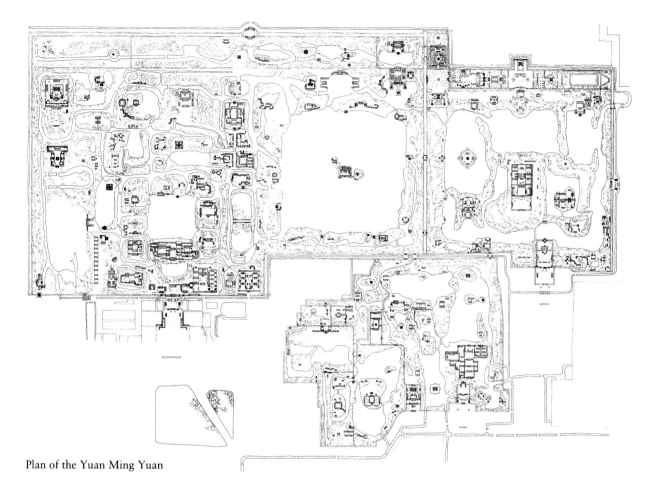

Plan of the Yuan Ming Yuan

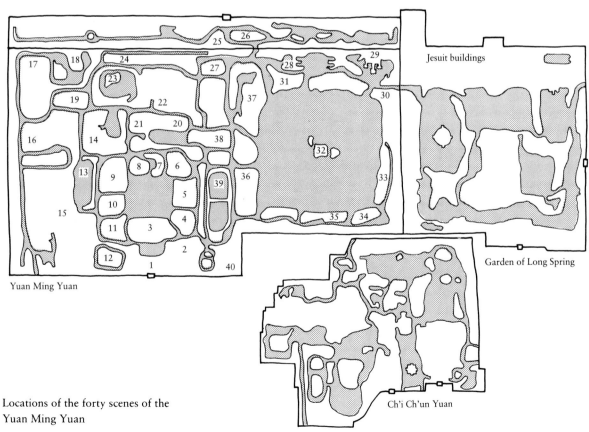

Jesuit buildings

Garden of Long Spring

Yuan Ming Yuan

Ch'i Ch'un Yuan

Locations of the forty scenes of the
Yuan Ming Yuan

4. *Engraved Moon and Open Clouds* included the *Terrace of the Peony.*

5. *The Picture of Natural Scenes* was a two-storied building behind a lotus-covered pool.

6. *The Library of the Topaz Wu-Tung Tree* was named for a tree rare indeed in North China and regarded as the only tree suitable for the landing of the fabulous phoenix.

7. *Merciful Clouds All Protecting* was a tower on a hook-shaped island.

8. *Heavenly Light Above and Below* was so named because the principal pavilion was built on piles over the water so that light reflected from below as well as shone from above.

9. *Springtime Hall of the Apple Blossoms* was backed by the highest hill in the garden and had a stone gateway leading to a peasant village.

10. *Tranquil and Vast* was a balustraded rectangular pond with a bridge leading to a pavilion called *The Bright Wind and Arrow Moon.*

11. The last of the nine islands was *Study the Old; It Contains the Present.*

12. Just west of the *Great Audience Hall* lay *The Prolonged Springtime Lodge of the Immortal.*

13. A swastika-shaped pavilion was *Peace and Harmony Everywhere.*

14. *The Springtime Coloring at Wu Ling,* in a hamlet called *Peach Blossom Village,* referred to Wu Ling, a Shangri-la in Hunan Province where the climate was famously mild. A number of buildings were included, called the *Pavilion of Leisure,* the *Hall of Spotless Jade,* the *Lonely Arcadia,* and the *Hall Where One Composes Poetry.*

15. *High Mountains and Long Waters* was a row of houses with a central pavilion, from which the emperor could watch the action on a large parade ground.

16. *The Dwelling of the Moon, Earth, and Clouds* was a Buddhist temple. The clouds were said to rise from the bronze incense burners.

17. *Vast Compassion and Eternal Blessings* is a picture of *The Palace of Peace and Assistance,* Ch'ien Lung's ancestral shrine.

18. Nearby was the *Library of Assembled Good Men.*

19. On another island, there was a Buddhist temple called *Sun, Heaven, Jade Roof.*

20. An island called *Placid, Contented, Peaceful, Quiet* showed a house in the shape of the ideogram for field.

21. Pavilions and kiosks set among gnarled pines were called *The Reflections of the Fragrant Orchid.*

22. On the largest island in this part of the garden was *A Stream, Trees, and a Bright Lute,* with a ceiling fan mechanically operated.

23. *Lien Shi* evokes a river in Hunan, where the climate is mild, and a famous mountain called the *Lotus Peak* looms over the river.

24. An island full of busy farmers and containing a painted pavilion to enhance the emperor's leisurely viewing of their labors was called *Crops as Plentiful as the Clouds.*

Scene 7: Merciful Clouds All Protecting   Scene 13: Peace and Harmony Everywhere

25. The palace *Fishes Leap and Birds Fly* came to have its own dishes, decorated with the four characters "Fishes Leap" and "Birds Fly."

26. Beyond the gate lay the *Village of the Distant Northern Mountains*, copied from a famous poem by Wang Ch'u.

27. The next island is called *The Beautiful Coloring of the Western Peaks*.

A later addition to the garden was a built lake, the *Happy Sea*, half a mile long and wide. It held thirteen more scenes.

28. *The Studio of the Four Complements*, which had to do with the four seasons, was renamed *The Garden of the Quiet Waves* when Ch'ien Lung had it remodeled into a copy of a famous garden in Haining. Between this picture and the next was a stretch with copies from Hangzhou's celebrated West Lake, including the *Sunset at Lei Fang Pagoda* and the *Peaceful Lake and Autumn Moon*.

29. *The Elevated Region of the Square Pot* is not so homely as it sounds: it is named after a celebrated mountain and rises near the *Three Fairy Lakes*. Barges as big as houses were rowed around the lake from here to, for instance, *The Moon Reflected between Three Pools*, which was copied from the garden in Hangzhou.

30. *To Cleanse the Body and Bathe in Virtue* was a place to bathe.

31. *The Calm Lake and Autumn Moon* was copied from an ancient dike on the West Lake in Hangzhou.

32. In the middle of the Happy Sea was a group called *The Fairy Islands and Jade Terrace*, copied from a T'ang painting by the famous artist Li Ssu Hsun.

33. *The Rustic House that Shelters the Beauty of the Mountains* was a library on the shore.

Scene 29: The Elevated Region of the Square Pot

Scene 32: The Fairy Islands and Jade Terrace

34. There was a water gate near the *Village of Grace and Beauty* that was called *There is Another Cave of Heaven.*

35. A poem by Li Ch'ing Lien inspired the name for a square pavilion in the middle of a stone bridge, just under the curious hand-fed waterfall. It was called *The Double Mirror and the Sound of the Lute.*

36. The western shore of the Happy Sea was a *Vast, Empty, Clear Mirror.*

37. *The Hall of Great Justice* had a pool fragrant with water lilies just outside the window from the emperor's couch.

38. The picture *The Resting Stone near the Stream* includes *The Garden of Universal Happiness,* with a village where eunuchs masquerading as storekeepers engaged the emperor and his ladies in make-believe village life. In the theater on the village street, *The Stage of the Tender Voice,* even the emperor sometimes acted.

39. Hangzhou was the source for yet another courtyard, *The Court of Fermented Liquors in the Midst of Lotus Flowers Stirred by the Breeze.* Wine was brewed in the Hangzhou original and consumed in great quantities in the emperor's copy.

40. The last picture is of the school of the young princes, *The Depth of the Vault of Heaven.*

The paintings of these scenes at first seem paradoxical to Western eyes: tiny buildings are shown nestled on the shores of seas amid towering peaks and ranges, but the site is, in fact, mostly flat and we know that the mountains could not have been more than modest artificial rockeries (the rubble of which remains on the site today). We have to imagine ourselves *inside* the buildings, looking *out* at the surrounding mounds and stones, with the peaks of the Fragrant Hills rising in the background. Through scenographic tricks we are given the illusion of being in a vaster scene— the one shown by the painter.

Scene 34: There is Another Cave of Heaven

Scene 38: The Resting Stone near the Stream

Scene 39: The Court of Fermented Liquors in the Midst of Lotus Flowers Stirred by the Breeze

So the great scenes of Ch'ien Lung's vanished youth were born again in a garden, and the lost garden is reincarnated for us in the forty painted scenes and their forty names—a labeled collection of memories of recollections, a faint but poignant reverberation of magnificence, like distant thunder.

Hadrian's and Ch'ien Lung's collections were made for the private pleasure of powerful men, and there was little effort to render the memories and references accessible to a wider public. The twentieth century has produced, by contrast, a few comparable collections that can be understood and enjoyed by all kinds of people. Portmeirion, on the west coast of Wales, is composed of salvaged buildings holding memories of an earlier era, set in gardens and painted amazing colors by Sir Clough Williams-Ellis, who devoted a long life to the assemblage and shared it with delighted paying guests. Other historical villages, less dominated by a single personality, have been collected at Sturbridge, Massachusetts, Greenfield Village, Michigan, and elsewhere. But the grandest collection of places, the only contemporary conflation of memories that can match in scale those of Hadrian and Ch'ien Lung, is the Magic Kingdom of the great populist Walter Elias Disney, first made concrete (though it had previously been constructed in the public's imagination by Disney's films) among the orange groves of Anaheim, California.

Anaheim is located in a particularly nondescript part of the vast Los Angeles plain. Disney perhaps chose it for some of the same reasons that took Hadrian to the viewless foothills of Tivoli. At nowhere in particular on that plain, at a point made even more featureless by one of the world's largest parking lots, lies the Magic Kingdom, which seems to be roughly circular. Disney's demesne is bounded by a berm, on top of which a train circles. The train (and the several other transportation systems in Disneyland) is among the most compelling attractions in the place—a fortunate development from Walt Disney's backyard electric train. All the rides help you use, even inhabit, the space by setting up something to *do,* just as the rules of golf help you use a patch of parkland by engaging in a ritual on it.

Entry is through a gate and under the berm, on which a smiling Mickey Mouse is laid out in flowers. Flowers and bushes and trees are everywhere, and they form a very important part of the fantasy, since, even though they are in southern California, they are *real,* they are *familiar,* and so bring the most exotic settings and hoked-up rides into remarkably close and believable connection with ourselves and our own memories and fantasies.

Just inside the gate is a square that serves as the beginning of *Main Street,* which heads straight for the plaza in front of *Snow White's Castle,* most of the way across the circular park. Main Street is a slightly miniaturized version (to make the visitor feel a little bigger and more important than usual) of an American Main Street of about 1910, recent enough and familiar enough to be what Henry James called the "palpable imaginable *visitable* past . . . the nearer distances and the clearer mysteries." Nor is it too long; in a short block comes a little cross street with cut flowers and

Main Street: "the palpable imaginable visitable past"

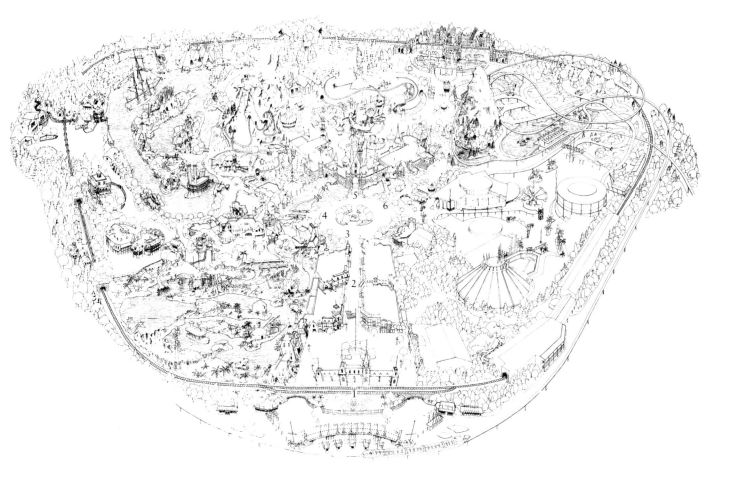

Disneyland, Anaheim

1. Entrance
2. Main Street
3. Adventureland
4. Frontierland
5. Fantasyland
6. Tomorrowland

shows, then another short block later is the central plaza, soft and green with olive trees in which tiny lights sparkle at night. Eateries resplendent in volutes and gingerbread flank Main Street, facing the plaza.

To the left is tropical foliage through which lies the entry to *Adventureland,* where a short street slips past a number of pleasingly sleazy tropical styles, suitable first for Timbuktu, then maybe the Caribbean, then what must be Beverly Hills, and then New Orleans. Across the little street is lush foliage, some of it real in front of the *Jungle Cruise,* some of it lifelike vinyl on the world's largest artificial banyan tree, which can comfortably be climbed to examine the dwelling of the Swiss Family Robinson.

Just beyond is a circular Mississippi River, on which New Orleans lies, the starting point for an indoor ride to view the misdeeds of the *Pirates of the Caribbean.* On the river plies the steamboat Mark Twain, which circles past frontier landscapes, most of them on *Tom Sawyer's Island,* whose flora is real but whose fauna is plastic and mechanized, which allows for the orderly repetition of moose fights and Indian massacres along the shore.

Extensive as Adventureland is, its shape, like a piece of pie, gives it only a short frontage on the plaza; so back on the plaza, walking clockwise only a few steps more the visitor finds the entrance to *Frontierland.* It has a stockade and old-time dance hall, and tacos, in a stereotypical Mexican village setting (by the shore of the Mississippi, somehow—and it *is* the

Mississippi, though that's not what they call it; Walt Disney was from Missouri). The dusty village plaza is made attractive by an arbor on which a magnificent bougainvillea grows. Nearby, another train goes by parts of the American desert on its way to disaster in a mine.

A little farther around the central plaza, a bridge across a pretty moat, with real rocks and fishes and swans, leads through Snow White's Castle to *Fantasyland,* with rides for small children partly surrounding a court in which a carousel spins. Behind the tiny miniature village, hillsides of succulents stay in proper scale. Hard by, a jungle backs up a pirate ship, and just to the left of that a picturesque Swiss hillside path leads to a chalet, which serves as the embarkation point for a skyride through the *Matterhorn* to *Tomorrowland.*

Once the skyride comes through the Matterhorn into Tomorrowland, on a kind of crazy spiritual *axis mundi,* it soars above a beautifully clear lake in which the world's ninth-largest submarine fleet travels, and touches down beyond it, in the midst of a fifties version of a streamlined hi-tech future. The rides draw great crowds, but the place is less convincing than the rest, partly because it doesn't seem at all clear to the designers what the landscape of the future might be (would bougainvillea grow on Venus or Mars?), so some very tacky constructions that look like fugitive elements from a fifties motel sign attempt to replace trees.

Past the Matterhorn and onto the plaza, a few more steps take us back to Main Street and a short walk takes us out of the park, for the long ride home. The collection of images has included something to please almost everybody, and the arrangement has juxtaposed the pieces so closely, then joined them with thick, real foliage so successfully, that the visit, whatever path you chose, has very tightly choreographed itself.

Much of the fascination of these collections resides in their connections to vivid lives—of a mighty oriental despot, of Hadrian and Antinous, and of a Midwestern genius who found fame in Hollywood. They remind us, too, that collectors' gardens (even our own modest ones) involve objects assembled from some point of view—dog roses because they remind you of English cottages you have enjoyed or palm trees because they recall a Raoul Dufy you admire or a favorite tropical beach or lunch at the Plaza, and also because, if you live in the right climate, there are enough kinds available to keep you collecting for a long time. But mostly, these collections say that there is excitement in memories, in recreating places and stories we have seen and enjoyed, changed to suit our means, our techniques, and the space at hand, even labeled so we can't miss the allusions. "Too flat-footed," architects of the last half-century would say, "such explicitness is barking on the heels of kitsch." "Nonsense," say these examples, "memories are the stuff of which collections, and gardens, are made, and there's power in being as literal, as specific, as clear as we can."

The Summer Palace

In 1860 an incident in the wake of the Opium War provoked the destruction of the Yuan Ming Yuan by an Anglo-French expeditionary force. The soldiers quite thoroughly pillaged its treasures and then burned it to the ground; today it is a sad, silent field of lotuses, spotted with anonymous heaps of rubble. For good measure, the invaders also razed the gardens that Ch'ien Lung had made in the Fragrant Hills and at Jade Fountain Hill some miles to the west of the Yuan Ming Yuan. They also destroyed The Garden of Clear Ripples, which he had constructed around Kunming Lake, not far from the western boundary of the Yuan Ming Yuan, on the occasion of his mother's sixtieth birthday. In the 1880s the Dowager Empress Cixi had it rebuilt as her Summer Palace. In 1902 she had to rebuild it again after it was devastated by Tsarist troops. Today, much restored to its former splendor, it is a reminder of the great Ch'ien Lung and his passion for scenery, an enormously popular sightseeing spot for the people of Beijing, and a place still haunted by memories of the extravagant, scheming Old Buddha herself.

It is a garden of distinct parts, but all of them carefully hinged together. You should follow on the map as we introduce them. Note particularly their relations to each other and to the sun.

The first part is the entrance complex to the east. Starting at the *pailou* (archway) of the *East Palace Gate* there is a formal, symmetrical sequence of three rectangular courtyards about an east-west axis, terminating with the splendid *Hall of Benevolence and Longevity*, where the Dowager Empress sat on her nine-dragon throne. The buildings here served as audience halls; foreign envoys could not come any farther into the palace and gardens without special permission. Behind the Hall of Benevolence and Longevity is a garden of small mounds, which divides the audience halls from the imperial household proper. You make your way through the gates and courtyards, where the views are bounded by close walls on all sides, and around the mounds to arrive, with sudden drama, at the shore of the broad lake, with long views opening up to the north, west, and south. Nearby, on a small island connected to the shore by a bridge, is an open-sided viewing pavilion called the *Pavilion Heralding Spring*. This is surrounded by willows and, as the ice of the lake begins to thaw in February and March, by blossoms of peach and apricot.

The second part (immediately to the north of the Hall of Benevolence and Longevity), consists of the imperial living quarters, arranged in the traditional Chinese way around courtyards on north-south axes. The principal buildings here are the *Hall of Jade Billows*, where the unfortunate son of the Dowager Empress, the emperor Guangxu, was confined by his mother after the attempted Wuxu Reform; the *Lodge of the Propriety of Weeding*, the sleeping quarters of the Dowager Empress; the *Hall of Happiness in Longevity*, living quarters around courtyards planted with magnolia; and the *Garden of Virtue and Harmony*, with a gold-lacquered throne, a stage for theatrical performances, and a clockwork bird in a gilded cage. In these quarters the Dowager Empress was attended by her hundreds of eu-

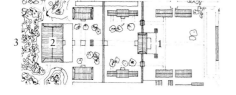

The Summer Palace's first collection of pavilions and courtyards: the entrance complex

1. East Palace Gate
2. Hall of Benevolence and Longevity
3. Rockery garden

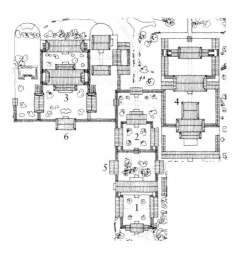

The second collection of pavilions and courtyards: the imperial living quarters

1. Hall of Jade Billows
2. Lodge of the Propriety of Weeding
3. Hall of Happiness in Longevity
4. Garden of Virtue and Harmony
5. Pavilion of Beautiful Sunset
6. Hall of Affinity between Wood and Water

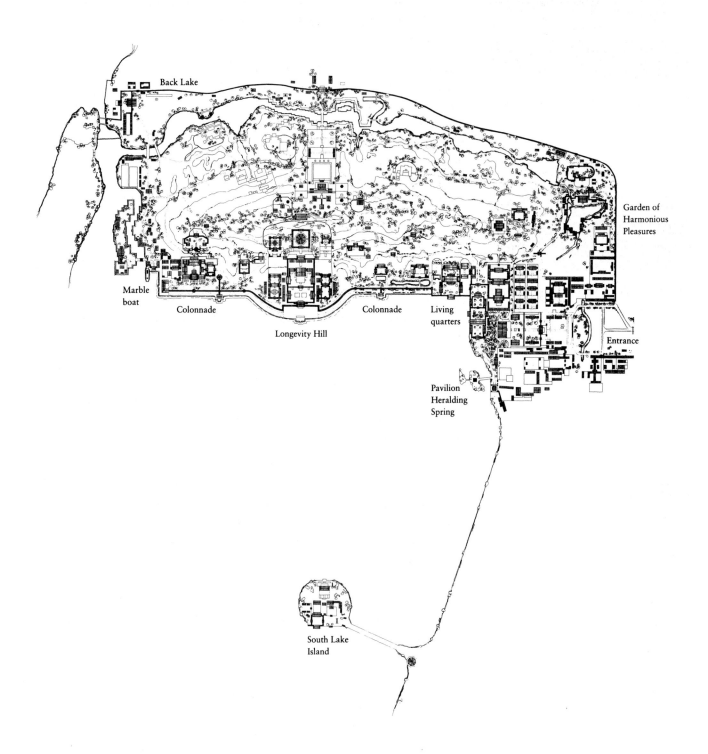

Back Lake

Garden of
Harmonious
Pleasures

Marble
boat

Colonnade

Colonnade

Living
quarters

Entrance

Longevity Hill

Pavilion
Heralding
Spring

South Lake
Island

The grid meets the edge of Kunming Lake

West Dike, bridge, and borrowed scenery on the opposite shore of Kunming Lake

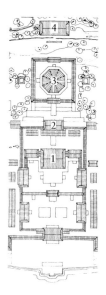

The third collection of pavilions and courtyards: Longevity Hill

1. Hall that Dispels the Clouds
2. Hall of Glorious Virtue
3. Tower of the Fragrance of Buddha
4. Sea-of-Wisdom Tower

nuchs, ate at a dining table with a hundred different dishes, and dressed splendidly (her wardrobe filled three thousand chests). Breaking out of all this, on the shore of the lake, are two modest pavilions: the *Pavilion of Beautiful Sunset,* which provides an elevated, breezy outlook to the west; and the south-facing *Hall of Affinity between Wood and Water,* a landing place for boats.

The third part of the garden, *Kunming Lake,* is nearly a mile long (from north to south) and about half a mile wide. Ch'ien Lung divided it into three distinct parts by the very long *West Dike* running from the northwest corner to the southeast and another, shorter dike dividing the western half in two. Within each of the three parts is an island, recalling the Taoist myth of Penglai, Fangzhang, and Yingzhou—the three islands of the immortals on the eastern seas. *South Lake Island* is connected to the eastern shore by the long, graceful *Seventeen-Arch Bridge:* standing on it are the *Pavilion of Eight Directions* and the *Hall of Forbearance and Humbleness.*

At the north end of the lake is the fourth part of the garden, the steep northern slope of *Longevity Hill.* This is an east-west ridge, about half a mile long and two hundred feet high, thickly wooded with pines and cypresses. The sunlight brings the intricate shapes of red, yellow, green, and blue buildings into sharp focus against the somber foliage; you can suddenly see the point of the famous remark by the painter Zheng Ji that buildings are the "eyes and eyebrows of the landscape."

The centerpiece of Longevity Hill is complex of courtyards, pavilions, walls, and stairs stepping up, first, to the *Hall that Dispels the Clouds,* named for some lines from the Jin Dynasty poet Guo Fu:

When fairies dispel the clouds and emerge,
The gold and silver terraces appear.

Next come the *Hall of Glorious Virtue,* the *Tower of the Fragrance of Buddha,* a rockery, and finally the *Sea-of-Wisdom Tower.* The axis runs north-south, continuing that of South Lake. This is a place of high outlooks over yellow-glazed tile roofs: down the lake to the south, to Jade Fountain Hill and to the Fragrant Hills in the west, to the Yuan Ming Yuan in the northeast, and to the lakes and palaces of Beijing (connected to Kunming Lake by a canal) far to the southeast.

Across the northern shore of the lake, at the foot of Longevity Hill, runs a long wooden colonnade. It is straight for a few hundred yards at either end, and in the center sweeps in an arc around the Hall that Dispels the Clouds. At the eastern end are the imperial living quarters, and at the western terminus is one of the most notorious follies of the Dowager Empress, the marble *Boat of Purity and Ease*—doubly infuriating to her detractors because, so the story goes, it was built with funds intended for the Chinese navy. The covered promenade serves as a device for connecting numerous pavilions scattered along the hillside and the shore. But more than this, it is a collection of scenes on an appropriately grandiose scale. There are fourteen thousand *painted* scenes (of famous landscapes, of birds and flowers, and from literature), and each of the 273 sectors frames a *living* scene to the north and another to the south. Cypresses and pines filter the light and the view on either side, and in spring there is the contrast of blossom against their dark foliage. The northern scenes are of pavilions and nearby shaded walls, while the southern scenes extend past foreground branches across glittering water to islands and dikes and distant hills.

Now there is a fifth, hidden part, a surprise. The shaded northern slope of the Hill of Longevity turns out to be covered with the ruins of buildings that have never been restored. They look down onto a long, narrow waterway called the *Back Lake*, along the northern boundary. This wilderness contains a garden within a garden—the walled *Garden of Harmonious Pleasures*, built around its own miniature lake. Characters inscribed on its white stone bridge (by Ch'ien Lung himself) recall a dispute between two ancient philosophers about whether or not fish know happiness.

The Jade Pagoda

The final element is in one sense not part of the garden at all, and in another its most essential part: the borrowed view of the hills to the west, far beyond the physical boundaries of the park. The trick is simple, but the effect is stunning. From the pavilions and promenades of the northern and eastern shores, the view across the water is always bounded by the lines of the West Dike and of the Seventeen-Arch Bridge. But these are not solid boundaries; the Seventeen-Arch Bridge allows you to catch glimpses of water beyond, and the line of the dike is also broken by several pretty, high-arching bridges. This device conceals the true boundaries and creates the illusion that the lake extends indefinitely to the south and the west—as far, perhaps, as the foot of Jade Fountain Hill, misty purple-gray against the dusk sky, with the softer gray of the Fragrant Hills beyond. On the ridge of Jade Fountain Hill, to invite the eye into the distance, is the tall, slim profile of the *Jade Pagoda*—like Proust's church steeple at Combray, a little finger of art tickling the clouds. The garden extends beyond the lake, beyond the pagoda, beyond the Fragrant Hills, to the sunset.

The horizontal axis of the long colonnade

The complexities of the Summer Palace overwhelm the imagination, but they result from the rich orchestration of just a few simple, powerful themes. The layout begins, like that of a *chahar bagh*, with cross axes oriented to the points of the compass. A north-south axis runs through the Hall that Dispels the Clouds and down the center of the South Lake, dividing the West Dike from the South Lake Island. This is intersected by the east-west axis of the long colonnade, running along the shore of the lake. The Tower of the Fragrance of Buddha marks the crossing with a strong vertical. Rigorously gridded arrangements of buildings and courtyards develop parallel to these axes: the Hall of Benevolence and Longevity complex to the east; the imperial living quarters; the courtyards and towers stepping up Longevity Hill to the crowning tower; even the marble boat pointing due south. Flowing through all this Confucian rigor, though, is the free-form breath of nature: the irregular outline of Kunming Lake; the dark, rugged profile of the Hill of Longevity; foliage and mists.

The vertical axis of the Tower of the Fragrance of Buddha

Intersections of nature and the grid become halls and pavilions, and the garden is an accumulation of these, gathered within the enclosing walls.

A pavilion for a mood: the marble Boat of Purity and Ease

All have evocative names, some moralizing, like the temples to various classical virtues in the eighteenth-century English gardens (Forbearance, Humbleness, Purity, Longevity, Happiness, Literary Prosperity, Glorious Virtue), some descriptive of natural beauty (Lotus Fragrance, Rosy Clouds, Jade Ripples, Golden Water, Clear and Far, Blessed Scenery, Beautiful Sunset), and others that speak of Epicurean moods (Watching the Moon, Strolling through a Picture Scroll, Listening to Orioles, Heralding Spring, Harmonious Pleasures). Often the name of a hall or pavilion is inscribed on a horizontal wooden tablet over the main entrance. In addition, there are vertical tablets on the columns at either side. These tablets, called *lian* (couplet) carry two lines of poetry, each with the same number of characters; architectural and literary symmetries coincide.

This enormous, complex agglomeration gains point and poignancy through its evocation of a particular personality at a particular moment in history. Each day the sun moving across the Garden of Clear Ripples still dances with the absence of the iniquitous old collector of pleasures. It rises over her distant capital (visible from Longevity Hill), shines into her face across the glittering waters of Kunming Lake, and drops down behind the Jade Pagoda to make her a sunset picture at the Boat of Purity and Ease.

Katsura Imperial Villa

For the German architect Bruno Taut, the Katsura Imperial Villa was a revelation, a stirring confirmation of the virtues of simplicity, sobriety, and purity of form that this early modern architect so highly prized. He brought the long-neglected garden to the attention of the world, and there can be few places on this planet that have been more admired since.

The place has a remarkable attribute: it reflects, for people of widely differing vision, just what those people want to see in it, everything from Taut's vision of purity to an almost kitsch expression of the popular taste of its time (by Naomi Kawa). The celebrated Japanese architect Kenzo Tange saw it as the highly charged collision of the *yayoi* and the *jomon*, two very different progenitors of the Japanese people turned into principles roughly parallel to the Chinese *yin* and *yang*, the one (*yayoi*) yielding, recessive, and enveloping, the other (*jomon*) macho and aggressive. His book on Katsura includes a chapter by Walter Gropius, the modern architect and educator, who saw the architectural principles developed in his Bauhaus and the modern movement vindicated in a far-off land. Akira Naito sees in the place a fascinating reflection of the tense and delicate relationship between the imperial family, in an era when its power was waning, and the Tokugawa shoguns, in the first flush of their power.

The descriptions are all, of course, correct, and it is doubtless the mark of a great work of art that it can encompass vast contradictions. Our drawing is meant to encourage looking at this house and garden as objects to be walked in and enjoyed, and the villa's inclusion here as a collection is meant to encourage examining the place as a set of references and recollections, far more spare and economical than Hadrian's or Ch'ien Lung's but still imperial. A portion of the four-hundred-year-old wooden

KATSURA IMPERIAL VILLA

Overview
·
Landform and water
·
Buildings and paths
·
Planting

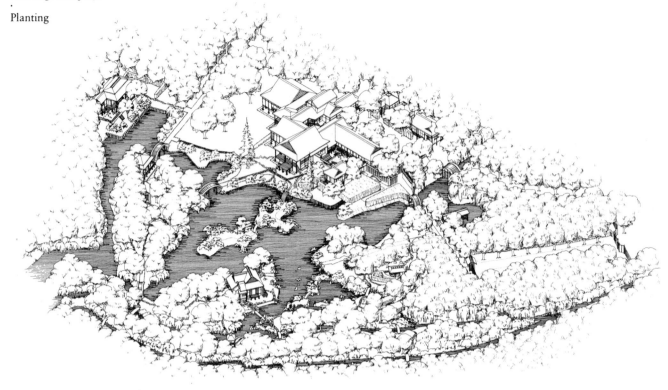

1. Gate
2. Pine tree
3. Mount of Maples
4. Sotetsu "mountain"
5. Rustic hut
6. Gorge (Oi River)
7. Cape with lantern
8. Amanohashidate
9. Shokin-tei
10. Valley of the Fireflies
11. Green Mountain Island
12. Shoka-tei
13. Orin-do
14. Shoi-ken
15. Lawn

villa itself, for instance, was lately disassembled for restoration, its component pieces stored in a series of bins until decayed members could be restored or replaced; there are, in this palace so long praised for its simplicity, over thirty thousand component pieces!

The first builder of all this was an imperial prince, Toshihito, born in 1579, the sixth son of the eldest son of the emperor. In 1586 he was adopted by the Napoleonic figure Hideyoshi, who had himself taken the precaution (in the same year) to be adopted into the Fujiwara clan, which had long held the reins of real power in a country where the imperial house traditionally had none. Hideyoshi's adoption of the young prince lost force when he had a son of his own, and the situation changed again when Hideyoshi died. After a civil war, Tokugawa Ieyasu founded a new warrior dynasty, which was to rule Japan for 250 years, until a member of the imperial house himself seized power. Prince Toshihito was seen, through the early years of the seventeenth century (for incredibly complex reasons, that read like the libretto of a terrible opera), as an important liaison between the real rulers and the imperial family and was therefore granted the limited means necessary to make, of a little teahouse in a melon patch outside the capital, an imperial villa extensive enough to assemble recollections of many distant places. This was in 1616.

Most of the buildings we know apparently date from a generation later, after 1640, in the time of Prince Toshihito's son, Prince Noritada, and are only now being restored and replaced. The planting in the garden, of course, has gone through faster cycles: tiny pines have become giants and powerfully changed the composition of the garden, then have died and been replaced by tiny ones again.

The simplicity of Katsura

The showiness of Nikko

Through its changes, Katsura's presence is so strong, it is so powerfully a work of art, that visitors assumed it must have been designed by a professional genius, most likely the great tea master Kobori Enshu. The design is now believed to have been done on a very careful budget and to have been the result of the prince's own intense and unending involvement with some intelligent and responsive low-caste carpenters and gardeners. But the style owes much to Enshu and his vision of a combination—or collision—of the illusion of the mountain hut and the elegance of the old imperial court life. "Beautiful sabi" is a partial translation of the name for the mood that it creates: the phrase is not fully renderable in English, but "elegant rustic" is a reasonably close parallel. The composition is, on the one hand, far more relaxed and complex, and vivid and popular, than the stones of Ryoan-ji but, on the other hand, far less voluptuous and showy and expensive than Nikko, the supersplendid memorial to the new Tokugawa shoguns, which was being built at the same time, and by some of the same people, in a style as curvily florid as Katsura was straight and, in its way, simple.

The garden is generally visited by moving clockwise around its central pond. The imposition of a definite sequence on the collection of scenes imparts extra meaning to the garden and allows the development and amplification of a composition in time—with rhythms, fast and slow, regular and irregular, and pauses, syncopations, diminuendos, and fortissimos. Attention shifts from one amazing object to the next, sometimes viewed up close and sometimes seen in long vistas across the water. The sequence does not, however, become a narrative like some of the pilgrimage gardens that we will visit later. It is, rather, a series of inflections of mood.

There are two entries. One, down a straight *allée*, through a gate, and along a straight route to the right, affords, just before the house, a view along a long, thin peninsula to a celebrated pine tree at its point. (The last fine old tree was replaced about thirty years ago with one not yet quite adolescent.) Then there is a turn to the left and quickly to the right, to the central gate of the villa. This was the imperial entrance. The ordinary entrance comes diagonally to a gate near the house and makes a pair of picturesque turns to the same central gate the emperor would come upon. The main living pavilions of the house stretch out in a stepped diagonal unlike anything in the West; all of them are high above the main lawn, with their views angled across it.

To tour the garden, we go back out the central gate and head to the right toward the peninsula with the pine tree at its end. A little later, after the *Mount of Maples*, we turn right onto a long axis with steps to the water and an unobstructed view of a large and elegant tea house called the *Shokin-tei* on the opposite peninsula. The path we follow almost immediately turns left off this axis and winds through dense woods with many groups of rocks, past the *Sotetsu "mountain"* to a rustic hut containing an outside resting place. A route so meticulously timed, like a piece of music, requires pauses.

Our path approaches the lake shore through a tiny recollection of the deep gorge of the Oi River and comes out at a little bay protected by a peninsula extended by bridges onto islands, which almost separate the bay from the larger lake. The peninsula and islands are named *Amanohashidate*, after such a spot, but far larger, where a celebrated naval battle occurred. Beyond Amanohashidate the *Shokin-tei* pavilion is in full view, but there are going to be many more wonders before we round the bay and cross the bridge to it. Most famous among them is a tiny cape of carefully selected stones projecting from the rocky shore, tipped by a small stone lantern which, lighted at night, causes the stone bridge at Amanohashidate to reflect in the water.

The *Shokin-tei* or *Pine-Lute Pavilion* is the main ornament of the garden and is shadowed and closed like a traditional farmhouse to counter the sunny openness of the main house. A passage in the eleventh-century *Tale of Genji* describes a moonlit night when the sound of lutes combined beautifully with the rustling of the pine trees, and Kenzo Tange opines that this passage was the inspiration for the Shokin-tei.

The pavilion is a fairly large structure, but its even grander scale is established by the unusually small tea house (six by nine feet, with a tiny extension) that occupies its nearest corner. The door to the tea room is half height, so the visitor has to enter on hands and knees. In the pond nearby

A stone lantern and the bridge of Amanohashidate

are three large rocks, where guests for the tea ceremony could have the surprising pleasure of washing their hands in flowing water rather than in the more usual still basin.

The largest (and original) rooms of the Shokin-tei merge into an L-shaped space, with views through open outside walls to the *Face of Light,* where thick trees make darkness fall early, in exquisite contrast to the bridge at Amanohashidate, which stays longest in the sun. Inside, perhaps the most striking sight is an alcove papered with large blue and white squares, which comes as a particular surprise among the soft earth tones of the building and the garden and carries the force the twentieth century produces with neon. The collision of moods on which Katsura depends is nowhere more apparent than here.

The route after the Shokin-tei, though more relaxed than the first part of the circuit of the pond, offers much variety still. Just before the bridge to the *Green Mountain Island* lies the *Valley of the Fireflies.* The island, which is linked to the mainland in three directions, has a dense (though small) forest of cryptomeria trees, in which a steep climb up no more than sixteen feet feels like a pilgrimage up a mountain. At the summit, the *Shoka-tei,* rustic under an open sky, is like a hut one might find at a mountain pass. But few mountain passes could match the surprising semi-aerial panorama of the Katsura Villa that opens up from here.

The route downhill leads to the *Orin-do,* a family memorial in the appropriately historic Chinese Buddhist style that one chronicler describes as "immaculate carelessness." An earth-covered bridge leads to a straight path lined with plum trees at the edge of the main lawn adjoining the villa. A turn left, away from the villa, leads to a squared-off bay in the pond, which is fitted with steps for the mooring of boats, to the *Shoi-ken,* which translates as *Laughing Thoughts Pavilion,* after a passage from the Chinese poet Li-Po:

When they ask me what I think
Of living in the azure mountains,
I laugh and do not answer
That my heart here finds rest—
The peach blossoms and the flowing stream
Go far, far away.
There is another universe
Where there are no men.

This cheerful pavilion was Prince Noritada's private study, a place of refuge from royal intrigues. The view is out across the fields of lower Katsura Village and the presumably simple world of the peasants.

A walk back across the lawn to the main building completes the circuit around the pond. The shape of the pond itself repays some careful study; it is not really very large (much larger than those found in most of our private gardens, but rather smaller than the ones in most parks) and there are no vast reaches of water, as there would be at the Yuan Ming Yuan, but each stretch, as seen from the shore, is special and quite unlike the piece that is coming next. Every turn of the path produces new views across the water, with an ever-varying distance to the opposite shore and a new sight to see there.

Katsura, then, is a collection choreographed into a pilgrimage route. It is the choreography that makes this large and elaborate garden a useful model for our more modest efforts in smaller places, for it suggests not only the collection of pieces (rocks or flowers or bowers or tea houses) but also the ordering of them in time. A garden you walk through, however small it may be, must be composed in time as well as space.

What Katsura does, perhaps more clearly than any of the other gardens we show, is to stage the amazing collision of the gorgeous and the ordinary: electric blue and earth tones; the Shokin-tei and rocks; the court and the peasants; the palace and the melon patch. Western garden history offers few models for the desire, which seems to be felt especially strongly in our own time (bluejeans and rhinestones), to conflate the practical and the glamorous, the plain and the fancy. There is a garden at Villandry, in the Loire Valley, elaborately laid out in geometric parterres full of vegetables, which acknowledges our need to feast our stomachs as well as our eyes, but Katsura and its sister garden across Kyoto, the Shugakuin, make the most out of weaving glimpses of the everyday into their meticulously concocted rhythms of dreams.

Sissinghurst

"Things of Beautie" in season at Sissinghurst

Francis Bacon is remembered today as a collector of practical knowledge, which he arrayed for the instruction of his readers, and as a sharp-tongued opponent of scholasticism and alchemy ("whereof the one never faileth to multiply words and the other ever faileth to multiply gold"). His facts are now out of date, of course, and scholars pursue different disputes, but the felicity of his style and the agility of his mind can still delight. One of the prettiest of his essays is "Of Gardens" (1625).

For Bacon a garden was, quite explicitly, a reconstruction of the biblical paradise, and fine gardening was an accomplishment of high civilization. The essay begins:

GOD Almightie first Planted a Garden. And indeed, it is the Purest of Humane pleasures. It is the Greatest Refreshment to the Spirits of Man; Without which, Buildings and Pallaces are but Grosse Handy-works: And a Man shall ever see, that when Ages grow to Civility and Elegancie, Men come to Build Stately, sooner than to Garden Finely: As if Gardening were the Greater Perfection.

His first principle of garden design is that "there ought to be Gardens, for all the Moneths in the Yeare: In which, severally, Things of Beautie, may be then in Season." To accomplish this the gardener must know the flowers that bloom and the trees that are in leaf for each month, so Bacon provides a convenient list. For example, "For March, There come Violets, specially the Single Blew, which are the Earliest; The Yellow Daffadil; the Dazie; the Almond-Tree in Blossome; The Peach-Tree in Blossome; The

Cornelian-Tree in Blossome; Sweet-Briar." When he reaches the end of the year, he pauses to comment that, "These Particulars are for the Climate of London, But my meaning is Perceived, that you may have *Ver Perpetuum*, as the Place affords."

Bacon was not the first to imagine a perpetually fruitful garden, in which crops and blossoms succeed each other unendingly. The *Odyssey*, for instance, had told how Ulysses came upon the garden of Alcinous, King of Phaecia. The beguiling couplets of Chapman's *Homer* enumerate its delights:

Without the hall, and close upon the gate,
A goodly orchard-ground was situate,
Of near ten acres; about which was led
A lofty quickset. In it flourished
High and broad fruit trees, that pomegranates bore,
Sweet figs, pears, olives; and a number more
Most useful plants did there produce their store,
Whose fruits the hardest winter could not kill,
Nor hottest summer wither. There was still
Fruit in his proper season all the year.
Sweet Zephyr breath'd upon them blasts that were
Of varied tempers. These he made to bear
Ripe fruits, these blossoms. Pear grew after pear,
Apple succeeded apple, grape the grape,
Fig after fig came; time made never rape
Of any dainty there.

But there is a difference. For Homer this ceaseless bounty was a splendid gift of the gods. Bacon, though, imagines how it might be the product of human knowledge and ingenuity; confident Elizabethan man is to take control of nature and make it serve his pleasure.

Not only must a gardener know the ordering of plants by their seasons, Bacon suggests, but also according to their qualities of scent:

And because, the Breath of Flowers, is farre Sweeter in the Aire, (where it comes and Goes, like the Warbling of Musick) then in the hand, therefore nothing is more fit for that delight, then to know, what be the Flowers, and Plants, that do best perfume the Aire.

He then classifies flowers and trees according to the strengths of their perfumes, the times when these perfumes are produced, and whether the scent is experienced as they are "passed by" or as they are "trodon upon and Crushed."

At Sissinghurst, in the Weald of Kent, there stands a red brick tower dating from Bacon's time. Around this Elizabethan relic a great garden was constructed (over a period spanning from the 1930s to the 1960s) by the famous literary couple Harold Nicolson and Vita Sackville-West. It is Bacon's ideal triumphantly realized: a place of blossoms and scents for all the months of the year, accomplished by the application of formidable knowledge.

The capabilities of the place, as Nicolson and Sackville-West found it in 1930, were well concealed. Sissinghurst Castle was a decaying ruin, the remnants of what had once been a grand Elizabethan mansion now being used as farm buildings. The site was nearly flat and roughly rectangular, with the long axis running east-west. At the northeast corner were the L-shaped, stagnant remains of a moat. A regular grove of nut trees defined the southeast corner. Four major fragments of Elizabethan brick construction remained: a wing running across the western boundary (now known as the Library), the high tower to its east, a fragment called the South Cottage, and another called the Priest's House. There were also numerous remnants of Elizabethan brick wall scattered about the site. All around were Kentish farmland hillsides dotted with trees.

The story usually told is that Nicolson was mostly responsible for laying out the skeleton of walls and enclosures and Sackville-West for populating the spaces with plants. Perhaps the roles were not quite so neatly defined; however, much of the fascination of this place, certainly, is that it is the work not of a single author but of two very different personalities who enjoyed a long and complex partnership.

The Sissinghurst tower

Nicolson set out on the ground a pattern of formal enclosures connected by long vistas. The Elizabethan walls were used to bound and shape the spaces wherever possible, augmented occasionally by some new brickwork and lengths of clipped hedge. From the tower the whole composition is revealed, like a cutaway aerial perspective of some ancient palace. The enclosures are roofless rooms, the openings between them and out to the surrounding countryside are treated as doors and windows, and the vistas through successive layers of walls and hedges are *enfilades*. Fragments of roofed indoor space are set within, so the result is neither pavilions standing in a garden nor garden courts enclosed by buildings, but an interweaving of garden and house, with each seeming to flow through the other.

A view from the tower

Two major vistas form the organizing skeleton. The first runs roughly east-west, from the archway under the tower, across the lawn in front of the tower, through a gap in a pair of yew hedges, across an orchard to terminate at a statue of Dionysius at the southern end of the moat. The second forms a cross axis to the first, meeting it at the center of the lawn. This runs from a statue near the northern extremity to another at the south. Several of the enclosures reflect this cross-axial scheme at a smaller scale.

Each enclosure is a discrete small garden, with its own particular shape, character, and name, like a chapter in a novel. If we begin at the front entrance and make a clockwise circuit of the grounds, we encounter them in the following sequence.

1. The *Front Courtyard* is a generous, trapezoid-shaped open space between the library and the tower.

2. The *Tower Lawn* is a formal rectangle of grass, bounded by walls and flower beds, the long horizontal of a yew hedge to the east, and the dramatic vertical of the tower to the west.

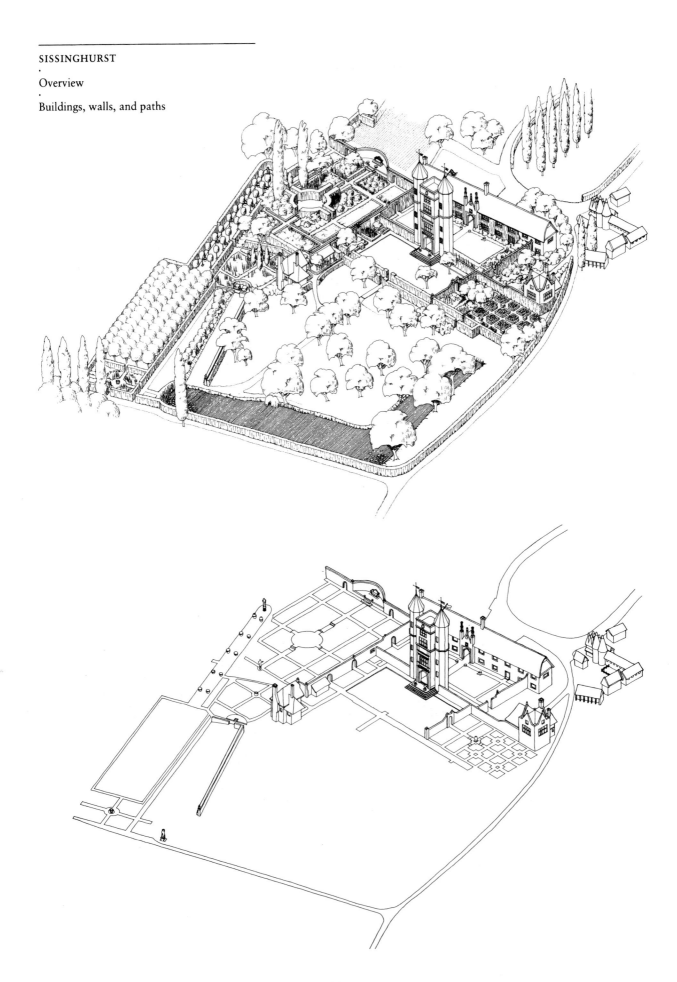

Planting
·
Key to the parts of the garden

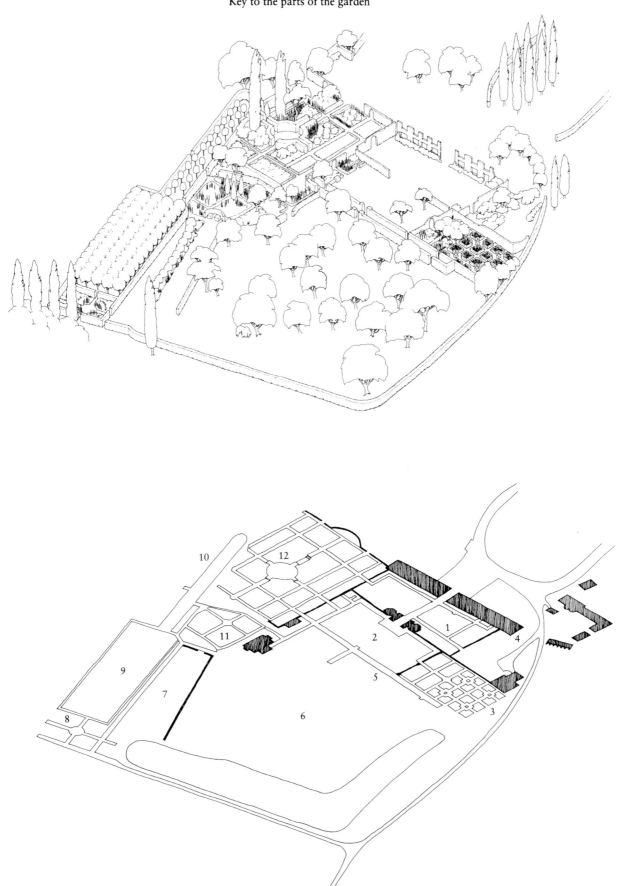

3. The *White Garden*, to the north of the Tower Lawn, is a foursquare, symmetrical enclosure filled with white flowers.

4. *Delos,* in the northwestern corner, behind the Priest's House, is a shady spot.

5. The *Yew Walk,* which forms the eastern boundary of the Tower Lawn and slices through the garden from north to south, consists of high, parallel, closely clipped yew hedges with a narrow path between.

6. The *Orchard,* beyond the Yew Walk, is a large enclosure filled with high grass, fruit trees, the songs of birds, and the buzz of insects. The old L-shaped moat forms the northern and eastern boundaries. The South Cottage dominates the southwest corner, and it is answered by a gazebo to the northeast, in the crook of the moat. A long vista runs from the Yew Walk entrance to the statue of Dionysius at the southeast extremity.

7. The *Moat Walk* runs west from the statue of Dionysius. There is a brick wall on the northern side and a border of shrubs and flowers to the south.

8. The *Herb Garden* occupies the far southeast corner.

9. The *Nuttery* is a long, formal grove of old nut trees, running west from the Herb Garden.

10. The *Lime Walk,* with parallel rows of pleached limes, extends (with a slight jog) the axis of the Nuttery.

11. The *Cottage Garden* stands between the South Cottage and the Lime Walk.

12. The *Rose Garden,* with its rondel of yew hedge at the center, occupies the southwest corner. From here you can complete the circuit by returning to the Tower Lawn and Courtyard.

With its inflected shapes and colliding axes, the pattern of enclosures is complex, but the vertical shaft of the tower is always there for orientation.

Sackville-West's planting fills the enclosures like a collection of paintings in the rooms of a museum. She was a collector and cultivator of enormous energy and resourcefulness, so in time the plant collection grew into one of the most remarkable in England. And, like a good curator, she catalogued and annotated it—from 1947 to 1961 in a popular Sunday gardening column in the London *Observer* newspaper and in books: *In Your Garden,* followed by *In Your Garden, Again,* then *More for Your Garden,* and finally *Even More for Your Garden.* Many visitors now come to Sissinghurst (no longer a private garden, but operated by the National Trust) to see its treasures and to enrich their stores of horticultural lore.

Just as Bacon had proposed, the plant collection is organized into "Gardens for all the Moneths of the Year." Sackville-West wrote of this intention:

One of the ideas we had decided on from the first was that the garden with all its separate rooms and subsections must be a garden of seasonal features throughout the year; it was large enough to afford the space, we could have a spring garden, March to mid-May; and an early summer garden, May-July; and a late summer garden, July-August; and an autumn garden, September-October. Winter must take care of itself, with a few winter-flowering shrubs and early bulbs.

This works out well in the south of England, where there are very pronounced seasons, but they are not too severe. Incidentally, it is one of many parallels between the garden traditions of the two island nations that the same idea had, long ago, arisen in Japan; the eleventh-century *Tale of Genji* tells how Prince Genji constructed gardens for his ladies—one for each season. Lady Murasaki had a spring garden, the summer garden was for the "Lady from the Village of Falling Flowers," the autumn garden for Lady Akikonomu, and the winter garden of pines and chrysanthemums for Lady Akashi. The plants in each are listed with care.

The seasonal planting of the Sissinghurst enclosures is arranged as follows. In spring the Lime Walk, the Orchard, and the Nuttery are filled with tree blossoms, and the effect is reinforced by carpets of spring flowers. In summer the most intensely concentrated masses of flowers are in the Rose Garden, the White Garden, and the Cottage Garden, while the Lime Walk, Orchard, and Nuttery become leafy green above and below and are filled with a lazy buzz of bees. In autumn the Moat Garden has its turn, becoming a mass of bright fall foliage. (The final chapters of Anne Scott-James's book *Sissinghurst: The Making of a Garden* chronicle these seasonal transformations in detail.)

Plants are grouped according not only to their rhythms of seasonal display, but also to color. This is most rigorously carried through in the White Garden, which is entirely restricted to white and almost-white blooms. Sackville-West wrote that she aimed for a "cool, almost glaucous" effect and meticulously described the planting:

There is an under-planting of various artemisias, including the old aromatic Southernwood; the silvery Cineraria maritima; *the grey santolina or Cotton Lavender; and the creeping* Archillea ageratifolia. *Dozens of the white Regale lily (grown from seed) come up through these. There are white delphiniums of the Pacific strain; white eremurus; white foxgloves in a shady place on the north side of a wall; the foam of gypsophila; the white shrubby* Hydrangea grandiflora; *white cistus; white Tree peonies;* Buddleia nivea; *white campanulas and the white form of* Platycodon Mariesii, *the Chinese bell-flower. There is a group of the giant Arabian thistle, pure silver, 8 ft. high. Two little Sea Buckthorns, and the grey willow-leaved* Pyrus salicifolia *shelter the grey leaden statue of a Vestal Virgin. Down the central path goes an avenue of white clinging roses, straggling up old almond trees. Later on there will be white Japanese anemones and some white dahlias.*

The White Garden

As she planted it she hoped that "the great ghostly barn-owl will sweep silently across a pale garden, next summer, in the twilight—the pale garden that I am now planting, under the first flakes of snow."

The warm-toned Cottage Garden she described as "a muddle of flowers, but all of them in the range of colors that you might find in a sunset." Delos is dominated by dark tones of green, brown, and gray, and the Orchard in Spring by the pastel of fruit blossoms. There are masses of blue and purple in the beds along the north side of the Front Courtyard.

The pattern of the planting, in contrast with the architectural severity of the enclosures, is informal and romantic. Shapes, textures, and colors are juxtaposed, with studied care, for picturesque effect. Sackville-West commented that "a sense of substance and solidity can be achieved only by the presence of an occasional mass breaking the more airy companies of the little flowers" and felt there should be "alternation between color and solidity, decoration and architecture, frivolity and seriousness." She clearly detested thinness and sparseness, and there is always a sense of overflowing, bursting profusion; not only are the beds filled with masses of foliage and blossom, but there are also pots hanging on the walls, creepers tumbling over the top, and glimpses through openings of yet more treasures in neighboring enclosures.

There is complexity of scent as well as of color and texture and shape. Some of the plants give out their aromas in the early morning, some in the heat of the day, and some in the evening. In the flower-filled enclosures, the scents are experienced as the blooms are "passed by." But the smells produced when plants are "trodon upon and Crushed" are not neglected; the grassy walks through the Orchard and the small Herb Garden provide this experience. All this, like the pattern of colors, follows the seasonal rhythms as the various species come into leaf and bloom.

A grassy walk through the sunlit Orchard

The character of the ground surface is varied from enclosure to enclosure, so that the feel, rhythm, and sound of a visitor's steps, too, are transformed as he moves through this garden. There are springy, flat, perfectly mowed lawns; rough, informal grassy walks mowed casually through the undergrowth of the Orchard; and formal stone and brick paved paths in various patterns.

The shaded, paved Yew Walk

Sensations of warmth and cool are varied as well. In the morning there are sunny corners to be found to the northwest of the White Garden and the Tower Lawn. The Yew Walk has bright and shady sides (like Hadrian's Poecile): sunny along the Orchard side in the morning, in its interior at noon, and along its Tower Lawn side in the afternoon. Delos is always cool and shadowy. There is the shade of a gazebo beside the water, a leafy bower at the center of the White Garden, and a sheltered circle in the Rose Garden, where you can catch the afternoon sun. If you want to feel the breeze, you can climb to the top of the tower.

Sissinghurst presents us with a fixed structure (of walls and enclosures) within which transformations of the collection unfold. There are daily cycles, of corners glowing in the warmth of the sun then falling into shadow, of morning dew and of bees buzzing in the stillness of noon, and of flowers propelling their scents into the evening air. As the seasons rotate, color visits the enclosures one-by-one: the White Garden has its miraculous summer moment, followed by the saturated autumn warmth of the Moat Garden, the interregnum of winter, and the spring pastels of the Lime Walk and the Nuttery. The presence of busy gardeners reminds us that the content of plant collections itself is not static: Sackville-West experimented and readjusted, pruned and removed, added and replanted for decades, and this work continues. Fragments of ruins and mementoes of Sackville-West and Nicolson connect us to the even longer cycles of history: an Elizabethan mansion metamorphoses into a farm, then a locus of glittering literary and political lives, the subject of a newspaper column, and finally a tourist attraction. Like the river of Heraclitus, Sissinghurst cannot be visited twice: it has always, in the meantime, become something different.

Some Botanical Gardens

A botanical collection in Spring (Oxford)

The first of the great European botanical gardens—in Padua, Leyden, and Montpellier in the sixteenth century, then in Paris, Uppsala, and Oxford in the seventeenth—were made after the discovery of the New World, in the age of expansion of the colonial empires. They formed images of the world by collecting specimens from its far corners—the spoils of exploration and conquest.

The motivation for this, as John Prest has suggested in his fine book *The Garden of Eden,* came from a curious piece of medieval reasoning:

The value of a Botanic Garden was that it conveyed a direct knowledge of God. Since each plant was a created thing, and God had revealed a part of himself in each thing that he created, a complete collection of all the things created by God must reveal God completely.

So the founders of the first botanical gardens made their plant collections not merely for pleasure, but as a means of attaining wisdom (in the sense of knowledge of God) and thus of regaining that dominion over nature which man had lost after the Fall. Man might recover Eden, it seemed, by carefully collecting and piecing together its scattered fragments.

In all of the early botanical gardens the collection is overlaid upon a map of the world. There is a square or rectangular walled enclosure (at Padua inscribed within a circle), which is divided into the traditional fourfold pattern of both Persian and medieval European gardens by four paths meeting at a central fountain. These four paths stand for the four rivers flowing out of paradise, and the four quarters represent the continents of Europe, Asia, Africa, and America. (Before the discovery of America the quarters had been identified rather more vaguely with the four corners of the world, and Australia and Antarctica had yet to make their appearance.)

Within the four quarters, specimen beds were laid out systematically to form a living encyclopedia, which could be used as a scientific reference. The parterres were subdivided into assigned places for each family of plants, then for the different members of each family.

The garden at Oxford, for example, still retains the essentials of its original organization. It fronts High Street to the north, and the Cherwell River runs along its eastern boundary. The square plan is about 130 yards on edge, so that about three and a half acres of ground are enclosed. An elegant neoclassical gate, designed by Inigo Jones, forms the entry from High

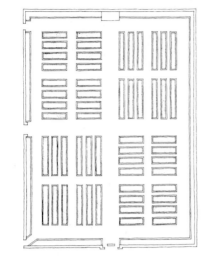

Leyden

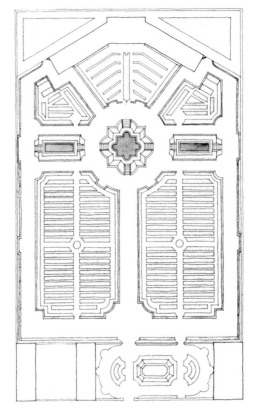

Uppsala

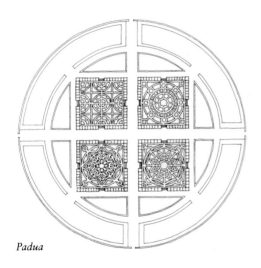

Padua

Paris

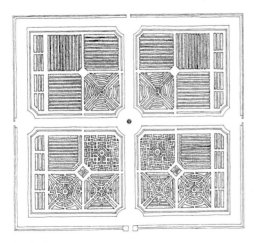

Oxford

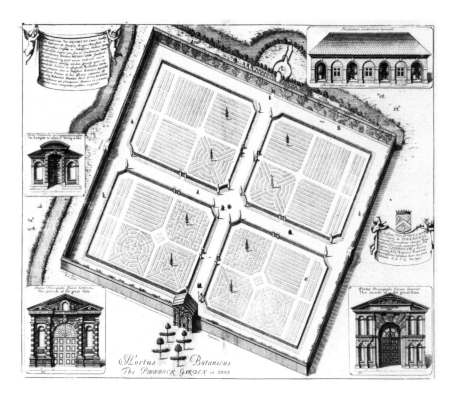

The Oxford Botanic Gardens

Street. The original fourteen-foot stone walls still surround the garden on three sides, but these have been replaced by the Old Botany School along High Street. The broad gravel paths meet at a shaded central fountain.

The four interior squares are now filled with long rectangular beds containing herbaceous plants and shrubs set out in family groups and by lawns with specimen trees and shrubs. Climbing plants cover the walls. The only concessions that botanical systematizing makes to the Genius of the Place are pragmatic. As the Royal Horticultural Society's guide dryly points out, "The walls themselves provide a variety of aspects for 300 different climbing plants, with tender shrubs against the southwest facing wall of the Old Botany School. Ferns, lilies, and ivies are planted in north-facing borders and new trees are planted wherever space permits between older specimens."

This is a garden made for the intellect rather than for the senses, to be studied rather than savored. For most of the year it has the quiet appeal of a scholar's library. But in May and June it is suddenly filled with blossoms and new ducklings, as the college courtyards are filled with the celebration of spring.

By the eighteenth century, when the Royal Botanic Gardens at Kew were founded, different ideas prevailed. At Kew the grounds were laid out not as a finite, closed, fourfold world, but as an English "natural" landscape with rolling, grassy slopes, picturesque clumps of trees, and meandering water—a setting attuned to the temper of liberal, self-confident, expansionary modern science, rather than that of medieval theology. One by one buildings emblematic of a worldwide empire made their appearance: the Far East was represented by a pagoda by Sir William Chambers, the tropics by Decimus Burton's Palm House, and eventually the Antipodes by the

Australian House. From Kew the great botanist Joseph Banks directed a vast enterprise of exploration, collection, cultivation, and classification, aimed not only at the expansion of knowledge, but also at meeting the empire's practical needs; he arranged, among other things, for the planting of tea in India and breadfruit in the West Indies.

Shoreline near Sydney

Southern flowers

As a young man, in 1796, Banks had sailed on the famous voyage of the *Endeavour*, with Sir James Cook, to observe from Tahiti the transit of Venus across the sun. ("Any blockhead can go to Italy," he reportedly told a friend who inquired about his plans for the usual Grand Tour of Europe, "Mine shall be around the world.") Accompanying Banks were his assistant Daniel Solander (a pupil of Linnaeus), and the botanical draftsman Sydney Parkinson. After leaving Tahiti the *Endeavour* continued to New Zealand, and from there southwest to the eastern shores of the huge, unexplored continent of New Holland. They landed at a place later known as Botany Bay (near where Sydney's airport now stands) at three o'clock in the afternoon of April 29, 1770. Cook and his men became the first Europeans to set foot on the eastern shores of Australia. Banks and Solander sighted curious fauna and carried numerous specimens of unfamiliar antipodean plants back to an astonished England.

Thus began an exchange: the southern continent sent flowers to London and London (after some time for thought) sent back 736 assorted highway robbers, petty thieves, sheep stealers, fences, swindlers, forgers, and other criminals. A decade after news of the landing at Botany Bay, the jails of a rapidly urbanizing England were jammed. Even the rotting, pestilent hulks along the Thames, which housed the overflow, could take no more. Mass executions seemed impractical (though a vast number were held for capital crimes), and, of course, the American colonies could no longer serve as a convenient dumping ground. So Botany Bay, on the farthest rim of the world, seemed a good place for a gulag. On May 13, 1787, Governor Arthur Phillip set sail with the First Fleet, of convicts and soldiers, to Australia.

The voyage (via Tenerife, Rio de Janeiro, and Cape Town) took 252 days. Forty-eight people died on the way. The fleet arrived at Botany Bay in midsummer 1788, but Phillip quickly decided that its blazingly hot sandy shore, scattered with grass trees and scribbly gum, the inedible wooden pear, and the flowering banksia, was no place for a settlement. He sailed a few miles northwest, entered a large protected harbor, and settled in what became the town of Sydney on the wooded hills along the shores of Port Jackson.

In the century of William Kent's famous leap, to see that "all nature was a garden," these unwilling pioneers found themselves in a wild land that had never known cultivation, surrounded by a fence of endless space that nobody could leap. The familiar cycle of the seasons was inverted, with Christmas falling at the height of summer. Swans, perversely, were black. The subtropical southern sun moved across a different half of the sky, so protective verandahs had to be placed along the northern sides of the houses. At night the Southern Cross and a brilliant splash of Milky Way replaced the reassuringly constant constellations of the north. In place of the soft green grass of home and the cool shady foliage of oaks and elms, the English found a dry, brown land with dusty gray-green, blue, and brown eucalyptus and wattle, whose sparse foliage cast only speckled, gauzy traces of shade upon the ground. (A popular poem by Dorothea Mackellar was later to describe Australia as a "sunburnt country.") The wattle trees blossomed brilliant yellow in wintry July, but the colors of autumn never disturbed the cyan constancy of the bush. Marcus Clarke, who wrote *For the Term of His Natural Life,* a famous novel of the horrors of the convict days, complained that "in other lands the dying year is mourned," but no bared limbs mark the antipodean fall. Kangaroos, emus, wombats, giant goannas, poisonous snakes and spiders, thousands of small black bush-flies, and bizarre parrots and cockatoos took the place of the familiar, gentle fauna of the English countryside. All around there were hostile aboriginals and the impenetrable ring of the Blue Mountains (not to be crossed for decades). And home was eight or nine months away, by uncertain voyage across half the world; most of the colonists would never see it again.

But Phillip had sailed with seeds and plants from England (loaded under the supervision of Sir Joseph Banks himself). In Rio de Janeiro he had added coffee, cocoa, cotton, banana, orange, lemon, guava, tamarind, prickly pear, eugenia, and ipecacuanha, and at the Cape of Good Hope he had purchased fig, bamboo, Spanish reed, sugar cane, vines, quince, apple, pear, strawberry, oak, myrtle, rice, wheat, barley, and Indian corn. Colonization was to be botanical, as well. By July 1788 Phillip had established a government farm at a place now called Farm Cove (just to the east of the settlement at Sydney Cove) and had nine acres under wheat. A small monument today commemorates it as the place where "the agriculture and horticulture of a continent" began.

A pioneer's house in the bush

Sydney grew as successive convict fleets arrived, and slowly, from their fragile imported plants and the fading images in their minds, the colonists constructed fragments of a remembered England. Georgian buildings were erected by Francis Greenway, a competent pupil of John Nash, who arrived (transported for forgery) in 1814. Gardens became patches of damp, shaded expatriate green among the native browns and olives. Even today in the Australian countryside the site of an old house is instantly recognizable in the distance as a patch of foreign color.

Georgian Sydney, drawn by
William Hardy Wilson

In his planning for the new town, Governor Phillip had provided for spacious gardens around Government House; these grounds were later extended by Governor William Bligh (the notorious former captain of the *Bounty*). In 1810 Governor Lachlan Macquarie built a stone wall around the Government House gardens and the fields of Farm Cove, and by 1816 he had completed Mrs. Macquarie's Road through this domain to a harborside rock seat now called Mrs. Macquerie's Chair. This marked the foundation of the Sydney Botanic Gardens, on the site of the continent's first cultivation and adjacent to the port for the long journey back to London. Like its contemporaries at Rio de Janeiro, Pamplemousses in

Sydney Botanic Gardens, adjacent to
Sydney Cove

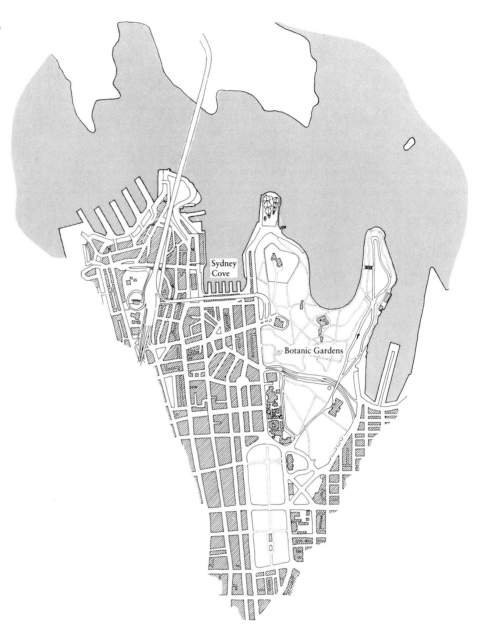

Sydney
Cove

Botanic Gardens

The end of the voyage to the Antipodes

Mauritius, Bogor in Java, Hobart in Van Diemen's Land (now Tasmania), and Melbourne in the colony of Port Phillip (now Victoria), it has become one of the great gardens of the South Seas.

It is made of smoothly shaven, astonishingly green hillsides that slope down to the sparkling blue waters of Sydney Harbour (rather than to a silvery lake, as they might in a Capability Brown park). Early settlers had often been reminded of English park landscape by the topography of Port Jackson, and the layout conspires with this vision. Enormous fig trees protect it from the sun: the native Port Jackson fig (some may be part of the original vegetation of the site), the Moreton Bay fig from the northern rainforests, and banyans from the islands. There are a couple of forest red gums surviving from pre-colonial days, and there is a line of very old swamp mahogany trees along Mrs. Macquarie's Road. Norfolk Island pines (from an even more terrible penal colony, far out in the Pacific) provide vertical contrast to the spreading masses of the figs, and there are the bizarre shapes of the dragon's blood trees from the Canary Islands, and the swollen Queensland bottle trees. Of English deciduous trees there are plenty, but they refuse to produce bright autumn foliage here; the most brilliant reds are the flowers that appear on the bare branches of the flame tree, from the tropical rainforests of the north. Old World flowers share beds with the natives.

Where the first botanical gardens had arrayed specimens of God's handiwork on an ancient diagram of the world, and Kew had situated great scientific enterprises in a noble park, Sydney's garden overlays native wonders on recollections of a lost, green home on the far side of the earth. Within the boundaries of this quiet and shady place the antipodes were connected; the breadth of the world was compressed into the compass of a Sunday afternoon's stroll, and the terror of distance (so much a part of the colonial Australian consciousness) was tamed.

Collections of plants can no longer summon faith in the possibility of paradise reassembled, or pride in far-flung empire, and distance has little power to oppress in a world of satellite links and jumbo jets. But the sight of a South Seas palm protected against the chill of the London winter by the great glasshouse at Kew, or of an English flower shielded against Sydney's summer sun by the spreading branches of a banyan tree, reminds us of the power of plants to move the imagination. A blossom can call up half-lost memories, and a fragrance can carry the imagination across oceans.

PILGRIMAGES

Settings and the pieces of a collection work like nouns—objects that stand, as metaphors or metonyms, for other things. "Pilgrimage" is also a noun, but one whose implications are altogether of action, or a verb. People *go* on pilgrimages, on quests, sacrificing to make them, perhaps enduring discomforts or hardships or even dangers along the way as the price that must be paid to reach a goal. Myths and fairy stories abound in quests, as Hercules performs his labors or young heroes search for something and eventually find it, and their manhood, or perhaps the hand of the princess. Gardens hardly ever contain (knowingly) any dragons or other mortal peril, but they can be choreographed to make a trip through them full of variety and excitement, with qualities that pull the pilgrim on to a goal and reward arrival there, perhaps with a resting place or a cool splashing fountain, even as a well-constructed narrative pulls us on to the climax and the end.

Pilgrimage gardens, like settings and collections, do not form a precise and exclusive category; most real gardens function in several ways at once and are likely to have settings along a pilgrimage route or collections revealed beside the way. Katsura, especially, which we have considered principally as a collection of moods and references, is also a carefully choreographed pilgrimage route around a pond.

There are close affinities between pilgrimage gardens and literary narratives, but they have differing economies of time and space. A narrative text unfolds in time, and its author must, somehow, suggest the space for its action. A pilgrimage garden *has* the space, but its designer must suggest the time dimension by establishing a sequence of movement through it. The pilgrim's path might lead to some end altogether different from the beginning, or it might circle back to where it began—like a fairy tale in which, however dragon-strewn the adventure, the young protagonist is certain to be home in time for tea.

Amarnath

Innumerable Shiva shrines and temples in Hindu Asia share a common diagram. Since the sacred mountain Meru is taken to be the center of the universe, and since Shiva is the supreme mountain god, there is a massive stone superstructure in the formalized image of a mountain. Cut into this is a small, dark cave of a sanctuary: the abode of Shiva. The traditional symbol of Shiva, an erect phallus called a lingam, is set within. The worshiper ascends the mountain to the cave, enters, and places offerings at the lingam.

We can find this pattern as far south as Prambanan, in Java, where the immense Larajonggrang Temple stands. Its four-sided stone superstructure rises from an elevated platform and is approached by four flights of steps. At the head of each flight is a dark chamber. One of these leads to the central sanctuary, while the other three contain images of Shiva, Ganesha, and Durga. We find the pattern, too, at the other edge of the Hindu world, in Kashmir. The miniature temple at Pandrethan (just outside Srinagar) stands within a moat. Four sets of steps lead into a single central chamber. Here there is a stone lingam, surrounded by offerings of flowers; water, like the lingam a symbol of vitality and fertility, drips onto it from above.

In the Himalayas to the east of Pandrethan, set among glaciers in a mountainside at nearly thirteen thousand feet, is a huge natural cave called Amarnath. Within there is a mystery: a five-foot ice lingam, formed in the summer months by dripping water. The story circulates that it waxes and

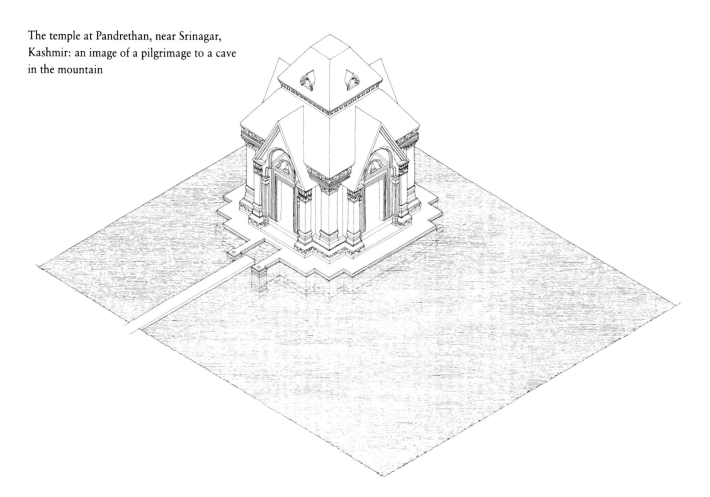

The temple at Pandrethan, near Srinagar, Kashmir: an image of a pilgrimage to a cave in the mountain

wanes with the moon and grows to its fullest stature on Sravana Purnima day—the time of the full moon in August.

Such a wonder could scarcely fail to inspire legend. Shiva, it is said, dwells in the cave, accompanied by two pigeons, and out of the nearby lake of Sheshnag the Lord Vishnu once appeared riding on a thousand-headed serpent. So powerful is the cave's symbolism that it was chosen as the spot to scatter the ashes of the assassinated Indira Gandhi. And every year at the full moon of August tens of thousands of pilgrims ascend to it, along the valleys and over the high passes, from the Vale of Kashmir.

The pilgrims come from every part of India, and they are of all ages and classes. There are naked, ash-covered *sadhus* (holy men), fat businessmen from Bombay clutching their briefcases, soldiers in uniform, young sari-clad women carrying babies, family groups with elaborate camping gear, imperious rich old women borne on litters, and a scattering of foreigners with rucksacks and cameras. The men of the local villages are Muslim and presumably have little regard for ice images of infidel gods, but they keep their peace and patrol the trails with scruffy mountain horses for hire.

In the years before the modern road network in the Vale of Kashmir was constructed, the pilgrims walked all the way from Srinagar. Now there are two much shorter foot trails. The traditional route begins in the Alpine meadows of a small resort town called Pahalgam, in the upper valley of the Liddar River to the east of Srinagar. A second, quicker route, begins farther north at the village of Baltal, in the valley of the Sind River at the foot of the Zojila Pass, which leads up into Ladakh. The two routes merge into one near the valley named Sangham, a few miles short of Amarnath.

The Baltal route (which you can follow in and out in a day, if you are fit) climbs southeast through the Kuth Pathar and Nagin Pathar mountains. It begins in pine forests, then emerges beyond the treeline onto granite and slate mountain sides. Deep in the canyons below are the camps of nomadic shepherds and glacial bridges crossing the streams. After crossing the pass at Brarimarg, there is a steep descent into the valley of Sangham, then an equally steep climb out again to meet the Pahalgam path.

Pilgrims usually take two or three days to walk in from Pahalgam, and they stay along the way in huge, crowded camps, where pundits recite the Sanskrit *Amarkatha*, which tells the pilgrimage's story. The route first leads northeast up the wooded valley of a mountain stream to the village of Chandawari. From here there is a steep climb up a spur of Pissu Ghati to the first pass of the journey. The trail continues along bare mountain sides parallel to the stream, but now is high above it, and eventually reaches the source in the green waters of Sheshnag Lake, from which Vishnu once arose. This lake, at an elevation of twelve thousand feet, is formed by glaciers descending from surrounding peaks of about sixteen thousand feet. There is a windy rest point called Warjan on the trail above Sheshnag, then still another climb of two thousand feet to reach the bleak, gray Mahagunas Pass. The Panchtarni Plain follows, and flower-filled valleys forming headwaters of the Sind River, until the track from Baltal is met near Sangham.

From the meeting of the two routes, the path continues upstream along the narrow valley of the small Amravati rivulet. For much of the time the Amravati flows beneath a cap of dirty snow. Then the wide mouth of Amarnath is seen ahead; it is set into a gypsum mountainside, at an elevation of about thirteen thousand feet, and looks out over an amphitheater floored with white gypsum dust and boulders. To one side, the Amravati cascades from its source. All around are glacial slopes, and peaks of sixteen to seventeen thousand feet.

In the traditional pilgrimage the worshipers reach the amphitheater on the evening before the full moon, then climb up to the cave at dawn the next morning. A crowded tent city assembles. By day, slow lines of pilgrims wind up to the cave to enter the sanctuary of Shiva, chant prayers, and place offerings on the ice, which slowly melts as the day goes on.

The return of the successful pilgrims, their foreheads marked with red sandalwood paste, is a quick and joyous one. They have endured hardship, but they have seen the god.

Amarnath is wild and beautiful, but surely not more so than other parts of the Himalayas; it is the yearly human *act* of pilgrimage, constantly reaffirming the legend, which makes it so memorable. Each year the place emerges from the impenetrable snow, to be seen briefly by thousands, then is reclaimed by the cold and silence once again. V. S. Naipaul has com-

Pilgrims rest by the trail

Descent into the Valley of
Sangham

The valley of the Amravati

The mouth of the cave

The camp in the amphitheater of the cave

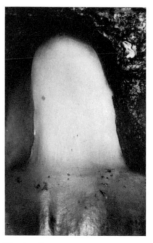

The ice lingam

mented (in *An Area of Darkness*) that Amarnath's mountains, lakes, and streams seem to have "only a qualified reality." He writes:

They could never become familiar; what was seen was not their truth; they were only temporarily unveiled. They might be subject to minute man-made disturbances—a stone dislodged into a stream, a path churned to dust—skirting snow—but as soon as, on that hurried return journey, they had been left behind they became remote again. Millions had made the journey, but the naked land carried few signs of their passage. Each year the snow came and obliterated their tracks, and each year in the cave the ice lingam formed. The mystery was forever new.

Lamayuru

An agricultural valley in Ladakh (Chendey)

If you take the road up from the floor of the Vale of Kashmir, past the approaches to Amarnath and over the Zojila Pass, you reach a high, hard, and dangerous place called Ladakh. It is the upper valley of the Indus River where, at an altitude of twelve to sixteen thousand feet, it begins to make its descent from Tibet to the plains of India.

A village in Ladakh (Zulidok)

A refuge on a peak (Chendey)

A refuge commanding the head of a valley (Trakthok)

This is a travelers' place; many have passed through, but few have stayed. For centuries, until very recently, it was the main caravan route between Tibet and India. It was also a tributary (connecting Yarkand to the Bombay coast) of the Silk Road. Due to its strategic position, it has always been subject to raids and incursions from Jammu and Kashmir on one side and Tibet on the other. For Rudyard Kipling it became the land beyond the Passes of the North that beckoned Kim from Lahore to play the Great Game. And it remains a land of Tibetan Buddhist faith—the land where Kim's lama companion ended his search, and his soul went free.

At the height of summer the valley landscape at Ladakh is trisected, with Euclidean precision, into vertical layers. The flat valley floor, irrigated by the streams, is covered by the bright green of crops. Cows, yaks, and sheep graze here, and there are hamlets and villages set among the fields. Then, where the irrigation stops at the feet of the surrounding mountains, there is a sudden change to forbiddingly bare brown rock and granite dust. The slopes are lifeless and motionless, silently reflecting the intensity of the high-altitude sun. Many thousands of feet above, far from the places of human habitation, the violently ripped and twisted profiles of the peaks are sharply outlined against the cloudless deep blue of the Himalayan summer sky. Heaven and earth are parallel planes of pure, perfect color, with the hostile mountains in between.

In winter, the malevolent fury of wind, snow, and ice is unsurpassed in any inhabited region of the world. The people of Ladakh can only retreat to their compact, thick-walled houses to cluster around tiny fires, on which teapots bubble, to wait it out.

The pattern of human habitation in these high valleys, then, is one of fortified refuges between which fragile webs of trails are spun. These refuges are of two kinds: old royal palaces (at Shey, Ley, Stok, Basgo, and Ting-mo-sgang) and citadel-like Buddhist monasteries dating from the fifteenth century and later. (There are some unfortified monasteries too, left from earlier, more peaceful times.) Generally these refuges are found, like Greek acropoli, at places that command the surrounding landscape and that can be defended. Around them are clustered villages and fields.

The royal palaces all stand on peaks that either rise from the valley floor or project out into it from the surrounding mountains. So do many of the

A refuge set into a mountainside (Shergol)

A protected courtyard lies at the heart of each monastery (Chendey)

A prayer flag stands against danger

Looking out from the safety of the refuge

monasteries: Mulbek, Ringdom, Lamayuru, Spikuk, and Phiyang, for example. Others, such as Hemis and Trakthok, command the heads of the valley. A few, like the tiny retreat at Shergol, are set back almost flush into sheer mountainsides.

The thick mud and rubble walls of these buildings are whitewashed, so in the sunlight they stand out brilliantly from the blue sky and brown peaks and announce their presence to travelers still many miles away. The windows are outlined by thick bands of dark paint and stare out large and lustrous, like mascaraed eyes. At the corners of the roofs stand gilded finials with shreds of cloth and tassels of yak hair fluttering in the breeze.

Each of these citadels contains a central courtyard: a sunny and protected place, usually surrounded by wooden verandahs, with buildings on several sides and with windows to look out over the fields and villages below. Here clusters of monks gather in warm corners to talk, pack donkeys are loaded and unloaded, firewood is stacked, and in deep winter elaborate dance festivals take place.

Everywhere in Ladakh the traveler making his way along the narrow, bumpy trails connecting the palaces, forts, and monasteries or through the winding, hillside streets of a village is accompanied by a silent but palpable chorus of endlessly repeated *mantras*. Monks sit in the monastery courtyards and patiently spin prayer wheels. And prayer wheels are also strategically placed where they can be given a turn by each passerby. Prayer flags flutter on vertical poles or are strung like pathetically vulnerable cobwebs between crags and peaks. Marking the approaches to settlements are rows of *chötens*: small, whitewashed *stupas* of complex significance; the religious historian Giuseppe Tucci describes them as buildings "designed to symbolise the ultimate essence of the Buddha and of any other created being who by virtue of asceticism has realised the body of Buddha." There might be just a handful at the approaches to a poor hamlet, or there might be a long, proud avenue at a more important place. Accompanying the *chötens,* very often, are *mani* walls, sometimes thousands of feet long. These are heaped with smooth, flat stones, each one inscribed with a *mantra*. Thus the approach to a settlement becomes a pilgrimage from *chöten* to *chöten,* in the constant presence of prayer.

The most moving of these approaches is to the great monastery of Lamayuru, via a narrow, steep-sided valley. The first sign of habitation is a single *chöten,* appearing suddenly around a bend. This turns out to be the first in a row of hundreds which, accompanied by a sinuous *mani* wall, line the remainder of the trail. The valley floor gradually broadens out, so that there is room for the fields upon which the settlement depends for its tenuous existence. You begin to meet a few travelers with yaks and donkeys and to see people working in the fields, but this sparse and transitory human presence seems scarcely noticeable compared to the awesome, eternal chorus of *mantras* inscribed upon tens of thousands of *mani* stones. The monastery appears ahead, on a peak that rises abruptly from the val-

The approach to Lamayuru

The valley leading to Lamayuru

The mani *wall*

Stones with mantras

The streets of the village

ley floor and has the houses of the village spilling down its slopes. The approach continues through the village streets, lined with prayer wheels, and you eventually reach a protected courtyard surrounded by halls in which flickering yak-butter lamps reveal images of gods and demons painted on *thangkas, mandalas,* gold and silver treasures, and the surprise of polaroid pictures of the Dalai Lama.

This landscape does not belong to the gods, like that of Amarnath; it has been claimed (however tenuously) for human habitation. The tracks of the traveler are not obliterated by the yearly snows, but are permanently marked by the line of the *mani* wall—beginning in wild nature, gathering fields and pastures about it as it goes, and eventually winding into the streets of a village. The goal is not a miracle of nature, but a construction of man; progress toward it is celebrated by the rhythm of *chötens*. And the thousands of *mani* stones lining the wall, each one placed in gratitude for a safe arrival, tell us that multitudes have passed this way.

Rousham

The countryside of England is a softly green and pleasant place, beautiful (in Burke's sense) rather than sublime like the Himalayas, and the gentlemen gardeners of the eighteenth century had little in common with Tibetan Lamaists or followers of Shiva, but they too made places for pilgrimage—on foot or on horseback, from one allusive scene to another. Their appeal is to a classically educated sensibility, informed by the landscape criticism of Alexander Pope and Horace Walpole.

Walpole's great work on gardening, *History of the Modern Taste in Gardening,* is a cheerful adventure tale, full of praise for heroes and accounts of their startling deeds and discoveries. And no episode in it is more dramatic than the appearance of the architect, painter, and landscape designer William Kent. "At that moment appeared Kent," wrote Walpole, "painter enough to taste the charms of landscape, bold and opinionative enough to dare and to dictate, and born with a genius to strike out a great system from the twilight of imperfect essays. He leaped the fence, and saw that all nature was a garden."

The garden Kent designed at Rousham House, beside the River Cherwell not far from Oxford, reveals the reasons for Walpole's excitement. He called it "the most engaging of all Kent's works." It is one of the best preserved of all eighteenth-century English gardens, matured now into quiet and splendid perfection. We can still follow its pilgrimage route, taking Walpole and Pope as our guides.

The site of Rousham extends along one bank of the Cherwell, at a point where the course of this modest stream makes a right-angled turn from south to east. Across the river are flat fields and hedgerows, with Cotswold hills making a distant boundary to a broad river valley. There is a very narrow strip of flat land along the Rousham bank, and above this the ground rises steeply to form north-facing and east-facing slopes. At the bend in the river, where the two slopes meet, is a hollow that originally contained a sequence of fish ponds descending from the west. Rousham

Looking back from the refuge of the monastery

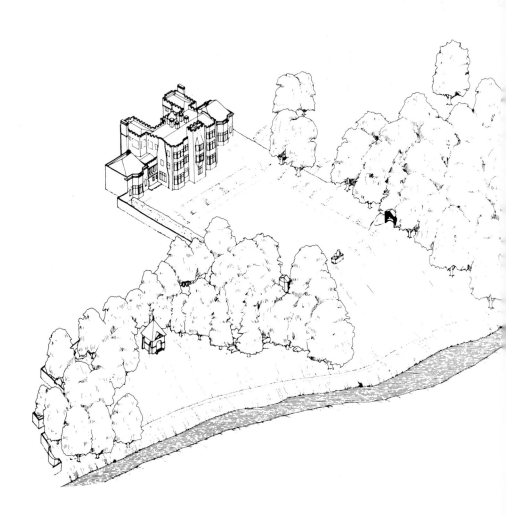

ROUSHAM

Water, landform, and buildings

Planting

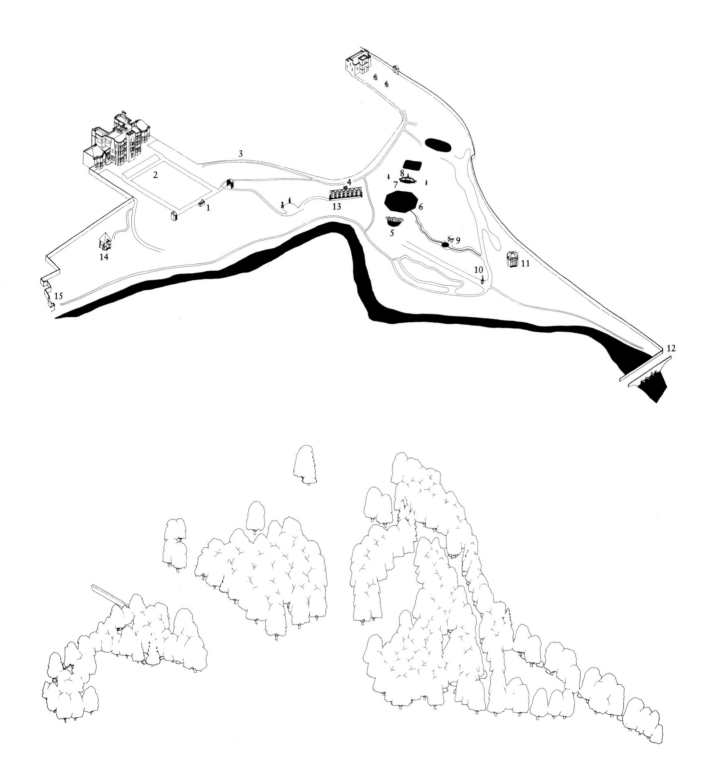

House, dating from the early seventeenth century, stands on a wide, flat expanse at the head of the north slope. The thirteenth-century Heyford Bridge across the Cherwell terminates the site to the north, and Rousham Village forms the eastern boundary.

Like many old gardens, Rousham is a palimpsest, a much-reworked surface of overlaid intentions and overwritten designs. To the east of the house are early formal gardens, reminders of the time before Kent's leap: a sunny, walled enclosure with a pigeon house and rose bushes, a medieval churchyard at the end, and a rectangular kitchen garden. Sometime around 1720 Charles Bridgeman produced an extensive design for the remainder of the grounds. Alexander Pope knew and admired Rousham at this stage, and it is sometimes claimed that he collaborated in Bridgeman's scheme. Kent apparently began working at Rousham in the early 1730s, inflecting the Bridgeman scheme into something radically new. His ponds and walks still remain, and his planting has waxed in majesty with the passing of two hundred years.

Horace Walpole may have consigned Bridgeman's Rousham to the twilight of imperfect essays, but, like Le Nôtre's Vaux-le-Vicomte of the century before, it did set the eye and the imagination in motion toward the distant horizon. Through riverbank woods, a vast rectangular Bowling Green opened up the northern view from the house to the hills across the Cherwell valley. This remains today, bounded by gravel walks and dotted with white daisies in the spring. Grassy banks parallel the east and west edges, and a lichen-encrusted statue of a lion attacking a horse (by P. Scheemaker, 1740) marks the axis of symmetry. Where the land falls away to the river, there is a concave grassy slope, planted on either side with masses of evergreens.

On the slopes to the northwest of the house, Bridgeman deployed a system of straight walks slicing through woodland to connect landmarks and rest points. At the hinge between the north and east slopes, the fish ponds were cast into formal, axially composed waterworks. A secondary system of narrower paths, made in rococo wriggles, was set up in contrast.

Kent's Rousham retains the Bowling Green, the chain of ponds, and the straight walk running north from their foot. But paths are reshaped, scenes are recomposed in a new style, and the visitor is now led from surprise to surprise in carefully established sequence. It becomes a demonstration of Pope's suggestion, made in the *Moral Essays*, that

He gains all ends who pleasingly confounds,
Surprises, varies and conceals the bounds.

We shall follow the circuit, much as Kent intended. The starting point is the *Bowling Green*. From here the axis through the house and *Scheemaker's statue* soars out high across the Cherwell Valley, literally leaping the fence, eventually coming to earth once more in the distant hills. At this point Kent placed a sham ruin (called the Eye-Catcher) on the skyline. It is nothing more than a flat piece of stone wall, shaped into a picturesque silhouette, but it serves to capture a broad expanse of countryside and make it part of a unified composition. Massed trees sharply define the

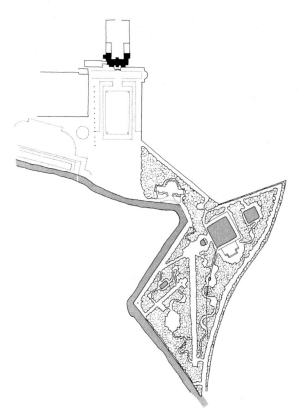

Sketch of Charles Bridgeman's scheme for
Rousham, about 1720

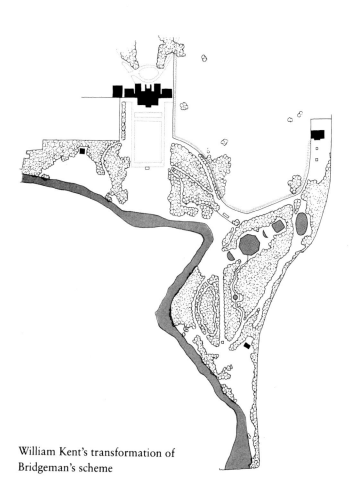

William Kent's transformation of
Bridgeman's scheme

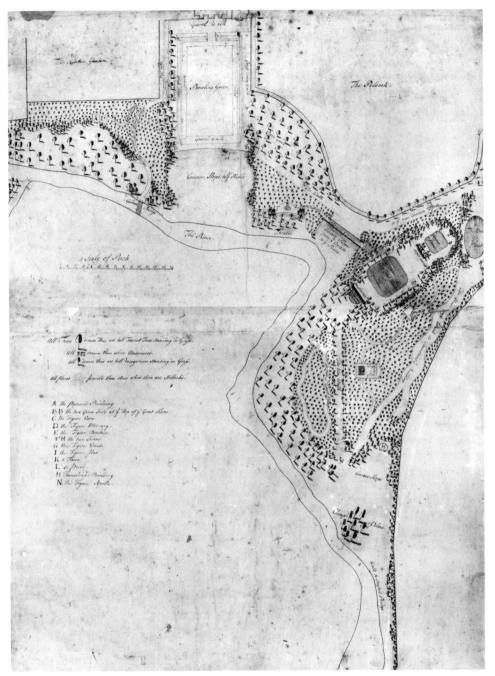

Kent's planting plan for Rousham

1. Scheemaker's statue of a lion attacking a horse on the axis of the Bowling Green

2. The Bowling Green flanked by gazebos

3. The ha-ha and paddock

4. The Dying Gladiator on the Praeneste Terrace

5. The lower cascade of the Vale of Venus

6. The octagonal fish pond in the Vale of Venus

7. The upper cascade of the Vale of Venus

edges of the view; and placed symmetrically on either side, backed up against the foliage, are two lacy white gazebos. In spring there is a delicate color harmony between the greens of the grass and trees, the white of scattered daisies and of the gazebos, and the sequence of encrusted stone surfaces disposed along the axis, first at the facade of the house, then at the statue, and finally at the Eye-Catcher.

This scene introduces a theme that will be repeated and varied at many later points. Its essentials are an axis conducting the eye out over hidden foreground slopes to a distant view, an evocative image placed on the axis, symmetrically disposed subsidiary features on either side, and parallel walls of foliage.

At the northwest corner of the Bowling Green is a wooded slope down to the river, and to the southwest is a large *grazing paddock,* separated from the house and gardens by a *ha-ha.* Kent's plan of 1837–38 shows a straight walk cut through the wooded area, with the zone between this walk and the paddock labeled an "open grove." This would have provided an afternoon stroller with views, through back-lit foliage, across the ha-ha and into the paddock. Walpole reported that Kent remarked how "loose groves . . . called in the distant view between their graceful stems, removed and extended the perspective by delusive comparison." Once more then, a view across a concealed boundary was captured as part of the garden. To-day the wood is dense and the path curves around the edge adjacent to the ha-ha, so this effect is largely lost. But there is a compensation if a visit is made in early spring, when the banks of the ha-ha are thickly overgrown with daffodils.

The first defined stopping point along the visitor's path is at a small, flat area called the *Praeneste Terrace.* Here there is a sudden opening of the woods to reveal a wide view out across the Cherwell Valley to the north-east and across the paddock to the southwest. It is here that we find the first variation on the theme introduced by the (much larger) Bowling Green. There is a statue at the center of the vista, in this case a cast-lead *Dying Gladiator.* The woods on either side are stopped formally by sym-metrically placed stone term-figures. In spring the ground is flooded with the surprising yellow of densely planted daffodils. A balustrade defines the northeast edge, and ground cover prevents one from approaching this too closely. This has the effect of cutting off any view of the foreground slope down to the river (very deliberately, as we shall see), but reveals the bend in the river and provides upstream and downstream perspectives.

From the path to the Dying Gladiator the main features of the garden are concealed by screens of trees; views across the ha-ha and paddock to the house make it seem a *ferme orné.* But now Kent makes one of his most dramatic moves: Bridgeman had led the visitor onward, to look down on the ponds from above, but Kent invites us down a steep descent, along a narrow path through the woods, to a tiny valley filled with ponds and cas-cades. We find ourselves at the foot of the *Vale of Venus.*

Walpole said of this little glade that "the whole is as elegant and antique as if the emperor Julian had selected the most pleasing solitude about

8. The statue of Venus

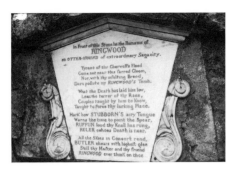

The inscription in memory of Ringwood

Daphne to enjoy a philosophic retirement." The lowest pond is a semi-circle fed by a rustic, arched cascade. Uphill from this is a wide, *octagonal pond.* Farther up a grassy slope, on axis with the ponds, is the upper cascade. This is crowned by a slightly overweight *figure of Venus* looking out over the water, backed up by a screen of branches. She is attended by swans and cuddly cupids at each side of the cascade, while Pan and a faun almost conceal themselves in the surrounding trees. Venus gazes out along an axis of symmetry to the distant hills—rehearsing the role that the visitor has already played twice, first at the Bowling Green and then at the Praeneste Terrace. An inscription at her feet turns out to be doggerel in memory of one Ringwood, "an otter hound of extraordinary sagacity." As at Katsura, there is an improbable but successful collision of moods: the Vale of Venus is ridiculously sentimental and convincingly magical at the same time.

We can see here the demonstration of Walpole's remark that "the great principles on which [Kent] worked were perspective, and light and shade." From the foot of the vale, foreshortening conceals the ponds, stacks up stone walls in successive layers, and produces a *trompe l'oeil* of descending cascades. In the long summer afternoons back-lit grass becomes almost incandescently green against a scrim of foliage. Water glitters, and there is the *chiaroscuro* of shadowy caverns contrasted with grassy slopes.

The slope to the north of the Vale of Venus is woodland, and it screens from view the wall and road running along the western boundary of the site. It serves, in Walpole's words, for "veiling deformities by screens of plantation."

9. The Cold Bath

Several paths lead north through the woods from Venus's Vale, eventually to reach a grassy hillside. Each reflects something of Bridgeman's earlier scheme, and each has its own character. The farthest from the river is an irregular grassy walk running along the boundary from the uppermost ponds (now gone) of the vale. Through the yew wood to the east of this is cut a graveled serpentine path leading from the octagonal pool. Then there is a straight, grassed, elm-lined walk rising from the foot of the vale. Finally, there is a gravel path running through clumps of trees on the flat land beside the river's edge.

Running along the serpentine path is a tiny, wriggling stream, which feeds the octagonal pond. Its smoothly inflected curves clearly anticipate Hogarth's celebrated "line of beauty." But more importantly, it invites us upstream, into the woods, on a journey of discovery. At the center is the garden's heart of shadows: the *Cold Bath.* There is a squat stone building beside a still, silent, densely overgrown octagonal pool. The few shafts of sunlight that filter through the branches overhead make intricate patterns among the dead leaves on the ground and glow in the murky water. We don't quite find darkness here, but we are reminded of the possibility.

10. The Elm Walk leading to the statue of Apollo

A second invitation to stroll onward from the Vale of Venus is issued by the sun, embodied as a colossal *statue of Apollo,* flanked by foliage and silhouetted against the sky at the distant end of the straight rise of the *Elm*

11. The Temple of Echo

12. The walk beside the Cherwell near Heyford Bridge

13. The seven-arched arcade under the Praeneste Terrace

Walk. Apollo has his back to us, which makes us curious to see what he is looking at. This turns out to be an open, grassy hillside sloping gently to the water.

The clearing here is approximately triangular, with southern and western edges formed by woods and a northeastern edge by the Cherwell. Although Rousham is a riverbank garden, this clearing provides the visitor following the established route with his first opportunity to approach the water. It becomes evident that Kent intended, as Walpole put it, "to make the richest scene more enchanting by reserving it to a farther advance of the spectator's step."

At the head of the concave slope to the water, backed by trees, is William Townesend's elegant little *Temple of Echo.* This introduces a new theme: a protected resting place looking out over the water to a carefully framed view. To the north the clearing narrows to an apex just short of *Heyford Bridge,* which terminates the view in that direction.

The path back from the bridge passes alternately through woodland and clearings that open onto the river. Kent's planting plan indicated deliberate and carefully controlled variation in the character of the woods that are traversed, from "tall forest trees" to "underwood" and "tall evergreens," and the spirit of this intention remains. The clearings open up a succession of low-angle perspectives along the river, broken at irregular intervals by clumps of trees, in contrast with the previous views down onto the water from above.

It soon becomes evident that the walk back will also provide a sequence of views back up to the high ground that complement and complete the earlier experiences of looking out from elevated vantage points. The visitor's relation to light and sky is reversed, and there are moments of astonishment as previously visited points are seen from new angles.

First, the riverbank path passes through a clump of elms, and the visitor can look back up to the classical temple. Then the path rounds a bend in the river to reach the foot of the Vale of Venus. A little way beyond, the view is terminated by a *seven-arched classic arcade,* seen at an oblique angle. As the visitor draws closer, the arcade surprisingly discloses itself to be the substructure of the Praeneste Terrace. It stands at the head of a very steep, grassy slope. The approach paths, though, are through trees on either side, past huge urns that formally terminate the foliage; it is intended to be seen receding in perspective, rather than frontally. Within are semicircular alcoves, with curved seats designed by Kent, which provide arch-framed views across the Cherwell Valley.

A glance at the garden plan reveals that Kent's handling of the Praeneste is an amazing *tour-de-force.* With a single gesture, he succeeded in creating, at a cramped and awkward neck in the site, two quite distinct resting places, in opening up sweeping vistas, in providing a picturesque surprise to enliven the return journey, and in inflecting the returning visitor's path from south to east. There could be no better illustration of Pope's principle (from "An Epistle to Lord Burlington"), "Start, ev'n from Difficulty, strike, from Chance."

To the east of the site of the Praeneste arcade, Bridgeman's plan showed a semicircular theater; this also appears in Kent's plan. Today the visitor finds only a faint recollection of it, conveyed by the shaping of the ground and the placement of statues half concealed in the undergrowth.

Farther east along the riverbank, the foot of Bridgeman's concave grass slope below the Bowling Green is reached. Scheemaker's statue now appears as a silhouette against the sky. This clearing also serves a pictorial purpose in the wider landscape. As Rousham is approached across the river from the north, the symmetrical south elevation of *Rousham House* is revealed on the skyline, with wooded banks stretching out on either side.

The mass of huge evergreens bounding this clearing on the east stretches almost down to the river, just allowing the riverbank path to squeeze by. As the visitor passes through this gap, Kent's final surprise presents itself. Here there is another triangular clearing facing onto the river, forming a counterpart to the opposite terminus of the site. In this case the uphill apex is filled not by a classical temple, but by a bizarre, pyramid-roofed stone pavilion called the *Pyramid House*. Kent's planting plan shows an open grove of trees in front of the Pyramid House, through which the view across the valley would have been "called in" to the visitor resting inside.

Concealed and shaded in the trees that come down to the river at the eastern apex is a mossy and decaying *classical seat*. This turns the visitor's steps back across the clearing and up along a path through trees to return to the pilgrimage's starting point on the Bowling Green. Here the variations are ended with a restatement of the original theme, oppositions reach a balance, and the symmetry of the experience is completed.

It is the sequential composition of Rousham that repays particularly careful attention and suggests most for the making of our own pilgrimage gardens. As in a musical composition, figures are introduced, transformed and varied, combined and contrasted, allowed to evoke associations and memories, and eventually brought together to create a unity. In the words of Pope, "Parts answ'ring Parts, shall slide into a Whole."

Stourhead

Stourhead, near Salisbury in Wiltshire, is, like Rousham, a well-preserved eighteenth-century landscape garden. It is also organized as a circuit from view to view, but is on a much larger scale, and it is an enclosed domain with extensive internal cross vistas rather than an outlook that achieves grandeur of scope by visually borrowing the surrounding countryside.

This difference is, of course, largely a consequence of the differing capabilities of the two places. Whereas the Rousham garden is stretched out along a high riverbank, the Stourhead garden is set into a basin surrounded by hills. Around 1755 a dam was built across the southwest egress of this basin, and the floor was flooded to form a roughly triangular lake about a quarter of a mile across at its broadest and about twenty acres in extent. The gardens occupy the band of sloping ground between the lake shore and the ridges of the surrounding hills.

14. View across the Cherwell Valley from the Pyramid House

15. The pilgrimage is completed at the classical seat

Although Stourhead has been in fairly continuous transformation for more than two centuries, the original scheme of its maker, Henry Hoare (a banker and amateur of the arts who inherited the property from his mother in 1741), remains clear. It is an eighteenth-century theme park—two hundred years before Disney, and with Virgil and Poussin (not Mickey and Donald) as its animating spirits.

The entrance is from the east, along a valley that descends through the village of Stourton from Colen Campbell's neo-Palladian Stourhead House. The village Main Street (English rustic-picturesque of course, not Norman Rockwell Midwestern like Disneyland's) conducts us into this Magic Kingdom. The street is a passage with one end grounded in the real and the other flying into fantasy, like the looking glasses and beanstalks, whirlwinds and backless wardrobes of literature.

The scenes of the garden are meant to be visited in a definite sequence, like those of a Disneyland ride (The Pirates of the Carribean, say), but Hoare didn't have twentieth-century mechanical contraptions at his disposal; we simply walk along a path that makes an anticlockwise circuit of the lake, starting out along the eastern shore, then returning down the western shore, and reaching completion via the southern shore.

The major points of interest along the way are:

1. The medieval *Bristol Cross*. This once stood in the High Street of Bristol but was brought to Stourhead and erected near the entrance in 1765.

2. A five-arched *stone bridge*, with a carpet of turf on top, crossing a short arm of the lake.

3. An urn, marking *Paradise Well*.

4. A tiny Doric *Temple of Flora*.

5. A *detour* from the main path which leads to another medieval relic called Saint Peter's Pump (now standing among sheep in a grassy pasture), a picturesque cottage called the Convent, and the tall, triangular, red-brick King Alfred's Tower, which marks the putative site of his battle with the Danes in 878.

6. A *grotto*, with statues.

7. A *rustic cottage*, with gothic detailing, standing in the woods by the shore.

8. The *Pantheon*, designed by the distinguished architect Henry Flitcroft. It is a miniaturization (though not a literally scaled-down version) of the original in Rome.

9. The *Temple of Apollo*, standing in a small clearing at the top of a steep, wooded rise. This too was designed by Flitcroft, around 1765. It is a reconstruction of the ruined circular Temple of Venus at Baalbec, as suggested by the magnificent plates in Robert Wood's *Ruins of Baalbec*, which had been published in London in 1757.

These elements, and their allusions, are woven into a complex narrative that calls for exegesis. This is not merely a matter of uncovering Hoare's intentions or revealing his prototypes (as garden historians have some-

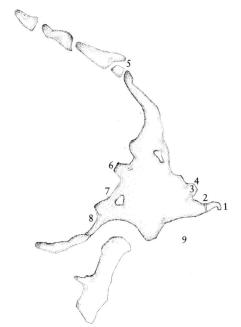

The points of interest along the Stourhead pilgrimage

STOURHEAD
.
Overview

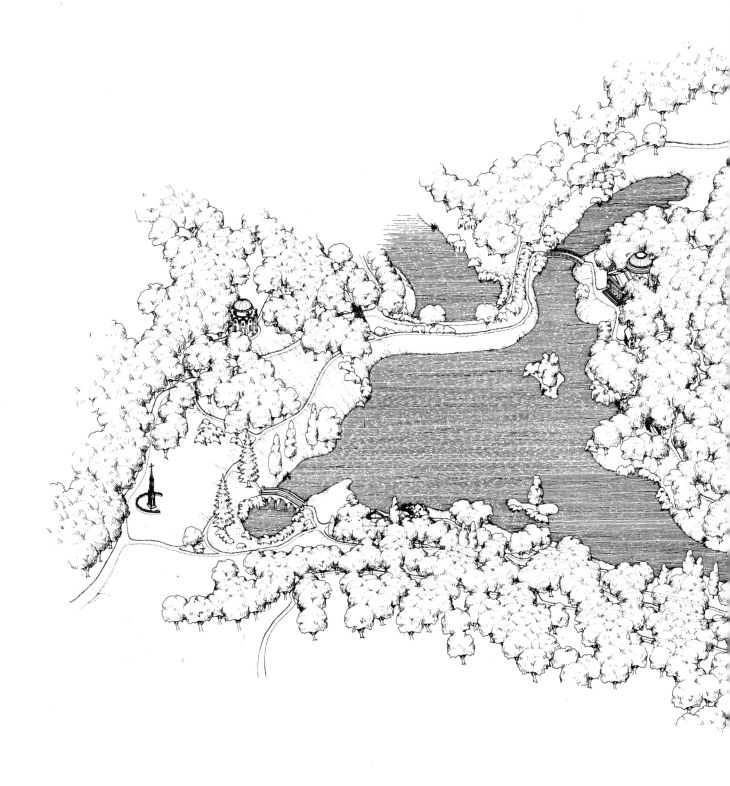

Landform
·
Water and buildings
·
Planting

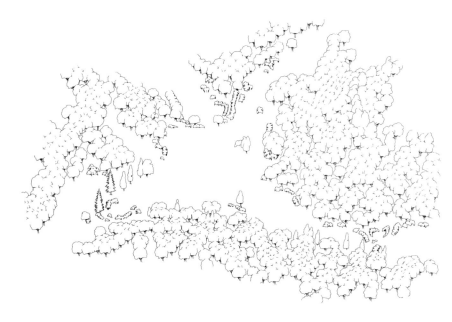

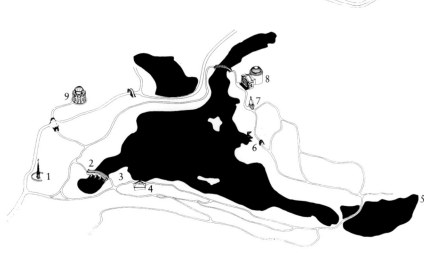

Henry Flitcroft's
Temple of Apollo on
a hilltop at Stourhead

The Temple of Venus at Baalbec, as depicted
in Robert Wood's Ruins of Baalbec

The Bristol Cross

View from the Bristol Cross

times supposed), for Stourhead certainly means more than its creator intended, and has significance for us beyond that. It seduces by offering the subtle pleasures of hermeneutics.

The key text is Virgil's *Aeneid,* which was more familiar to Hoare's classically educated contemporaries than to most of us. It tells the story of the great Trojan Aeneas, who fled with his men from the devastation of Troy, wandered through the Mediterranean, and eventually reached Italy—there to found the Roman Empire. Along the way he had many adventures, including a tragic entanglement with Queen Dido of Carthage, a visit to a temple on the island of Delos, where he received an ambiguous prophecy of his destiny, and a descent into the underworld at Avernus.

The *Aeneid* is first invoked by the panorama that presents itself when you enter the garden and stand by the Bristol Cross. It is a composition in the manner of Claude Lorrain. (Pope had suggested, in the "Epistle on Taste," that "All gardening is landscape painting.") Grassy banks and the arcaded stone bridge create a foreground; the lake occupies the middle distance, and the Pantheon, backed by trees, forms the focus in the distance. In morning light the Pantheon's facade is cast into brilliant contrast with the dark surrounding foliage and produces a clean, sharp reflection in the still water. Claude had made a series of six paintings illustrating episodes from the *Aeneid,* and it seems almost certain that one of these, *Coast View of Delos with Aeneas,* was the direct prototype for this garden scene.

If we follow our progress in the text we find ourselves, at this point, at the beginning of Book VI. Aeneas and his men have fled Carthage (leaving Dido to her death) and have made their way to Delos and drawn their boats up on the beach. Virgil tells us (in Allen Mandelbaum's translation) that Aeneas

seeks the peaks where high Apollo
is king and, in a deep, enormous grotto,
the awful Sybil has her secret home,
for there the seer of Delos so inspires
her mind and soul that she may know the future.

We enter the Claudian scene, with the Temple of Apollo looking down from the peak on our left and the grotto ahead.

When the Sybil was found, and prevailed upon to speak, she prophesied:

O you who are done, at last, with those great dangers
that lie upon the sea—worse wait on land—
the sons of Dardanus will reach Lavinium's
kingdom (for you can now be sure of this)
and yet shall wish that they had never come.
I see wars, horrid wars, the Tiber foaming
with much blood . . .

But Aeneas had another question to pose:

One thing I ask: since here is said to be
the gateway of the lower king and here

Claude Lorrain, *Coast View of Delos with Aeneas:* "there the seer of Delos so inspires her mind and soul that she may know the future"

the marsh of overflowing Acheron,
may it be granted me to go before
the face and presence of my dearest father?

He was speaking of Avernus, the Greek underworld from which Orpheus recalled the spirit of Eurydice. Virgil's narrative continues:

And so Aeneas prayed, clasping the altar;
the prophetess began: "Born of the blood
of gods and son of Troy's Anchises, easy—
the way that leads into Avernus: day
and night the door of darkest Dis is open.
But to recall your steps, to rise again
into the upper air: that is the labor;
that is the task . . .

The Temple of Flora: "easy the way that leads into Avernus"

As we continue our walk around the lake we find, chillingly, Virgil's words "facilis descensus Averno" inscribed over the door of the Temple of Flora.

We pass on through woods and cross a narrow, marshy, tree-lined valley. The text tells us that the Sybil warned:

A bough is hidden in a shady tree;
its leaves and pliant stem are golden, set
aside as sacred to Proserpina.
The grove serves as its screen, and shades enclose
the bough in darkened valleys. Only he
may pass beneath earth's secret spaces who
first plucks the golden-leaved fruit of that tree.

"Shades enclose the bough in darkened valleys"

Aeneas found the golden bough and so, we must imagine, have we.

Now the mouth of the grotto suddenly appears before us. Virgil describes it:

There was a wide-mouthed cavern, deep and vast
and rugged, sheltered by a shadowed lake
and darkened groves; such vapor poured from those
black jaws to heaven's vault, no bird could fly
above unharmed . . .

We descend into its darkness.

The chambers of the grotto house the springs that feed the lake and constitute the original source of the River Stour. Here the Virgilian allegory becomes overlaid with others, as dramatically illuminated figures appear.

"There was a wide-mouthed cavern"

The first figure is of a reclining nymph, lit from above by an oculus in the domed roof of her chamber and by a small gap in the rocky wall opposite, through which she looks out across the lake toward the morning sun. The dim and directional light that results is just sufficient to reveal the boundaries of the place and to cast a gentle gleam onto the flowing water. The east wall forms a dark and jagged mouth to a lake view, seen in the morning through back-lit mist rising off the water. These lines by Pope are inscribed nearby:

Nymph of the Grot these sacred springs I keep
And to the murmur of these waters sleep;
Ah! Spare thy slumbers, gently tread the cave,
And drink in silence or in silence lave.

The arrangement of the grotto also recalls that of the celebrated one in Pope's garden at Twickenham.

The nymph of the grotto

From the center of the nymph's chamber, the statue of a river god can be glimpsed, framed by successive layers of arches. To reach it we must first pass through a low, dark tunnel, then into a contrasting splash of open sunlight, then finally into the god's cave itself. The god's head and shoulders are brightly outlined against the dark background by light from above, and in the dimness at his feet water flows out from an overturned urn. There is an inscription from Virgil nearby. This tableau brings to mind Pliny's description of the source of the River Clitumnus at a lakeside spring, with a nearby temple containing a statue of Clitumnus, the river god.

The river god

These figures personify the Genius of the Place, so that it can have a voice and address us directly. This was a common enough device of eighteenth-century poetry; Pope invoked Father Thames (explicitly recalling Virgil's Father Tiber) in "Windsor Forest," for example, and Gray invoked him in his poem "On a Distant Prospect of Eton College." Disney was to employ personification as well, but he didn't have to rely on immobile stone statues and inscriptions; with twentieth-century technology he would animate his statues of cartoon characters and American presidents and make them speak out loud.

Aeneas, of course, did find Anchises in the underworld, and Anchises completed the prophecy of Delos by telling how Aeneas would go on to found Rome. Aeneas then returned, through the ivory gate of Sleep, to the sunlit

The Roman empire:
the Pantheon

The British empire:
Alfred's Tower

world above. We too climb out of the grotto and embark on the path to the Pantheon.

Overlaid on the sequence of Virgilian scenes is a collection of medieval buildings and monuments, carrying references to England's past, most notably to the almost legendary King Alfred, a hero of the foundation of the British Empire as Aeneas was of the Roman. In self-confident, expansionary eighteenth-century Britain it would have seemed natural to compare the two empires, and it seems oddly fitting once more now that both have disappeared into the history books. The Latin tale is given medieval English cadences, as in Chaucer's translation of Virgil.

Within the story of "The Thousand and One Nights," Queen Scheherezade begins to tell the same story once again, so that she will eventually arrive back at the night upon which she begins to tell it; we have a dizzying glimpse of the narrative cycling endlessly. So it is with Stourhead. The path closes back upon itself at the Bristol Cross (symbol of arrival and departure, when it stood in High Street of that old town), and the cycle (birth and death of men, and of empire) ends and begins again.

Writers have often thought of a narrative progressing in time as a path moving through space; Laurence Sterne drew a convoluted squiggle to describe the plot of *Tristram Shandy*, and Jorge Luis Borges wrote a metaphysical detective story, full of puzzles of time and space and human destiny, called "The Garden of Forking Paths." Henry Hoare reversed this; he created a path that tells a tale.

The Villa Lante

Sacheverell Sitwell, the marvelously traveled younger brother of Dame Edith, the poet, and Osbert, the essayist, wrote, "Were I to choose the most lovely place of the physical beauty of nature in Italy or in all the world that I have seen with my own eyes, I would name the gardens of the Villa Lante." He notes elsewhere that a part of their fascination comes from the people who have appreciated them through the centuries, and we would add that certainly some comes from the inspiration and imitation this garden has engendered around the world. Our axonometric drawing limits itself to the formal terraces of the garden, in order to show the details of the fountains, but one of the exciting innovations of the place is the connection, more developed than in any of its predecessors, between the formal terraces and the wild woods beside them, cut through by straight allées that lead to benches, monuments, and fountains.

Rumor, confident but unproven, has the great architect Vignola beginning the gardens in 1566 for Cardinal Gambara on a beautiful site that the city of Viterbo had given to its bishops for their summer residence. Cardinal Gambara did not succumb to pressures from the Holy See to deed it to Rome, though he did give in to the austere San Carlo Borromeo (whose family would build Isola Bella), to the extent of not building the second casino. His successor, Cardinal Montalto, reversed this decision, building the second casino and giving the property to the papacy, which traded it to the Lante family in 1655.

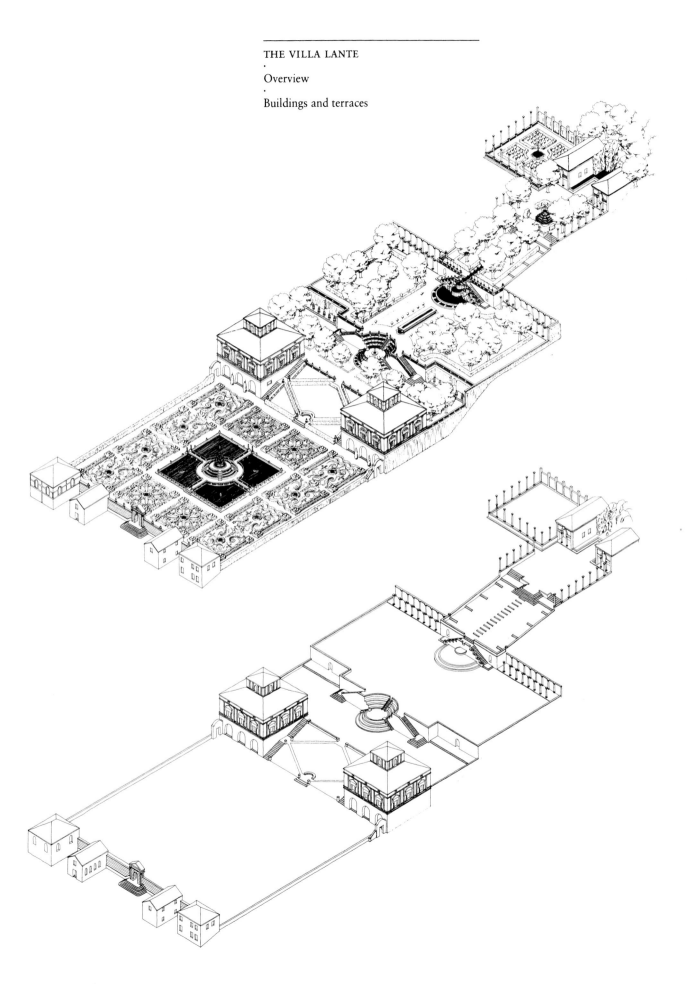

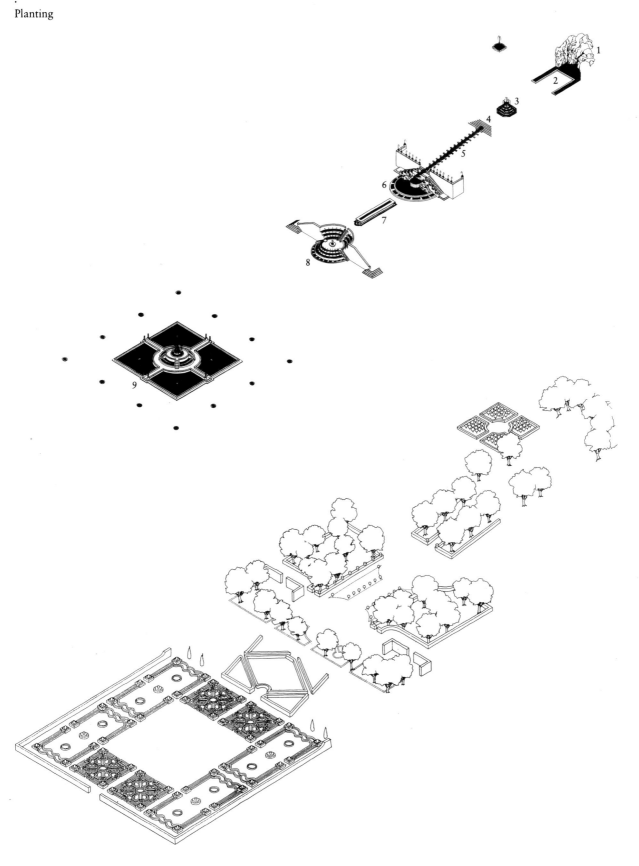

The garden is a continuous series of triumphs. The most evident among them is the coup of creating not one house to hold the central position in the garden, but rather two identical casinos flanking the central axis. Rather like the tower at Sissinghurst, these casinos, in their size and their positioning, remain splendid parts of the garden and do not compete with it.

The main glory of the garden is its axis of water. It is long, stretching well out of sight of the casinos, and needs to be visited as a pilgrimage. As in the days of Cardinal Montalto, the journey is a curious one, since it starts most of the way down the axis, and the goal is ambiguous—either the source up the hill or the magnificent fountain below, toward which the water drops.

Let us go by way of the relics, up through the wilderness, so as to start at the top. A *fountain* comes falling right out of the wild forest, down into a *pool flanked by pavilions,* flanked in turn by secret gardens (only one is left, to show in our axonometric) enclosed by a balustrade and colonnade with an old-fashioned foursquare parterre and central fountain. Forward along the axis, a marvelous fountain spouts water from *masks and vases and dolphins.* Just below it, a cascade issues from under the pavement and splashes down the center of a gentle, *stepped ramp,* which has a scroll that pushes the water into shapes that at once flash and sparkle and recall the crawfish (*gambero*) of Cardinal Gambara's arms. The water flows on into a grand *fountain with cascades* and steps and flanking river gods.

Below that, a long *stone dining table* carries the axis; its middle is a stream for cooling wine and, we have to presume, for floating the dishes along the table. Below that lies the *Fountain of Little Lamps,* a sloping circle bisected by the terrace, with an island in the middle, in the center of which is a small fountain. The slope between the casinos has ramped access to the balustraded square lake in the middle of its square garden, surrounded by twelve parterres (shown simple in an early drawing, but curvily ornate by now). Four bridges across the square lake lead to a circular island, which contains an inner basin crossed by four more bridges to the fountain platform, where four boys hold up the *Cardinal's arms* in a mist of spray. Below all that is a wall and a gate and the town of Bagnaia. Or we can end our pilgrimage by returning, perhaps by way of water games set up to amuse the guests by systematically drenching them, to one of the casinos.

Why did Sitwell so admire the Villa Lante's garden? Partly, certainly, because the stone fountains and frames for the cascades are so richly beautiful and complete, but mostly (and this is what is in it for us) because it is so focused, so completely in service to a central idea—the notion of water coursing down a central channel, moving in all kinds of ways, sliding and splashing, vanishing and reappearing, running down the middle of a long table, so that what was seconds ago a cascade is now a wine cooler, fixing to break loose again in a second, and go coursing on down the hill. At the bottom the four-part lagoon is at once a continuation of the axis and the place where it comes to rest. Even the water jokes squirting the unwary near the right-hand casino are recognizable as errant offspring of the watercourse, and the twin casinos, as they flank it at a very respectful distance, pay perhaps the most profound obeisance of all.

A part of the quality that those paired casinos produce is a sense of utter luxury: inside one is to give parties, relax, and frolic. They are not meant to house laundry, hold storage, or serve any such sober function; they mark, like sundials, only the sunny hours.

City Gardens: Isfahan and Beijing

The attraction of complementary opposites has often found expression, in gardens, in liaisons of the formal and the natural. In England, for example, we discover the precise, symmetrical geometries of Palladian houses set in parks by William Kent or Capability Brown, and in fourfold Persian gardens the forms of rose bushes and fruit blossoms soften the otherwise square severity. At a larger scale, we can often see the same sorts of balances and tensions in the fabrics of cities.

Isfahan's gardens are islands of calm, symmetrical clarity amid the bustle of the city: the Hesht-i-Behesht, drawn by Bertram Goodhue

Many visitors to the Middle East, for instance, have been struck by the contrast between the complexities of bazaars and residential streets, with their compression and bustle and noise, and the quiet, clear, symmetries that open in gardens and the courtyards of mosques. These islands of order in the human tangle all round are places for formal manners and prescribed ritual.

Nowhere is the contrast clearer than in the plan of the Safavid city of Isfahan, in Iran. This was laid out during the reign of Shah Abbas I (1589–1627), and, though it has become a large modern city and suffered the depredations of highway engineering and urban renewal, still retains much of its original form. To the south is a river, the Zayandeh Rud, and to the north is the intricate sprawl of the bazaar. Between is a famous quarter of gardens, mosques, and palaces.

The Chahar Bagh in the early nineteenth century, drawn by Eugène Flandin

Three important axes, which collide and create overlaid patterns, organize the plan of the garden quarter. The first of these is the line of the main artery, running almost due north from Allahavardi Khan's spectacular thirty-three-arch bridge over the river. This grand boulevard had a canal (featuring onyx basins filled with rose petals) along the center, and was named the *Chahar Bagh* after the fourfold gardens that lined it on either side. The squares of the gardens and their cross axes created a rigorous grid that contrasted with the smaller-scale, much less regular, cellular fabric of the *suqs* to the north. (The gardens are now gone, and the Chahar Bagh has become a modern street lined with trees.)

The second axis is that of the *Maidan-i-Shah* (Royal Square). This grandiose, rectangular open space lies to the east of the Chahar Bagh. Its axis is twisted about fifteen degrees from the other, and it knits together a commercial center (the bazaar at its northern end, and the shops surrounding it), an entrance to the royal palace to the west, and the important *Shah Mosque* opening off the southern end. Palace gardens, running between the Chahar Bagh and the Maidan-i-Shah, resolve the collision of the two grid systems.

The gridded gardens of Safavid Isfahan

1. Garden of the Dervish
2. Garden of the Vineyard
3. Garden of the Throne
4. Garden of the Vazirs
5. Chehel Sutun
6. Hesht-i-Behesht
7. Garden of the Mulberries

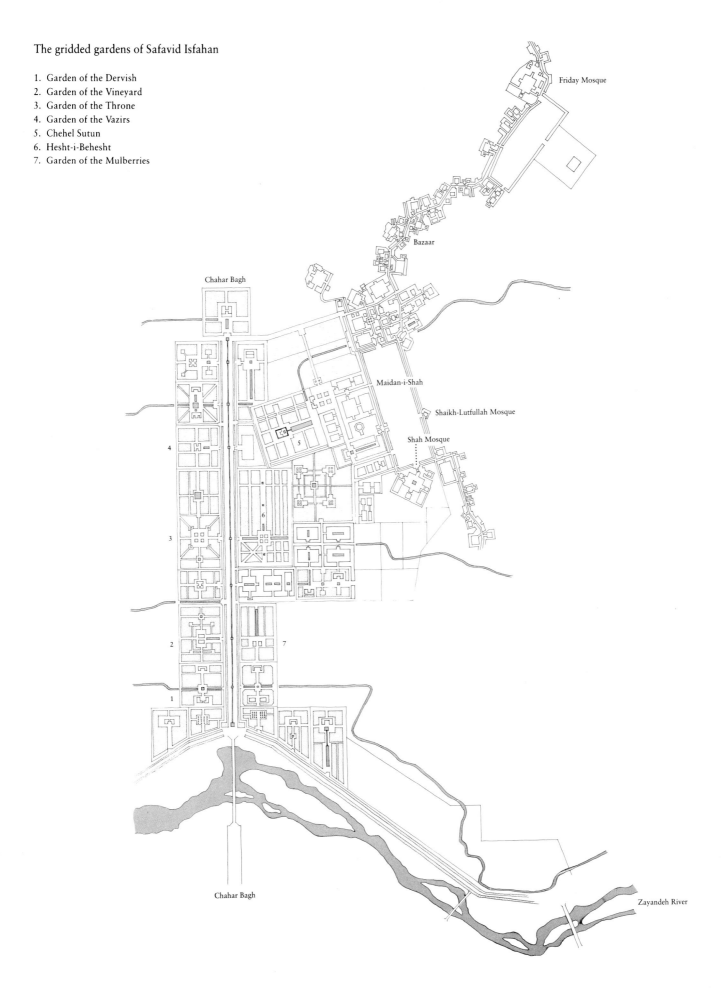

Friday Mosque

Bazaar

Chahar Bagh

Maidan-i-Shah

Shaikh-Lutfullah Mosque

Shah Mosque

4

3

6

2

7

1

Chahar Bagh

Zayandeh River

A sybaritic center of symmetries: crossing of the axes in the Hesht-i-Behesht, drawn by Pascal Coste

The third axis is determined by the direction of Mecca, to the southwest; this is the axis of the mosques. The Shah Mosque is rotated forty-five degrees from the southern side of the Maidan-i-Shah, and the resolution of the intersecting axes by means of portal, vestibule, and *iwan* is a famous architectural *tour-de-force*. The much smaller, but enchanting, *Shaikh-Lutfullah Mosque* is a domed square, colliding at forty-five degrees with the eastern edge of the Maidan. The enormous, old (mostly pre-Safavid) *Friday Mosque* is an astonishing accretion of labyrinthine alleys and column-gridded halls, all merging into the dense surrounding fabric, but at the center there is a spacious rectangular courtyard, with its *iwans* and fountain clearly marking the Mecca axis.

Compare the route through the bazaar with that along the axis of the Chahar Bagh, the Maidan-i-Shah, the Shah Mosque, or the Friday Mosque. One is an exploratory pilgrimage, twisting between close walls, amidst the noise of artisans and merchants, the aroma of spices, and the dust and jostle of crowds, with picturesque surprises and accidents of human commerce along the way. The others are straight-line progressions across symmetrical open spaces, with clear and certain ends in view.

The lust for order that motivated the symmetrical splendor of the Chahar Bagh is no less evident in the layouts of traditional Chinese cities. The ancient city of Suzhou, for example, was a rectangularly gridded walled rectangle. A broad canal surrounded it, and the interior was divided by streets, alleys, and canals. The plan of today is still recognizably a descendent of that shown on a famous thirteenth-century carved stele: the old walls are mostly gone now, and the city has sprawled far beyond their rectangle, but fragments of the traditional fabric still remain. Whitewashed walls of houses, relieved by brown wooden doorways and balconies, present a continuous front to the street. Sycamores arch over and cast dappled shadows onto the white planes. Canals flow past the backs of the houses. Narrow alleys run between the street and the canal, and sometimes become footbridges over the water. But hidden behind the walls is another world of zigzags and meanders, shadows, reflections and illusions—that of the celebrated gardens of Suzhou.

In addition to the grid, traditional Chinese planning makes use of the principle of axial progression. At the intimate scale of a house, for example, alternating rooms and open courtyards might be strung along an axis of circulation to create a rhythmic sequence of doorways dividing the light from the shade. At the vast scale of an ancient imperial capital, the whole city of Beijing is organized in a similar way—as the dwelling of the emperor. The plan has resulted from the overlay of successive rebuildings, from the twelfth century to our own time, but through all of this the basic idea has remained remarkably constant. The main central axis runs due north-south. The plan is, essentially, a composition of four walled, rectangular enclosures (products of rebuildings and additions) threaded onto this axis. At the center is the imposingly symmetrical, red-walled complex of the Forbidden City—the old Imperial Palace, dating from the fifteenth century (Ming dynasty). The main entrance is to the south, and all the major buildings face south so that, symbolically, the emperor's face would be

The Suzhou grid

A Suzhou street

A Suzhou alley

A Suzhou canal

The Suzhou gardens

Axial progression at an imperial scale:
the Forbidden City at the heart of Beijing

Axial progression at a
domestic scale: a house at
Yang Bay, near Suzhou

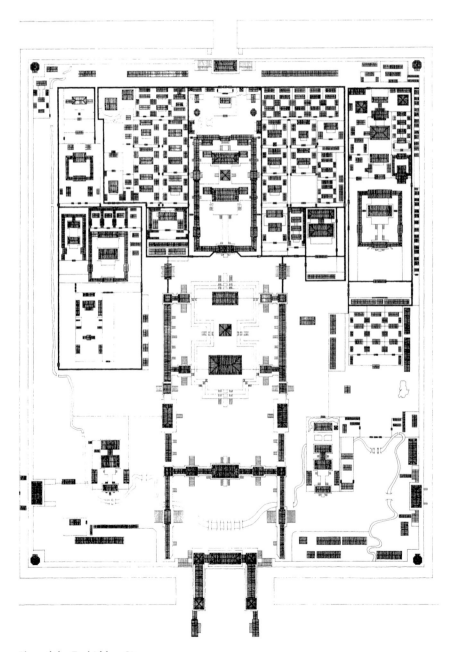

Plan of the Forbidden City

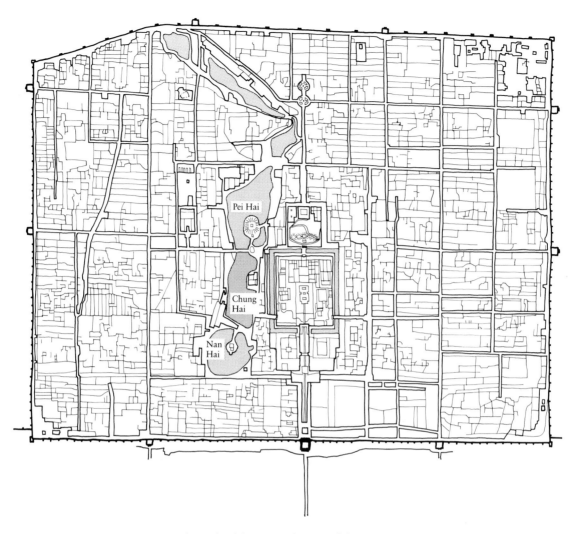

The grids of the Imperial City and the Inner
City surround the Forbidden City

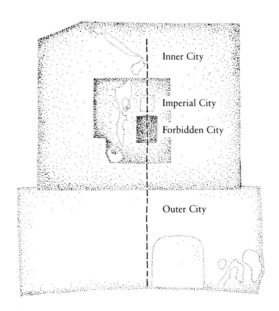

The north-south axis and the four walled
enclosures of Beijing

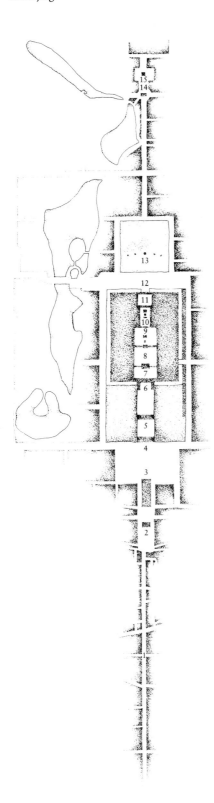

Events along the north-south axis
of Beijing

in the sun. Surrounding the Forbidden City is the Imperial City, then the Inner City. Farther to the south, abutting the Inner City, is the Outer City. The fabric between the Forbidden City and the outer walls was filled with a grid of streets, alleys, and courtyard houses: the street grid is still mostly intact, but much of the old housing is gone.

Two principles are combined here to create a hierarchy of space that focuses the composition on the center of political power, and the intermediary between earth and heaven: the emperor. The first principle is progression along the central north-south axis, through successive gateways, courtyards, and pavilions; the second is nesting of enclosures, one within the other.

Since China saw the last of the Manchus, and the Republic was established in February 1912, no emperor has wielded power from behind the high, red walls of the Forbidden City (although the last of them was allowed to stay there for a while). But the ancient axis is still there, and a walk along it, through layers of Chinese history, is perhaps the most thrilling urban pilgrimage in the world. Here, from south to north, is the five-mile sequence of gates, squares, and pavilions.

1. *Yongding Men* (Gate of Consolidation) is the southern gate of the Outer City and the starting point for the pilgrimage. From here, *Qian Men Road* leads north along the axis.

2. *Qian Men* (Front Gate) is the monumental southern gate of the Inner City.

3. *Tian'an Men Square,* the enormous rectangular open space that follows, is the focus of modern Beijing. It was here, on October 1, 1949, that Mao Zedong proclaimed the People's Republic of China, here that the Red Guards rallied in the sixties, and here, too, that the people rose against Jian Qing's radicals after the death of Chou En-lai in 1976. On axis are the *Chairman Mao Zedong Memorial Hall* and the *Monument to the People's Heroes.*

4. *Tian'an Men* (Gate of Heavenly Peace) rises at the center of the northern side of the square, across a small stream. This marks the entrance to the Imperial City. Imperial edicts were issued from here, and now the gate tower, with its red walls and yellow tile roof, has become the emblem of the People's Republic of China.

5. *Tuan Men,* across a small rectangular courtyard, is a high, red gate, similar to Tian'an Men.

6. *Wu Men* (Meridian Gate) is a huge, U-shaped building at the end of a long, narrow, rectangular enclosure with an avenue of trees down the center. Here you cross the moat and the walls (with guard towers at the corner) of the Forbidden City.

7. *Taihe Men* (Gate of Supreme Harmony) is approached across a paved rectangular courtyard (wider than it is long) and a curving stream with five marble bridges. This gate takes the form of a pavilion and is the antechamber to the important space that follows.

8. *Taihe Square* is the largest open space in the Forbidden City and forecourt to *Taihe Dian* (Hall of Supreme Harmony), a great hall at the center

1. Qian Men Road

2. Qian Men

3. Tian'an Men Square

4. Tian'an Men

5. Tuan Men

6. Wu Men

7. Taihe Men

8. *Taihe Square and Taihe Dian*

12. *View to Jing Shan from the North Gate*

9. *Zhonghe Dian: a ceremonial palace*

13. *Jing Shan*

10. *Qianqing Gong: a private palace*

14. *View north from Jing Shan to Gu Lou*

11. *Pavilion of Imperial Peace in the Yu Huan Yuan*

15. *Zhong Lou terminates the axis*

Beijing's gardens oppose the free-flowing curves of nature to the Confucian rigor of the grid: twisted cypress trunks in the Yu Huan Yuan

of the northern side. It climaxes the progression of rectangular enclosures, of varying scales and proportions, that began with Tian'an Men Square.

9. *Three Ceremonial Palaces*, raised on a great three-tiered terrace, occupy the next courtyard.

10. *Three Private Palaces*, which were the imperial private living quarters, follow next.

11. *Yu Huan Yuan* (Imperial Rest Garden), the final and most intimate open space in the Forbidden City, was a private garden. It is filled with ancient, twisted cypress trees, and with splashes of color from wisteria, peonies, and plum blossom. Ch'ien Lung kept his library here, and the Dowager Empress built a rockery tower against the back wall so she could look over it to the streets beyond.

12. *The North Gate* carries the axis across the outer wall of the Forbidden City and over the moat.

13. *Jing Shan* (Coal Hill) has a symmetrical line of five pavilions, the center one on the axis. Before modern buildings this was the highest point in Beijing. It provides a view south, back down the axis, and north to what is still to come.

14. *Gu Lou* (Drum Tower), a considerable distance north, terminates a street running from the foot of Jing Shan.

15. *Zhong Lou* (Bell Tower), just beyond, terminates the axis at a point a little south of the Inner City walls.

This is a Confucian hierarchical order at its most inexorable. But, if you look at the map of Beijing or look west from the height of Jing Shan, you will see that something else intrudes. Three large, irregularly shaped lakes—*Pei Hai, Chung Hai*, and *Nan Hai*—splatter themselves across the grid. Around each is a park, with meandering paths along the shore: a pilgrimage in consonance with the Tao of nature.

Pei Hai became an imperial garden a thousand years ago, during the Liao and Jin dynasties. It was much frequented by the garden-loving Ch'ien Lung, and after 1949 it was renovated to become modern Beijing's major public park. At its center is Resplendent Jade Island, with the tower known as the White Dagoba. Around the island is a circuit made of curving covered walks and rockery paths. A second circuit winds around the lake shore, under the branches of willows. There are the felicities of lotuses, ducks, pavilions, a smaller walled garden within the garden (as at the Summer Palace), borrowed views of Jing Shan's pavilions to the east, and a wall with nine brilliantly colored dragons. Here the grid cracks open, for a moment, and the gentle breath of the winds and waters flows through.

In both Isfahan and Beijing you can walk through the city along an axis, with symmetry all round, or you can take a more labyrinthine route that affords the pleasures of the picturesque. But in Isfahan the gardens create the axial geometry, while in Beijing the gardens oppose it.

The foursquare block

PATTERNS

Garden forms, like literary ones, differ in both scale and shape. Just as some gardens, like the plots of fascinating tales, lead us by way of interesting events to exciting surprises, so some others hold us with their form, with their symmetries and repetitions and variations and completions, like rhymed verse.

The basic symmetrical pattern for gardens is, as we have seen, the foursquare block, with water or sculpture at the center; paths for people or water going straight north, east, south, and west; a regular boundary substantial enough to keep out the wild world; and gardens in the four squares created by the paths, which might themselves be split into four squares, which might again be divided into four squares, and so on. This pattern existed at least as early as Sassanian times (third to seventh centuries A.D.) and was synonymous with gardens through the Middle Ages in the West.

A sonnet's symmetrical frame of rhyme and meter is of little interest in itself, but poets bring it to life again and again by clothing it with their own words and images. So it is with the patterned gardens. We are fascinated not by the simple and quickly grasped rules that govern them, but by the endlessly varied and thrilling games that the rules make possible.

The Symmetries of the Ram Bagh

Babur, first of the Mughul emperors, had little good to say about India. He wrote in his *Memoirs:*

Hindustan is a country of few charms. Its people have no good looks; of social intercourse, paying and receiving visits there is none; of genius and capacity none; of manners none; in handicraft and work there is no form of symmetry, method or quality; there are no good horses, no good dogs, no grapes, musk-melons or first-rate fruits, no ice or cold water, no good bread or cooked food in the bazars, no Hot-baths, no Colleges, no candles, torches or candlesticks. . . .

Except their large rivers and their standing-waters which flow in ravines or hollows there are no waters. There are no running waters in their gardens or residences. These residences have no charm, air, regularity or symmetry.

Even he could not put such an unsatisfactory place in order, but he *could* make himself a refuge within it by constructing a garden. This he did on the banks of the Jumna at Agra, and he has left us an account in his *Memoirs:*

One of the great defects of Hindustan being its lack of running waters, it kept coming to my mind that waters should be made to flow by means of wheels erected wherever I might settle down, also that grounds should be laid out in an orderly and symmetrical way. With this objective in view, we crossed the Jun-water to look at garden-grounds a few days after entering Agra. Those grounds were so bad and unattractive that we traversed them with a hundred disgusts and repulsions. So ugly and displeasing were they, that the idea of making a Char-bagh in them passed from my mind, but needs must! As there was no other land near Agra, that same ground was taken in hand a few days later.

The beginning was made with the large well from which water comes for the Hot-bath, and also with the piece of ground where the tamarind-trees and the octagonal tank now are. After that came the large tank with its enclosure; after that the tank and audience-hall in front of the outer residence; after that the private-house with its garden and various dwellings; after that the Hot-bath. Then in that charmless and disorderly Hind, plots of garden were seen laid out with order and symmetry, with suitable borders and parterres in every corner, and every border rose and narcissus in perfect arrangement.

The garden today called Ram Bagh is probably the remnant of the garden Babur described in this passage. It is located on the opposite side of the Jumna from the now more famous Taj Mahal. This part of the town is still (perhaps more than ever) "charmless and disorderly," and few of the visitors who come to see the Taj take the slow and dusty bicycle-powered rickshaw ride to see this most ancient of Mughul gardens. But on holidays the Ram Bagh is a crowded and festive place, with families and groups of friends spreading out rugs to sit in the shade, smoke, eat, and drink, much as Babur must have done. There are parrots and monkeys in the trees, and the smell of cooking rises from dozens of fires. Pavilions overlooking the Jumna still provide a refuge when the hot *loo* blows and the dust swirls around.

The grid of the Ram Bagh, Agra

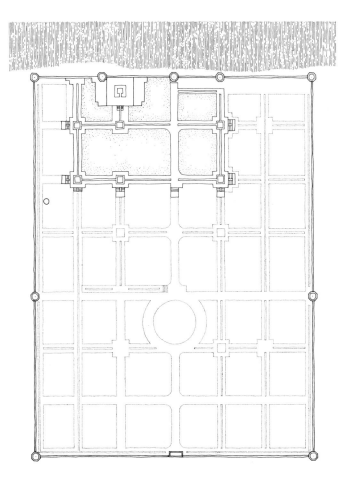

Babur carried with him memories of fourfold paradise gardens (*chahar baghs*) in Persia and Samarkand (which he had conquered, from time to time), and the plan of Ram Bagh is an elaboration of this pattern into an extensive square grid of canals. The part beside the river is raised to form a terrace, crisscrossed by canals with stone platforms (*chabutras*) at their intersections. You can still see where trees were planted in orderly rows. On the western edge of the terrace, two pavilions overlook the river, and between them there is an island-platform in the center of a large water tank; here Babur sat amid his borders and parterres. (His own name for this place was the Bagh-i-Gul Afshan, "Flower-Scattered Garden"; Ram Bagh is a corruption of a later name, Aram-Bagh, "Garden of Rest.") Formal chutes (*chadars*) at the edges of the terrace carry water from the canals down to the next level. These have steps on either side, and there are small pools at the bottom. From here the canals continue as stone channels.

The "lack of running waters" was remedied by digging a well beside the river at the southwest corner. Persian waterwheels (*rehats*) were used to raise water for storage in a tank, and from there it was distributed by the canals. In the northwest corner is a large storage tank, with underground baths (*hammams*) and cisterns nearby.

The ruined Ram Bagh that we see today can only hint at former splendors, but the plan still repays careful study. It is remarkable for the way that it integrates pavilions, pleasure grounds, and a cunningly engineered irrigation system into a unified, symmetrical composition. The architecture extends into the garden at the same time as the garden slides into the architecture, and the flow of water knits them both together.

Babur urgently sought both abundant water and "order and symmetry." But what, precisely, did he mean by this? We can infer a good deal from the regularities of the Ram Bagh, but we should also remember that Babur was heir to the artistic traditions of Islam, within which, for centuries, almost every possible form of symmetry had been explored.

First, there is symmetry about a point. Objects like waterwheels have rotational symmetry about a point, and a leaf (usually) has reflective symmetry about a single axis. The number of axes of reflective (and similarly, rotational) symmetry about a single central point may be multiplied indefinitely: a rectangle has two, an equilateral triangle has three, a square has four, a flower may have many, and a circle has an infinite number.

The square *chahar bagh* has four sides, four canals, four quarters, and four axes of symmetry. If we elongate it into a rectangle, its symmetries are reduced to two. Then, if we shift the crossing point toward one end, the symmetries reduce to one. Finally, if we shift the crossing off-center, there is no symmetry left. The opposite game is to increase the number of axes of symmetry. The Persians and Mughuls had good reason not to do this (there were only four rivers flowing out of paradise), but Renaissance and Baroque planners (at Karlsruhe, for instance) felt free to multiply symmetry axes for the sake of grandeur.

Rotational symmetry

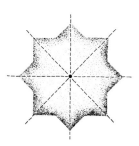

Axes of reflective symmetry passing through a point

The symmetries of the *chahar bagh*

The four axes of symmetry of a square chahar bagh

The two axes of a rectangular chahar bagh

Bilateral symmetry

Frieze symmetry

The quincunx

A second kind of symmetry arises from regular repetition along an axis. This is often called frieze symmetry. The simplest version appears when trees are planted at regular intervals along a straight path. Reflect the row of trees across the path, to form an *allée*, and you have a second sort. Offset the two rows and you obtain a third. Altogether there are just seven possibilities.

If the trees spread out to form an orchard and are regularly spaced at equal intervals in orthogonal directions, a square grid results. This was the basis of the Ram Bagh. A related garden form that became popular with the later Mughuls was the *char-chenar*: a square of closely planted chenar trees forming a shaded room, sometimes with a stone *chabutra* at the center. At Nasim Bagh, in Kashmir, the Mughul emperor Shah-Jahan was to multiply *char-chenars* to form a huge rectangular grove, set out on a square grid of approximately ten meters. Here the room grew into a palace.

We can stretch or shrink a square grid along one of its axes to generate rectangular cells. The groves of the Patio of the Orange Trees in Seville, for instance, are set out on a rectangular grid; the spacing in one direction is determined by the spread of the branches, and in the other by the needs of irrigation and access.

A further possible transformation of the grid is to offset each row so that the repeating spatial unit becomes an oblique parallelogram rather than a rectangle. If the offset is made to be exactly half a unit, then a pattern traditionally known as the quincunx is produced. It is so called because each point is surrounded by four neighbors, making a group of five like that on dice. This pattern became popular for fountains in Mughul garden tombs.

Seventeenth-century orchards in England (contemporaries of some of the great Mughul gardens) were often set out in regular quincuncial grids, and this pattern came to occupy a special and curious place in the history of gardening. The seventeenth-century English philosopher Sir Thomas Browne wrote a treatise entitled *The Garden of Cyrus*. It was subtitled "The Quincuncial, Lozenge, or Network Plantations of the Ancients, Artificially, Naturally, Mystically Considered." In it Browne suggested that Cyrus, like other ancients, was a "splendid and regular planter." He further argued that the pattern of ancient plantations was the quincunx, and that in its perfect regularity the quincunx was a revelation of the "mystical mathematics of the city of Heaven."

A quincuncial grid is the superimposition of two square grids. This is the planting pattern followed in the grove of the Mosque of Cordoba, where one square grid is planted with palms and another square grid of orange trees grows in the shade they provide.

The fifth and final regular grid of points is produced by stretching a quincunx such that a pattern of equilateral triangles is formed. Since the centers of close-packed, uniform circles dispose themselves at the vertices of equilateral triangles, this turns out to be the most efficient pattern for the green circles formed by center-point irrigation systems. In this arrange-

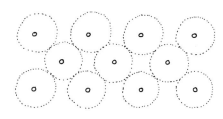

Minimum spacing of circles

Grid of trees

ment, the area of left-over, unirrigated land is minimized. Since most trees are roughly circular in the spread of their branches, this triangular grid is also the pattern that allows the densest planting of trees in an orchard.

Patterns with wallpaper symmetry, such as those in the tilework of mosques, are all constructed over one of these five regular grids of points. Geometry texts demonstrate that there are just seventeen different kinds of wallpaper symmetry. Persian, Mughul, and Moorish decorative artists found them all, explored the variations possible within each, and carried them into gardens on the walls of pavilions and tombs. On the ground, they became paving patterns.

These regular patterns in space play much the same role in garden design as regular sound patterns in poetry: the seventeen-syllable (five-seven-five) symmetries of the *haiku*, alliteration and assonance, euphony and rhyme, iambi and trochees, anapests and spondees. Alexander Pope disapproved, and said so (in iambic pentameter rhymed couplets, of course):

No pleasing intricacies intervene,
No artful wilderness to perplex the scene:
Grove nods at grove, each alley has a brother,
And half the platform just reflects the other.

Pope insinuates that symmetrical gardens follow mindless formal rules, with predictably dull results. But masters of the formal garden, like masters of regular verse, know how symmetries and correspondences can support structures of meaning by creating equivalences and contrasts between parts of a design, how deviation from a pattern or variation within it can be used to give special significance, and how a patterned fragment can suggest a larger whole. Without the rules, these games could not be played, and could never, never be won.

The Waters of Kashmir

Babur was able to create for himself an orderly, symmetrical, and shaded paradise at the Ram Bagh; his successors were to gain a more complete refuge from Indian heat and chaos: the valley of Kashmir north of Agra and Delhi in the Himalayan foothills. Kashmir is about ninety miles long and is ringed by high peaks and ridges. It falls away to the southwest and is drained throughout by the River Jhelum, which eventually emerges through a gorge in the Pir Panjals onto the plains of the Punjab. On the valley floor there are two large, shallow lakes, Wular and Dal, edged with thick beds of reeds and lotuses. The emperor Jahangir wrote of it in his *Journal:*

Kashmir is a garden of eternal spring, or an iron fort to a palace of kings—a delightful flower-bed, and a heart-expanding heritage for dervishes. Its pleasant meads and enchanting cascades are beyond all description. There are running streams and fountains beyond count. Wherever the eye reaches, there are verdure and running water. The red rose, the violet and the narcissus grow of themselves; in the fields there are all kinds of flowers and all sorts of sweet-scented herbs—more than can be counted.

Map of Lake Dal

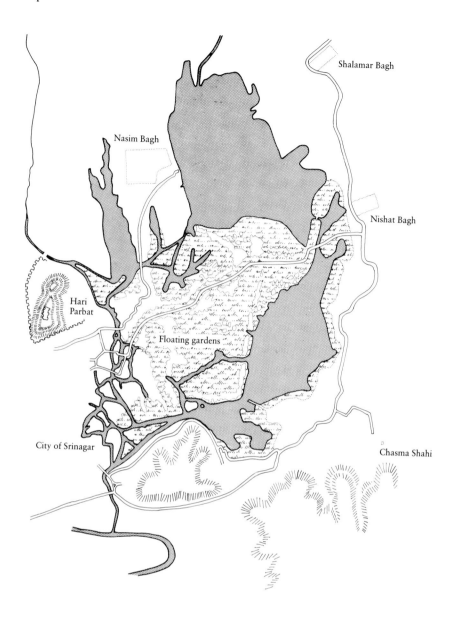

The surface of Lake Dal

Reeds and floating gardens

Lotus beds

Reflections of clouds

The emperor Akbar was the first to make expeditions to subdue Kashmir, then Akbar's son Jahangir and his successors made their permanent summer homes there. In the spring, when the snows had cleared sufficiently from the passes, they would make the long ascent from the plains of the Punjab to the cool green highlands. Then they would return south before the first snows of winter closed the passes once more.

Babur's vision of paradise, though, had included not only running water but also symmetry. So the Mughuls perfected this place by building pleasure gardens in which the Alpine meadows became patterned fields of flowers, the lakes became formal pools, the streams became canals, and the cadences of the bul-bul's song echoed through shady pavilions.

But the garden sites were hillsides, from which streams flowed down, not flat ground where water flowed from a pool or well. Logically, then, the source of water moved away from its traditional location at the center of the *chahar bagh* to the uphill end. The square became a downhill rectangle, with reflective symmetry only about its central water axis.

The landscape of Kashmir cast into a regular pattern at Vernag

A natural pond and meadow in Kashmir

A symmetrical pond and meadow at Achabal

The ground, no longer flat, was cast into a series of descending terraces. Where Babur had been able to use only modest *chadars* to descend from his low riverside platform to the ground, there was now the opportunity to make a grander sequence of cascades where the central canal crossed the terrace walls. There was more water, too, and better water pressure, so the cascades could flow swiftly, and (by means of pipes) gravity-fed fountains could be made to spurt at their feet.

The fall of water was intricately choreographed. Sometimes it descended in glistening, transparent sheets, revealing shadowy niches or flashes of color behind. Sometimes it became fine, drifting spray, and sometimes it jiggled and plopped in globs. The surfaces of the *chadars* were carved in relief patterns—formalizations of pebbly mountain stream beds—carefully shaped to produce shiny, glissading films of moisture, writhing standing waves, frostings of tiny bubbles, frothy flecks, interwoven spurts, bumps and hollows, flying droplets, splatters, rills, dribbles, or amazing foamy chaos.

Instead of a single pavilion set at the crossing of the water axes or fourfold pavilions at the ends, there could be a whole sequence of symmetrical pavilions and thrones straddling the now dominant central axis and stepping up the hillside. Alternatively, pavilions or thrones might be paired symmet-

A Kashmiri stream flowing
from its mountainside
source

A symmetrical stream at Vernag

Natural hillsides descend to Lake Dal

Garden terraces descend to Lake Dal
at Nishat

A mountain cascade

A symmetrical cascade: a *chadar* at Achabal

A symmetrical cascade with *chini kanas*
at Shalamar

Natural patterns of mountain stream water

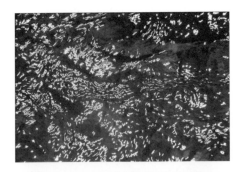

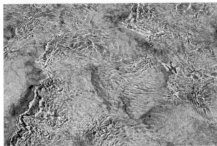

Symmetrical surface
patterning of a *chadar*
at Chasma Shahi

Symmetrical surface
patterning of a *chadar*
at Chasma Shahi

A natural stepping stone

Symmetrical stepping stones at Shalamar

rically on either side of this axis. Of course they would be placed to best effect—usually close by the sight and sound of falling water and within the range of its cooling spray. Crossings could be cast into marches of regular stepping stones.

The central canal, with its greater volume of water, needed to be enlarged and sometimes multiplied, while the cross canal was reduced in importance and sometimes eliminated. Chenar trees could be planted in regular rows, on either side of the central canal, to balance the continuous horizontal flow of water with an insistent, percussive rhythm of verticals.

The downhill (valley or lakeshore) end of the garden was usually the more accessible, so this became the entrance. From here there was a progression uphill and upstream, through successive enclosures formed by the terrace walls, which could be used to organize a progression from public to private. The most public terrace was on the bottom, by the entrance, and the most private (usually the *zenana*, the harem) was at the inaccessible top.

Our drawings on pages 168 and 169 show plans of those Mughul pleasure gardens extant in Kashmir. Shalamar is a splendid royal garden stepping down to the shores of Lake Dal, begun in the reign of the emperor Jahangir and extended by his successor Shah Jahan. Nishat, more steeply terraced, was built by the empress Nur Jahan's brother, Asraf Khan, along the lakeshore to the south of Shalamar and nearer to the city of Srinagar. These are the two greatest of the Mughul pleasure gardens in Kashmir, and later we shall explore them in more detail.

The minor gardens (but still worthy of note) are Chasma Shahi, Achabal, and Vernag.

Chasma Shahi (Royal Spring) was built to the south of Nishat, perched high on a mountainside overlooking the lake, by Shah Jahan's governor Ali Mardan Khan. It is much more intimate in scale than either Shalamar or Nishat—little more, in fact, than a terrace forecourt to the *baradari* housing the spring—and its glory is one great *chadar* running down its central axis.

Achabal is a place of forested hillsides and abundant water, and there is a garden dating from the time of Jahangir. The *chadars* here become roaring waterfalls, and there are places to sit and listen to their sound: a two-storied *baradari* that straddles the axis, another on an island, and huge stone *chabutras* shaded by ancient chenar trees.

The simplest of all the remaining Mughul gardens in Kashmir, and the most isolated, is at Vernag ("place of a snake"), near the head of the Banihal Pass to the plains of India. The site is a gently sloping meadow at the foot of an abrupt, pine-covered mountainside. Water wells up from underground to be collected in a deep, transparently blue octagonal reservoir, where schools of carp circle. The pool is surrounded on all sides by a cool stone arcade, so that the only views are to the mountain rising against the sky and along the outfall. From the outfall the water flows strongly into a straight canal, running a thousand feet through the meadow to empty into a trout stream. Parterres and quiet lawns stretch out on either side.

The Kashmir pleasure garden game: plans
drawn to the same scale

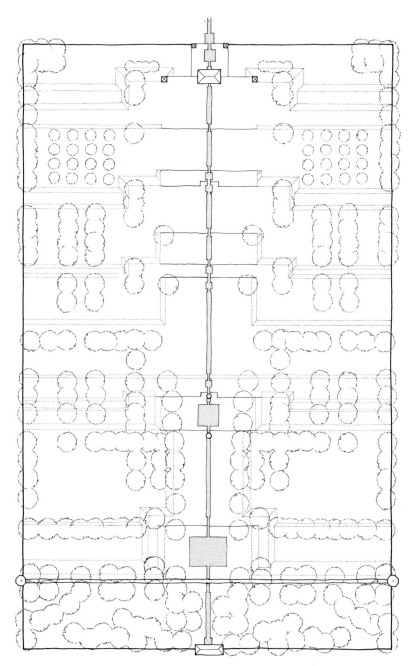

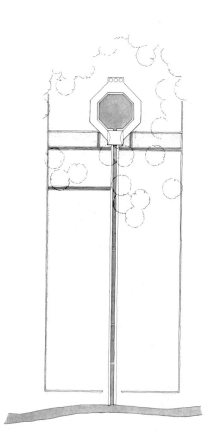

Nishat

Vernag

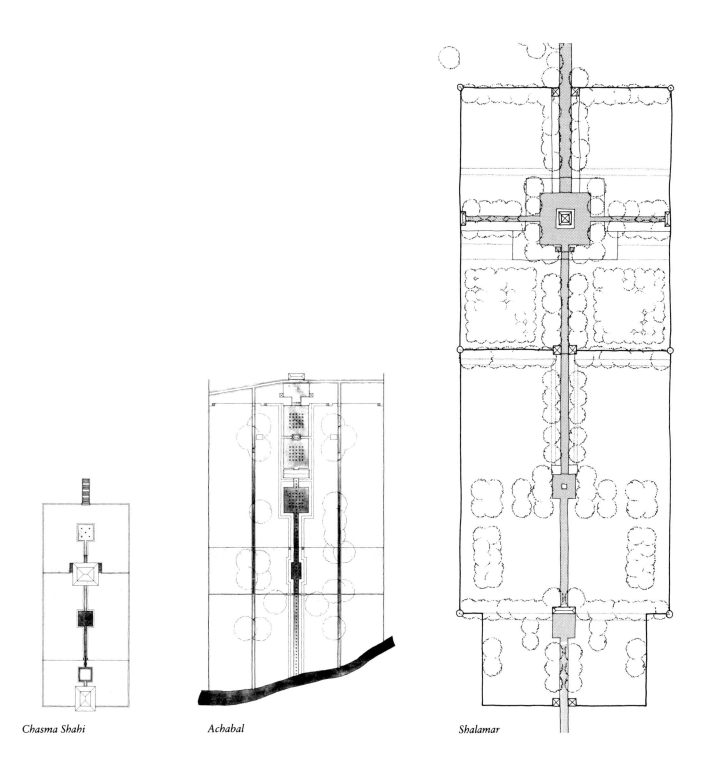

Chasma Shahi   *Achabal*   *Shalamar*

Jahangir, the great garden builder, died in a pass very near Vernag in 1627, on his annual return to the plains. His last wish was to be returned to Vernag and buried by the spring. But, like Rousseau, he was destined for a grander tomb. Apprehensive that the snows were about to close the passes, his followers carried his body on to Lahore, where Nur Jahan erected the marble Shadhara.

Each of these gardens grows from the same simple, symmetrical diagram. Their makers played a game with rigorous rules, and so, up to a point, we know exactly what to expect. The uniqueness, and the pleasure, of each one comes from the particular way that it engages these expectations— sometimes confirming, sometimes confounding, always conspiring to adumbrate the Genius of the Place in the grace of moving water: splashes and trickles at Chasma Shahi; rush and roar at Achabel; swirling, transparent depth at Vernag; delicate waterfalls down to the lotus-filled lake at Shalamar and Nishat. Each garden is a poetic renewal of the idea.

Shalamar Bagh

Approaching Shalamar

Shalamar ("abode of love" in Sanskrit) is the most renowned of all the gardens of Kashmir. Jahangir himself described the capabilities of its splendid site:

Shalamar is near the lake. It has a pleasant stream which comes down from the hills and flows into the Dal Lake. I bade my son Khurram dam it up and make a waterfall, which it would be a pleasure to behold. This place is one of the sights of Kashmir.

The layout of the garden here was begun by Jahangir in 1619, at the same time as the founding of the nearby city of Srinagar, and in 1630 it was extended toward the north by Governor Zafar Khan on the orders of Shah Jahan. Later, Pathan and Sikh governors used it as a pleasure resort, and European visitors began to appear during the reign of Ranjit Singh (who housed them in its marble pavilion). Eventually the Maharaja Hari Singh installed electric lights. Today it is a much-frequented public park.

It was appropriate enough for Jahangir to construct an Abode of Love. His scandalous past included a liaison with the beautiful slave girl Anarkali (Pomegranate Bud). It ended badly when his father Akbar caught Jahangir and Anarkali exchanging smiles in a mirror and had her entombed alive. Then, in Lahore, Jahangir encountered the Persian beauty Mehr-ul-Nisa. After quickly disposing of her husband Sher Afgan, the emperor married her in 1611, and she took the name Nur Jahan (Light of the World). She was to accompany him on his annual pilgrimages to Kashmir.

Shalamar sits astride a shallow ravine, around which the mountains rise sheer to the sky, and the snows of Mahadeo form the backdrop. Just as Kashmir is a bounded place, so the garden is an enclosed domain. Originally there were three square precincts. The lowest, which has now been truncated by a modern road, was the place of entry. At its head stands the *Diwan-i-Am* (Hall of Public Audience), a *baradari* where the emperor would sit enthroned before the public. Next comes the *Emperor's Garden,* which contained the *Diwan-i-Khas* (Hall of Private Audience), to which members of the court would be admitted. (This building has been destroyed, but its stone footings remain.) Finally comes the *Zenana* (ladies') *Garden,* with the magnificent *Black Pavilion* built by Shah Jahan. This was apparently used by the Mughuls as a banqueting hall.

The natural fall of the ground has been formalized into a succession of terraces that step down to the lake. Level changes between terraces are slight, and they are formed by low walls.

The mountain stream that Jahangir ordered dammed up has become a broad straight canal, which rolls down the central axis of the garden and empties into the lake. Square pools form below the pavilions, recalling the broadening of rivers into lakes on the Kashmir valley floor. Secondary axes cross these pools in the Emperor's Garden and the Zenana Garden, so that these take on the classical Persian *chahar bagh* form.

Water jets mark the center of the canal, and an array of jets covers each pool. Today they are feathery sprays, but they would originally have been solid plumes of water. They were clustered most thickly at the bottoms of cascades, where the head of water was sufficient to assure a noble spurt.

At each point where the canal crosses the retaining wall of a terrace there is a cascade. A smooth sheet of water is projected clear from the face, into which is cut a pattern of small recesses (*chini kanas*). These recesses are filled with flowers on special occasions, and in the past they would have held oil lamps at night. The head of the canal in front of the Zenana Garden's black pavilion is surrounded by cascades on three sides, making a splashy place that seems always to be filled with naked children.

The main pathways are placed at either side of the canal. This means, of course, that you cannot walk on the axis but are always slightly offset from it. Points of crossing the axis are few, and they are marked with great ceremony. The first is at the Diwan-i-Am, where the emperor's shaded marble throne stands in the center of the canal, at the top of the cascade, and is reached by stepping stones from either side. Next is the throne of the Diwan-i-Khas, which is reached by causeways. The Black Pavilion of the Zenana Garden is reached by narrow stone bridges threaded into the field of fountains. Only the ducks cross the axis without formality.

The walks are shaded by regular avenues of gigantic chenar trees, and on either side there are flat irrigated meadows filled with grass, flowers, and fruit trees. The basic organization of water and irrigated land is exactly the same as that still found throughout Kashmir in much more modest and informal fruit and vegetable gardens. Today Shalamar's meadows are patterned in an informal way, but in Jahangir's time they were organized with geometric precision, like planted fields.

To visit Shalamar it is best to avoid the buses and taxis from Srinagar, and instead take a *shikara* (the local kind of boat) from Nasim Bagh on the opposite shore of Lake Dal. The *shikara* pushes its way through lotus leaves, each of which is covered in quivering lenses of water after the

SHALAMAR BAGH
·
Overview
·
Buildings and terraces
·
Water
·
Planting

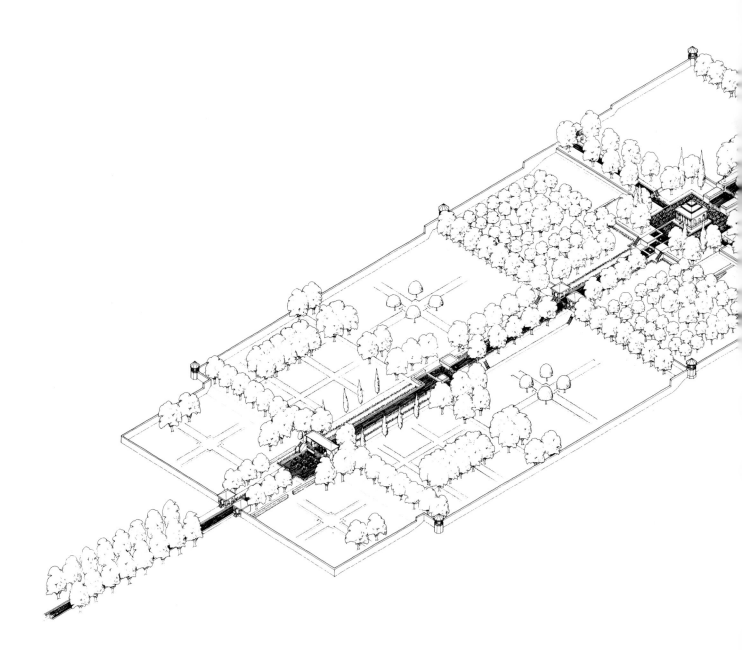

Pilgrimage through a pattern to the source
of water

1. Canal from Lake Dal
2. Entrance
3. Diwan-i-Am
4. Diwan-i-Khas
5. Entrance to Zenana Garden
6. Black Pavilion

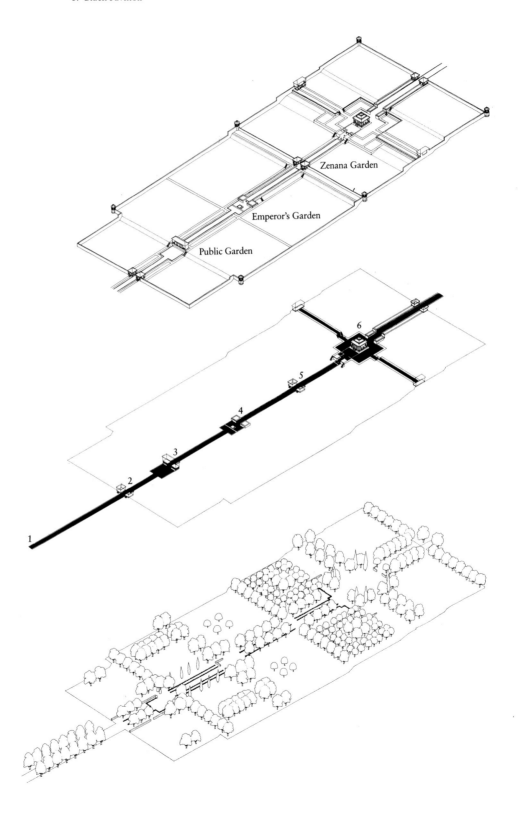

morning rain, into the dead calm at the center of the lake. Sometimes there will be boats with families going to the important mosque at Hazrat Bal, or fishermen casting nets for the carp that live in the weeds, but they scarcely disturb the reflections of the mountains. On the approaching shore, Shalamar and Nishat are revealed as rectangular blocks of chenar green, dark against the hillside. Near the shore a marshland with a maze of channels separated by islands of rushes as tall as a man must be traversed, then the *shikara* enters a mile-long straight canal: the formal approach to Shalamar. After passing between rows of chenars, watched by old men and children on the banks, you reach the foot of the garden.

The Black Pavilion

Inside the lowest precinct, the Diwan-i-Am stands revealed, lotus-flower pink at the end of the canal. Then there is a gently, shaded ascent, past the throne of the Diwan-i-Khas and two small guard pavilions flanking the canal to the climax of the Black Pavilion. This rises above its field of spray to complete the progression that began among the lotuses on the opposite shore. Within it there is a deep shadow and the sounds and reflections of water. Views open four ways, while cool air gently flows off the pools and cascades.

When a fourfold paradise garden is made on flat land, the focus, and the place to be, is usually the pool or fountain at the center. Such a garden recreates in miniature the experience of desert people coming upon and penetrating the heart of an oasis. But on Shalamar's hillside the central axis elongates, and the heart of the garden shifts to the uphill end. Here the micro-choreographed experience recalls that of the Mughuls' annual pilgrimage to Kashmir itself—with its beginning in the outside world, the crossing (by the passes) into an enclosed domain of fields and flowers and fruitful trees, the ascent to a cool refuge by the water, and the eventual return to the lowlands.

Nishat Bagh

Nishat is a garden of the same type and scale as Shalamar, originating in the same diagram, and made with the same materials in the reign of the same emperor, on a nearby site. But since Nishat was not a royal garden, it did not require the same ceremonial hierarchy of space as Shalamar. There are just two parts: the lower pleasure garden and the upper Zenana Garden.

Approaching Nishat: reflections in Lake Dal

The site is steeper than that of Shalamar, and it is more intimately related to the lake; no fields and marshes intervene. This allows for an entrance lagoon, and it means that the terraces must be higher, narrower, and more numerous. There are twelve of them, corresponding to the signs of the zodiac.

The terraces of Nishat

Transitions in level are made not by wide, low cascades backed by *chini kanas* (as they are at Shalamar), but by narrow, tall *chadars*. The inclined surfaces of these stone chutes are intricately carved in low relief with regular geometric patterns, formalizations of the textures of mountain stream beds. When they are dry, they create a delicate pattern of light and shade;

when they are moist, they glisten and glitter and shine; and when the water flows, they sculpt it into lacy white spurts and froths. Flanking the *chadars* are steps, and above them, spanning the canal, are stone thrones.

Nishat, like Shalamar, is a pilgrimage as well as a pattern. As in rhymed verse, then, its symmetries unfold and complete themselves in sequence. The poem begins with the approach, by *shikara,* from the groves of Nasim Bagh on the opposite shore of Lake Dal. The route passes by floating gardens (tomatoes and melons growing thickly on rafts) and mid-lake spots for swimming. A pointed, single-arched stone bridge set in an encircling bund, with an answering image in the still water, is the entrance to the lotus-filled lagoon. The green, gray, and lotus-pink garden terraces stack up dramatically on the shore.

A *baradari* (dating from the time of the Maharajas) once stood at the head of the entrance terrace. We have shown it in our drawing, and Constance Villiers-Stuart, writing in the early decades of this century, has left us a charming description:

The baradari *on the third terrace of the Nishat Bagh is a two-storied Kashmir structure standing on the stone foundations of an earlier building. The lower floor is fifty-nine feet long and forty-eight feet wide, enclosed on two sides by wooden latticed windows. In the middle there is a reservoir about fourteen feet square and three feet deep, with five fountains, the one in the center being the only old stone fountain left in the garden. On a summer day there are few more attractive rooms than the fountain hall of this Kashmir garden house. The gay colours of the carved woodwork shine through the spray in delightful contrast to the dull green running water. Through a latticed arch a glimpse is caught of the brilliant garden terraces and their waterfalls flashing white against the mountain side. Looking out over the lake which glitters below in the sunshine, the views of the valley are bounded by faint snow-capped peaks, the far country of the Pir Panjal. Climbing roses twine about the painted wooden pillars, and nod their creamy flowers through the openings of the lattice. All the long afternoon a little breeze ruffles the surface of the lake and blows in the scent of the flowers, mingling it with the drifting fountain spray; for the terrace below the pavilion is planted after the old custom with a thicket of Persian lilac.*

Beyond the *baradari,* the zodiac terraces of the pleasure garden climb toward the high wall of the Zenana Garden. From below they are foreshortened, seeming to become one gigantic waterfall. As you ascend, the garden opens up, plane by plane, like a flower in the morning. At each stage you can rest on the stone throne (where the Mughuls would have spread their tents and carpets), hear the sound and feel the spray of the *chadar* at your feet, look down on the brilliant parterres, and look out across the widening sweep of the lake. Finally comes the high stone wall, decorated with an arcade and flanked by octagonal gazebos. The Zenana Garden is a dense, shady grove with a view over the water to Akbar's fortress of Hari Parbat, which rises on a hill beyond the far shore.

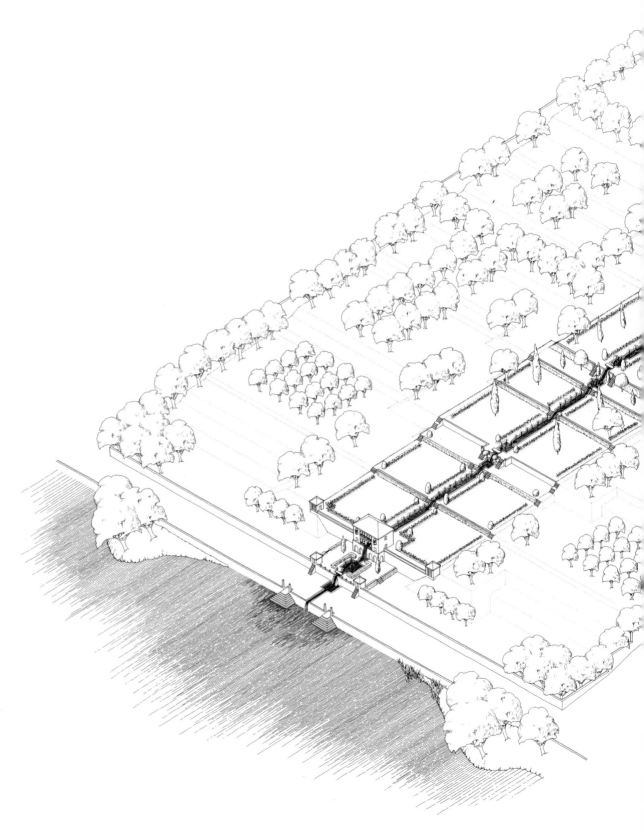

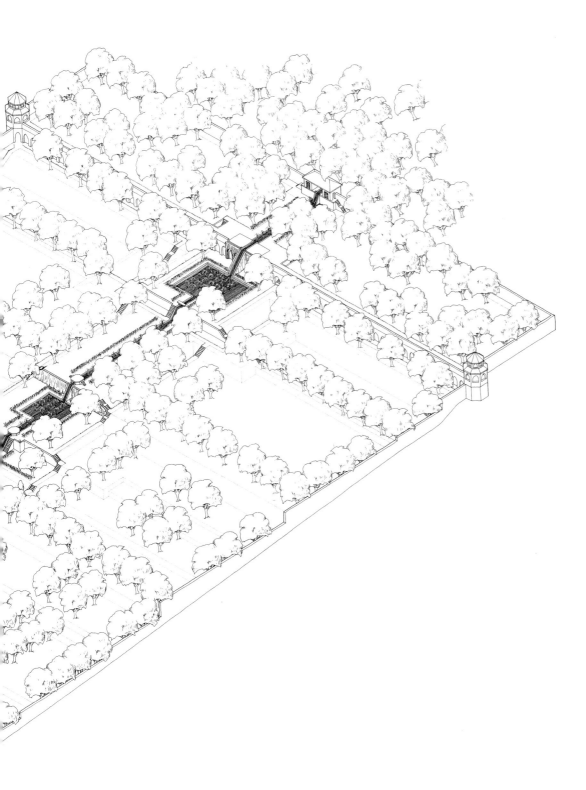

NISHAT

· Buildings and terraces

· Water

· Planting

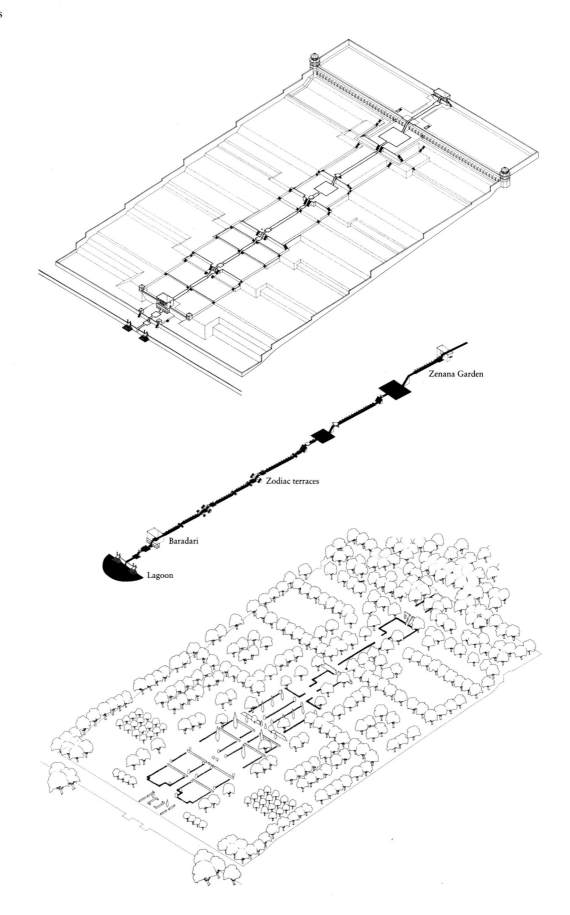

Zenana Garden

Zodiac terraces

Baradari

Lagoon

The stone mausoleum in the *chahar bagh*

Tomb of Humayun, Delhi

Tomb of Akbar, Sikandra

Tomb of I'timad-ud-Daula, Agra

The Taj Mahal, Agra

The twelve symmetrical zodiac terraces, climbing the mountainside from the blossoms of the *baradari* to the shadows of the Zenana Garden, are closed and completed by a couplet—clouds with their reflections in the lotus-strewn lake. Nishat Bagh is a sonnet to the sky.

Mughul Tomb Gardens

The Koran promises that the faithful shall dwell in a cool, fruitful paradise and gives details of the attractions that await them there. Sura 76 specifies that they shall "recline upon couches" and shall see "neither sun nor bitter cold." Sura 47 describes "rivers of water unstalling" plus rivers of wine, of milk, and of honey. Sura 55 tells of gardens, green pastures, palm trees, and pomegranates, and of "houris, cloistered in cool pavilions."

The great Mughuls built tombs within gardens constructed in the image of this promised paradise. During their owners' lives these gardens were used as pleasure grounds, then after death they became entrances to paradise. By this device the realms of heaven and earth were connected.

Babur, first of the Mughuls, began this tradition of burial in a garden. He was initially buried on the banks of the Jumna at Agra (probably in the Ram Bagh). After some years the body was taken to Kabul and reburied in a modest grave within a favorite hillside garden. As he had directed, the grave was originally "open to the sky, with no building over it, no need of a door-keeper," but it has now been covered by a modern superstructure, and all trace of garden has disappeared.

The tombs of Babur's son Humayun, and of several later Mughuls, are much more magnificent. All of them are variants of the same basic pattern; each is an elaborate stone mausoleum set in a *chahar bagh*. Several traditions meet in this form. Magnificent tomb building had been a tradition of the Mughuls' Timurid ancestors, and Timur's own domed tomb still stands in Samarkand. The *chahar bagh,* as we have seen, diagrammed the four rivers that flowed from paradise; furthermore, Hindu mythology (of which the Mughuls certainly were aware) tells of the sacred mountain Meru, from which streams also flow north, south, east, and west, forming a cosmic cross. At the Ram Bagh, Babur had demonstrated how pavilions, terraces, and a water system could be put together to form a unified composition.

But these Mughul tombs were of much grander dimensions than ordinary garden pavilions and did not fit easily into the middle of a *chahar bagh*. The rules of the game presented a formal problem that had to be resolved—just as Greek architects had to struggle with the problem of taking triglyphs around a corner, Byzantine architects were faced with the contradiction of circular domes over square rooms, and architects of the Italian Renaissance puzzled over how to combine a classical facade with the basilican nave of a church.

Humayun's tomb in Delhi illustrates one solution. It is a massive red sandstone and white marble pavilion, raised upon a high, square platform, and surmounted by a bulbous dome. Smaller cupolas, supported upon columns, flank the central dome. To remain in proportion, the surrounding *chahar bagh* was laid out at a matching monumental scale. If only the traditional four irrigation canals at the center had been employed, the corners of the garden would have been left far from any source of water. So the four major squares were each subdivided by a grid of canals into nine smaller squares. Each part of the garden thus became a miniature of the whole, with its own four canals and stone platform at their crossing. This recursive division of space became a characteristic feature of Mughul tombs.

Water was supplied to the canal system from a well located at the north gate. But the volume of water flowing from it would never have been sufficient to fill large pools and canals. Furthermore, the garden is almost flat, and of course there were no high-powered pumps, so there was no way to circulate large amounts of water. There was thus a mismatch between the grand scale of the designer's conception and the comparatively meager supply of water. This difficulty was resolved by making the canals narrow and shallow, little more than incised lines in a stone surface, but surrounded by broad, slightly raised, red sandstone causeways. These boldly mark out the grid of canals, establishing its significance in the scheme, while the delicate channels give maximum importance to every ripple and trickle of water.

Akbar's tomb at Sikandra, like Humayun's tomb, has the mausoleum placed at the center of a *chahar bagh*. But the scale is even more enormous; the garden is over two thousand feet on edge, compared to about twelve hundred feet for Humayun's tomb. Here, too, the layout was generated by the ramification of squares, but according to a different rule. In this case the squares were located concentrically, one within the other. The mausoleum itself is a stepped pyramid of diminishing square, red sandstone tiers, centrally placed at the intersection of the cross axes of a square enclosure. Water tanks are placed at four locations, where another square would intersect the cross axes. The tanks themselves form patterns of concentric squares, miniatures of the whole plan. At the center, the horizontal axes of the *chahar bagh* intersect an invisible vertical axis running from Akbar's burial chamber, which is concealed below ground, to a white marble cenotaph within a square cloister, open to the sky, on the topmost tier of the mausoleum. At the corners of the cloister, and clustered on the lower tiers, are astonishingly delicate, open *chhatris,* cupolas supported by four stone columns—pavilions upon a pavilion.

The garden is not a two-dimensional pattern, like that at Humayun's tomb, but is modeled in high relief. The causeways are raised several feet off the ground and are broad enough to accommodate large crowds. (Akbar's son Jahangir described, in his *Memoirs,* how holy men assembled there for "singing and dancing and practicing ecstacies.") Originally the edges of the causeways were lined with cypresses, symbols of death and eternity, while the garden squares were planted with groves of fruit trees, symbols of life. There are high gates with minarets, from which you can look out over the garden and feel whatever breezes stir on that hot plain,

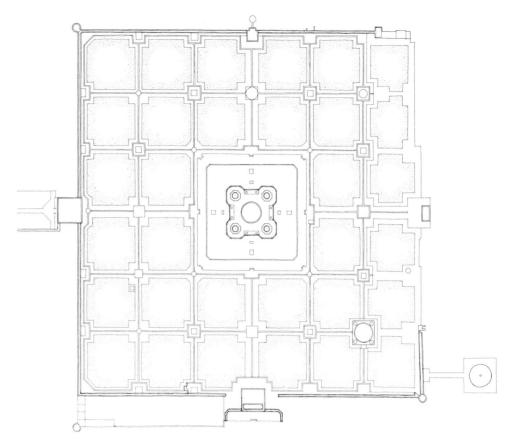

Geometric construction of Humayun's tomb

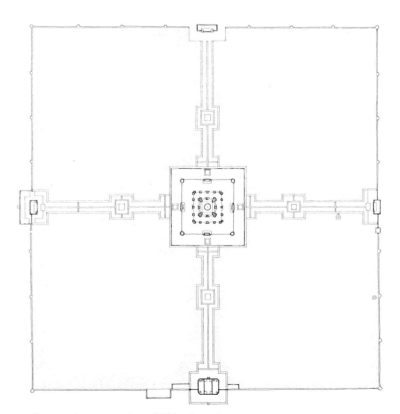

Geometric construction of Akbar's tomb

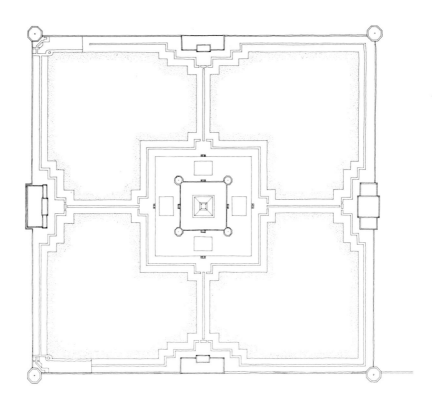

Geometric construction of the tomb of
I'timad-ud-Daula

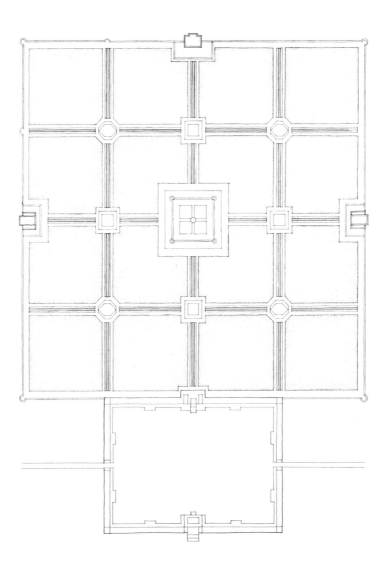

Geometric construction of Jahangir's tomb

and you can do the same from shaded eyries on the mausoleum itself. (Fathepur Sikri, a nearby city founded by Akbar, is also famous for its breeze-catching architecture.)

The next notable Mughul tomb was built at Agra on the banks of the Jumna, during the reign of Jahangir, for I'timad-ud-Daula. This is not a royal tomb. I'timad-ud-Daula was a Persian, Jahangir's prime minister, and father of Jahangir's wife Nur Jahan, who supervised the construction.

Here, since royal grandeur was not required, the contradiction of scale could be resolved by reducing the mausoleum rather than by enlarging the surrounding *chahar bagh*. The mausoleum becomes a delicate marble miniature, consisting of a square stone platform, raised upon a low plinth, topped by a canopied pavilion containing the cenotaphs of I'timad-ud-Daula and his wife. Octogonal towers stand at each corner of the mausoleum and also at the corners of the outer enclosing wall. As usual, pavilions mark the intersections of the cross axes with the outer walls. The east pavilion is the gatehouse, and the rest are false gates. Since the *chahar bagh* is quite small (about five hundred feet on edge), in scale with the mausoleum, a recursive network of canals is unnecessary. Canals along the two axes and around the perimeter suffice to ensure that no part of the garden is far from water.

The tombs of Humayun and Akbar are surfaced in red sandstone and white marble, but the mausoleum of I'timad-ud-Daula is startlingly different; it is completely covered with *pietra-dura* work—semiprecious stones inlaid in marble to form intricate patterns—and the openings are screened with delicate marble latticework. This dematerializes the surface and allows it to change with the colors of the sky, so that the mausoleum seems not a great, splendid mass, but a tiny fragile thing.

There is another striking difference. This garden does not stand upon a uniform plain, but, like other Mughul gardens in Agra, backs to the River Jumna. The main axis runs from the gate to the river. Three sides of the garden are enclosed by walls, and the fourth is formed by a high terrace from which you can look out over the broad muddy waters to the city.

After Jahangir's death in 1627 and Shah Jahan's accession to the throne, the widowed Nur Jahan set again to tomb building. The white marble mausoleum that she erected for her husband in Lahore was similar in style to that which she had made for her father, but appropriately larger. The garden is yet another canal-scribed square.

In 1631 Mumtaz Mahal (Chosen One of the Palace), wife of Shah Jahan and granddaughter of I'timad-ud-Daula, died while giving birth to her fourteenth child. Shah Jahan, with the energy of great grief, the resources of a great empire, and the help of a mature architectural tradition, built her the most splendid and beautiful tomb of all—the Taj Mahal. Work began, on the banks of the Jumna in Agra, in 1632. Sixteen years later the mausoleum was complete. Shah Jahan was eventually deposed by his son Aurangzeb and imprisoned in Agra's Red Fort, to spend his last sad years staring at the white domes across the Jumna's waters. When he died in 1666, his body was carried to where his thoughts had long rested, and he

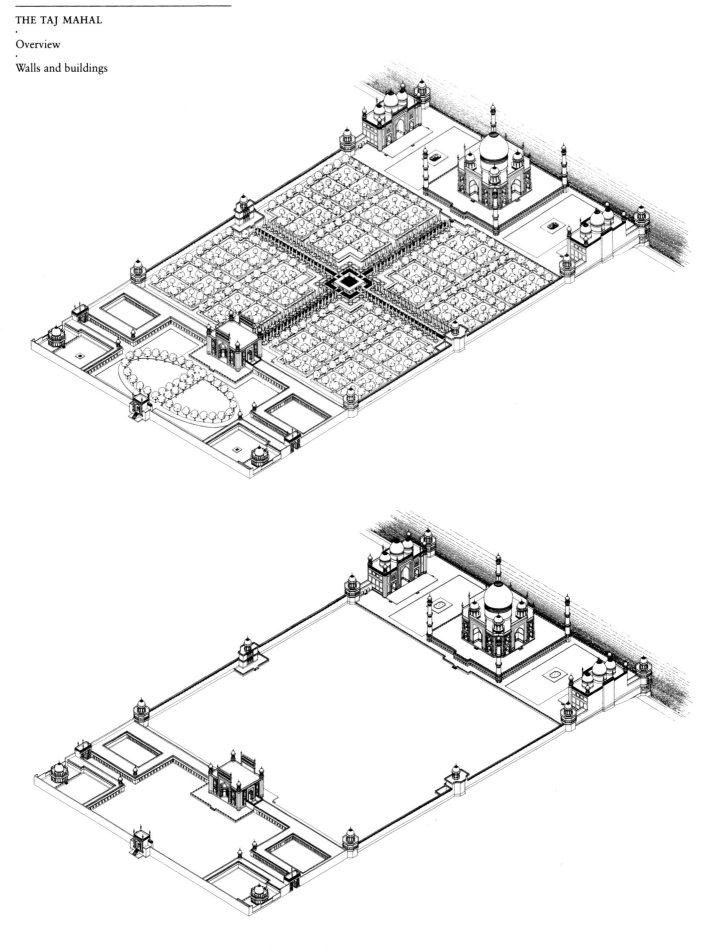

Water
·
Planting

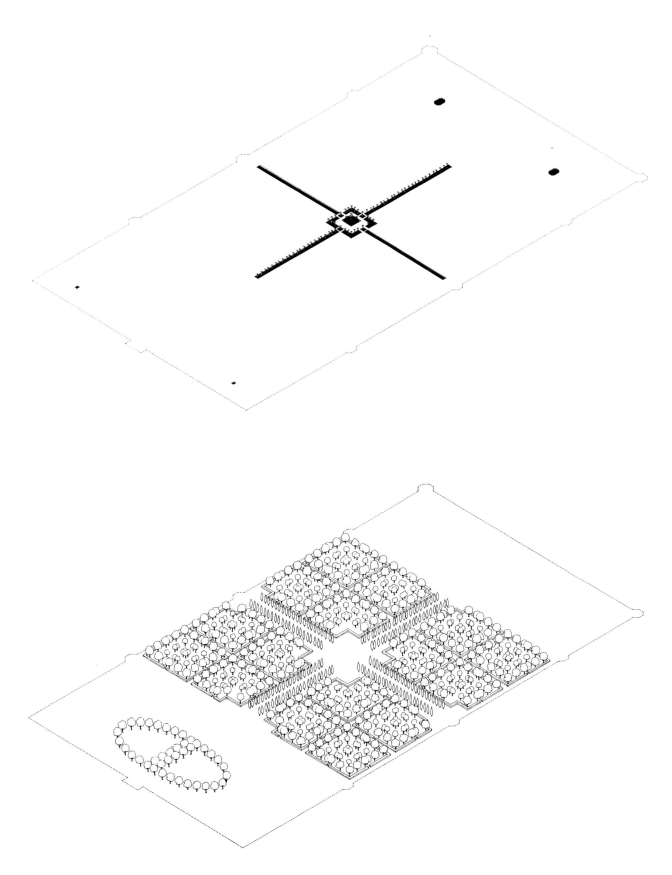

was buried beside his wife. The French traveler Jean-Baptiste Tavernier embellished this ending with a report (for which no evidence can be found) that Shah Jahan had planned for himself, on the opposite bank, a black marble replica of the Taj. But the parsimonious Aurangzeb, so the story goes, declined to print that three-dimensional negative.

It is hard to look past the accretions of anecdote and to see afresh a building whose image is so often repeated (even on the labels of beer sold in Indian restaurants), but it is worth trying, for the Taj is a remarkable architectural innovation. Its siting on the Jumna is similar to that of the tomb of I'timad-ud-Daula, and so is its construction of marble and *pietra-dura*. The relation of the mausoleum to the *chahar bagh*, though, comes as a breathtaking surprise. Here the mausoleum has been shifted from the crossing of the axes to the riverbank terrace, and the crossing is celebrated simply by a small reflecting tank. This neat sidestep breaks the connection between the size of the mausoleum and that of the *chahar bagh*, so that the troublesome contradiction simply disappears.

The *chahar bagh* is roughly one thousand feet square. It is divided into four quarters by the conventional axial causeways, then each quarter is redivided by smaller causeways. In the garden as it exists today the process of recursive subdivision stops here. But the plan of the garden prepared by the Surveyor General of India in 1828 shows that the process of division was originally repeated twice more, so that the *parti* was a grid of 256 squares, constructed by a recursion four levels deep. Position in the recursive scheme was indicated by breadth of the division between squares. The main cross axes have broad canals with fountains, a parterre on either side, then paved walks at the outer walls with narrow irrigation canals at the sides. The next level of division was formed by simple, narrow walks, and the final level appears to have consisted of little more than lines on the surface of the ground.

Repeating this theme, the plan of the mausoleum itself is recursively constructed. A square (with corners cut off) is divided into quarters by axial passages, and an octagonal space is located at their intersection. Then each quarter is in turn divided by crossed passages with an octagonal space at the center.

Worth noting is that the tall minarets, which we might expect to be at the corners of the mausoleum itself, are moved to the corners of the wide rectangular terrace. This increases the apparent size of the mausoleum without adding to its weightiness (so that it almost appears to float above the garden), matches the width of the mausoleum to the width of the garden, and captures a patch of sky to serve as the mausoleum's setting.

The earlier Mughul tomb gardens straightforwardly combined the fourfold plan symmetry of the *chahar bagh* with the infinite symmetry of a dome about its vertical axis and the bilateral elevational symmetry of the mausoleum. The symmetries of the Taj, though, are more complex and subtle. The garden and the mausoleum each have fourfold symmetry about their own (now noncoincident) central axes. The mausoleum stands upon a rectangular platform, with its minarets shifted to the corners; this

Recursive subdivision of space in the plan of the Taj Mahal mausoleum

The tomb garden game: plans drawn to the
same scale

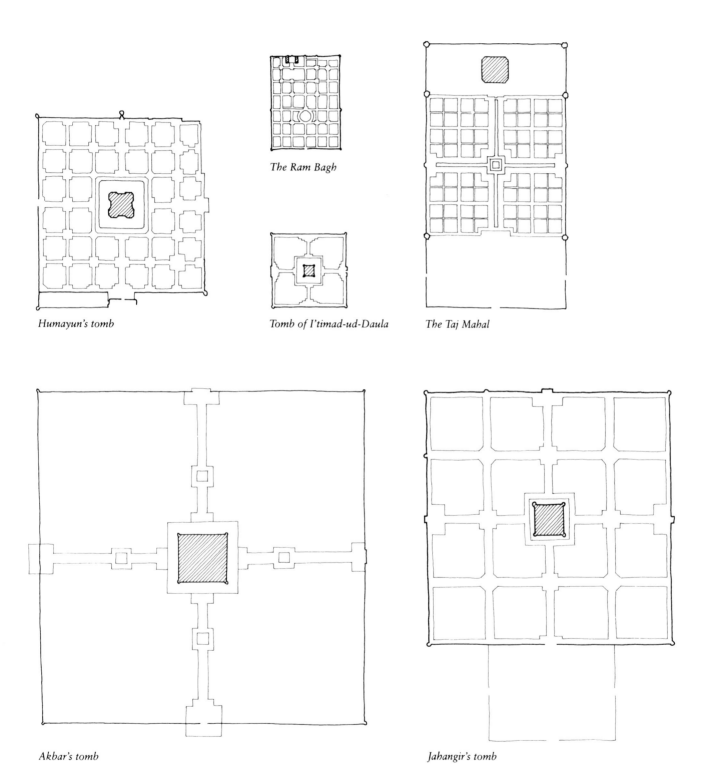

The Ram Bagh

Humayun's tomb

Tomb of I'timad-ud-Daula

The Taj Mahal

Akbar's tomb

Jahangir's tomb

ensemble has two axes of symmetry. The whole composition is bilaterally symmetrical about a single central axis, which also forms the axis of movement from the entry to the reflective pool, the mausoleum, and eventually the view of the Jumna. However, we don't walk quite *on* the axis, but to the side of the water, and the stairs up to the terrace go off to the sides as well; conspicuous avoidance gives the axis added importance. Finally, there is symmetry about the ground plane, as the mausoleum is reflected in the pool and so is brought back, inverted and immaterial, to the heart of the garden from which it had been removed.

When Aurangzeb's turn at tomb building came, he constructed, for *his* wife, a mausoleum that was much like the Taj, but without the same generosity of proportion or felicity of composition. Like Babur he ordered that his own resting place should be a simple, earth-covered grave, open to the sky. This brought the cycle of great garden tomb building to an end, although there were to be eleven more Mughul emperors before the last of them was removed by the British after the revolt of 1857.

Perhaps, though, it wasn't quite the end. When Sir Edwin Lutyens designed the great Viceroy's House as the focal point for the capital of the British Raj at New Delhi, he chose (despite his open contempt for Mughul architecture) a subtle transformation of the *parti* of the Taj. He was put up to it by Lady Hardinge, wife of a former viceroy, who had fond memories of Mughul gardens in Kashmir.

The Viceroy's House designed by Lutyens now stands at the termination of the major formal axis of the city. The axis becomes a magnificent street lined with canals, so that the approach to the symmetrical, pink sandstone house recalls the garden approaches to the Mughul tombs, but the scale is much vaster. Surprisingly, the axis continues through the house, and threaded upon it are, first, an elaborate garden in the Mughul style (known as the Rashtrapati Bhavan), then echelons of tennis courts, and finally a pretty little circular flower garden. Thus the house and the garden stand in much the same relation as the mausoleum and garden at the Taj, except that the house turns its back on the garden, so that the garden now provides a destination rather than an approach. Not only is the house much larger in scale than any Mughul mausoleum (as the British Raj surpassed the greatest heights of the Mughul empire), but the recursive subdivision of the garden also exceeds in sheer intricacy that of any of its predecessors. There are bougainvilleas and flower beds and over four hundred varieties of roses. But at its center, a place that had been occupied by the tombs of great emperors, then dramatically vacated at the Taj, there is nothing but a simple square of alien English lawn.

This has been a story of (to adapt a phrase of Sir John Summerson's) an aesthetic adventure, provoked by a problem that had to be solved. Such adventures become possible, and interesting, because designers agree (at least for a while) to certain conventions of vocabulary and syntax, and the internal logic of the conventions generates a design problem, just as some set of axioms and inference rules may generate a mathematical problem. It's not the conventions themselves that are interesting, but the adventures of the imagination they set going.

Mausoleum and minarets

The Taj Mahal

Tomb of Aurangzeb's wife

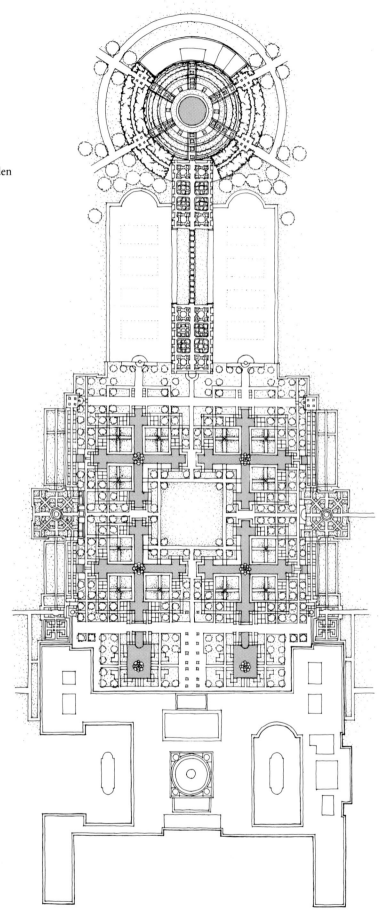

Plan of Sir Edwin Lutyens's Mughul garden
for the Viceroy's House, New Delhi

The Alhambra

The rough and defensible exterior of the Alhambra, drawn by F. O. C. Darley for Washington Irving's *The Alhambra*

On a spur of the Sierra Nevada just above the ancient city of Granada is a red fort, rough and defensible on the outside, but inside, sparkling like the center of a geode, lies a sybaritic pleasure palace of beguiling delicacy and dazzling splendor. It is not at all clear to those who have studied it why it is even there: no other palace gardens anything like it have come down to us from the rich and powerful capitals of Islam. Why would this insignificant and beleaguered principality have constructed this royal masterpiece?

Though its provenance is shrouded in mystery, its splendors are very much in evidence, hidden only partially by the swarms of tourists who cover its surfaces. It has been showered with appreciations since Washington Irving came to camp with the gypsies and brigands within the walls and recorded (or invented) resident tales of adventure and romance.

Granada's place in history derives from its being the last seat of a Moorish princedom in Spain. Boabdil, its last ruler, fled his palace on January 2, 1492, with laments that are still sung (the popular "La Golondrina" celebrates the flight). Granada was never a major capital: power during the early centuries of the Moorish occupation had been centered in Cordoba, but as the Christian monarchs gradually pressed the Moors into the south, the center collapsed and only a group of minor city-states was left. One by one the Christian kings of Leon and Castille and Aragon picked them off, until only Granada was left, under attack for years, defended without much spirit, and finally occupied by the Catholic monarchs Ferdinand and Isabella. Though they were glad to get it, it is unlikely that they were prepared to appreciate their new palace. Certainly the vast, dour, unfinished square palace with a round courtyard that was commissioned by their son Charles V betrays a minimum of sympathy for the lush delicacy it was superseding.

What we see now are remnants of the garden palace plus much newer garden terraces very similar to the originals. The walls of the Red Fort enclose considerably more than this; the remaining space must once have contained dependencies of the palace, protected by its defenses. The composition is not cast into the single foursquare pattern of ancient Persian rugs or gardens, but is a collage of several patterns only barely tied together. A typical pattern might include covered spaces, often roofed with elaborate faceted vaults, opening onto a central courtyard where a fountain plays. A tiny opening might then lead through a dark, irregular passageway into another pattern, arranged around another court.

The separate patterns are very different from each other, and except for the baths and the mosque, there is very little that would let us assign particular uses to the separate places. It is perhaps most useful to think of the courts as elaborate and beautiful campsites, made inviting and colorful by patterned carpets, with braziers for warmth and cooking and soft cushions to lounge upon. Now, of course, all the paraphernalia for living has vanished, but the walls and ceiling are so richly covered with patterns of tile and paint and plaster blocks that the spaces seem as full and as alive as they must have in the days of their inhabitation.

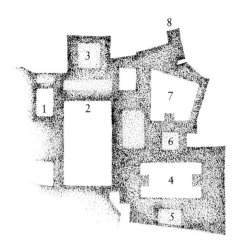

Major courtyards and related rooms

1. Cuarto Dorado
2. Court of the Myrtles
3. Hall of the Ambassadors
4. Court of the Lions
5. Hall of the Abencerrajes
6. Hall of the Two Sisters
7. Patio of the Daraxa
8. Peinador de la Reina

Our axonometric on the next page shows the heart of the palace, the adjoining gardens, and the palace of Charles V looming in the background. A tour should concentrate on maybe five of the collaged patterns: the Cuarto Dorado, the Court of the Myrtles and its adjacent rooms, the baths, the Court of the Lions and the rooms adjacent to it, and the Patio of the Daraxa. Just beyond (to the left) are the gardens of the Partal and some lower pavilions. Each has distinct spatial qualities, but all share an attachment to a delicate but relentless elaboration of surface—the intricacies of which, in the nineteenth century, the English architect Owen Jones was to draw in similarly relentless detail.

The *Cuarto Dorado*, the first patterned space inside the present public entrance to the palace, is a small rectangular court. Its marble floor is absolutely plain except for three steps near the south facade and an octagonal depression in the center, which holds a round fountain basin with scalloped edges that catch the rings of water coming from a central source and reflect them back and sideways in sparkling complexity. On the north face of the court, three layers of wall, complexly patterned, lead to a long room overlooking the valley. The south face of the court, richly decorated in tile and stucco, offers an altogether ambiguous pair of identical openings, the one leading back to the entrance, the other leading into the Court of the Myrtles and the rest of the palace.

The *Court of the Myrtles*, at 77 by 120 feet, is about four times as large as the Cuarto Dorado. It has a 24-by-114-foot pool in the center, whose stillness is emphasized by the water splashing into it down little chutes from circular fountains at the two ends of the pool. The end elevations of the courtyard are high and regular; the south facade of three stories is backed by the palace of Charles V; the north arcade (whose pierced stucco casts dancing patterns of sunlight onto the wall behind, to overlay the rippling light reflected from the water below) is even more formidably backed by the rough masonry of the Tower of Comares, the largest of the Alhambra's towers, which contains the *Hall of the Ambassadors*, a striking room with tile and stucco on the walls and a ceiling made of 8,017 pieces of wood.

The long sides of the Court of the Myrtles seem not to be composed at all, but they contain, very much played down, the openings that lead to the other patterned groups of spaces. One undistinguished opening leads to the baths, which are at a much lower level than the large courtyards they lie between in plan, so that they connect with the *Patio of the Daraxa* and the belvedere called the *Peinador de la Reina,* which looks out over the valley. Another modest opening in the same wall of the Court of the Myrtles leads through a tiny dark passage to the most celebrated of the patterns, the rooms around the *Court of the Lions.*

Spatially, this is by far the most complex of the Alhambra's areas. The court is rectangular and much smaller than the Court of the Myrtles (about 52 by 94 feet). It is surrounded by a portico that becomes a projecting pavilion on each of the two ends. Behind these pavilions are long narrow rooms, on axis; the one on the west is quite plain, the one on the

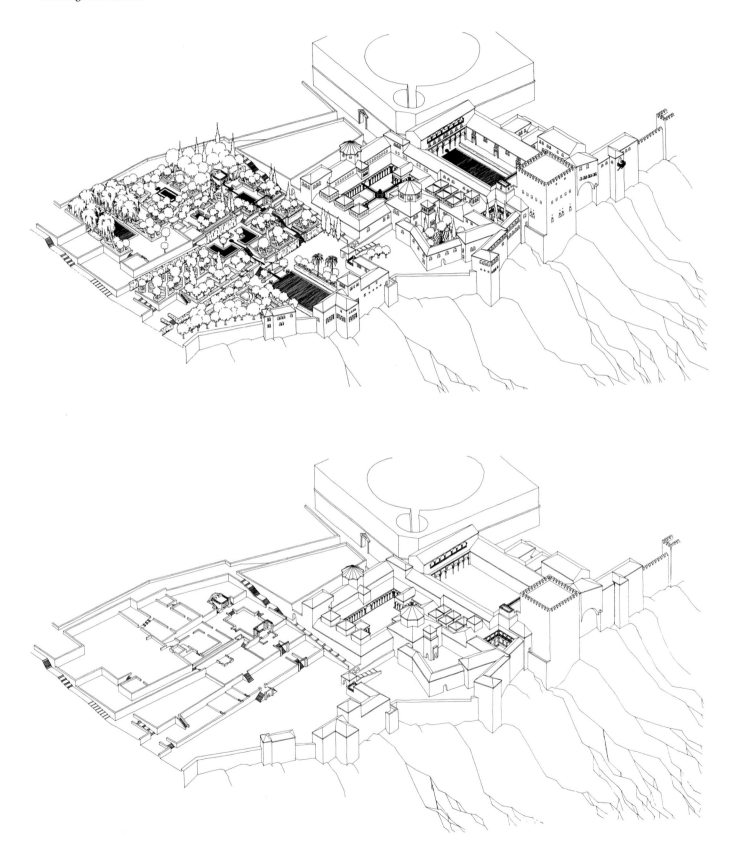

Water
·
Planting

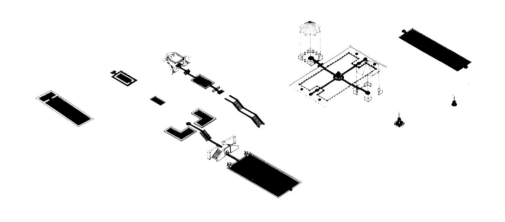

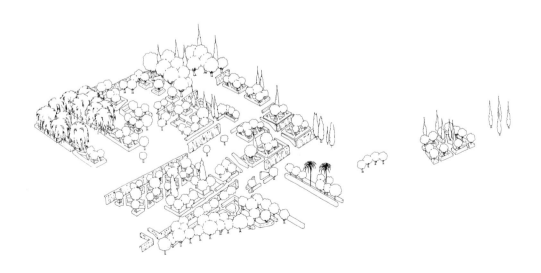

Tile and stucco patterns: illustration by
Owen Jones of the Court of the Myrtles

east, the Hall of the Kings, is composed of three squares, each with a
dome of stucco blocks and rectangular, flat-ceilinged spaces between.

On the north side of the court is the most splendid room of all, the *Hall of
the Two Sisters,* a room with an intricate cupola of stucco blocks set over
an octagon. Around it are three rectangular spaces, the northern one with
a pavilion overlooking the verdant Patio of the Daraxa, where trees and a
high jetting fountain push upward past the level of the viewing pavilion.
On the south side of the court is the *Hall of the Abencerrajes,* a square
room flanked by rectangular ones, with another cupola of stucco blocks
over the center forming an eight-pointed star. From each of the four directions, the two end pavilions and the magnificent rooms of the Two Sisters
and the Abencerrajes, marble channels fed by little fountains slip down
steps and to the center of the court, where another sparkling fountain is
rather extraordinarily held aloft on the backs of lions. Arguments continue about the appropriate surface for this court. It was overgrown in
Washington Irving's time, then became chaste crushed rock, and has recently been planted again. It is a garden nonetheless, with or without the
plants.

Just east of the Court of the Lions, the gardens open up in geometric patterns, but with fewer buildings and more greenery. A portico stands on top
of the fortification wall, with a view north over the valley and south over a
large pool, whose ripples send reflections dancing up into the richly
wrought wooden ceiling of the porch. There is a single tower and a beautiful little oratory set at an angle to the rest, facing Mecca, which makes for
an almost giddy disorientation from inside the dark room to the bright,
skewed world outside. Two rough towers along the ramparts have tiny,
delicate pavilions inside, repeating in miniature the splendors of this
stucco geode.

This patterned place strikes a responsive chord in the modern visitor in
part because of our sense of how it was used. Camping is one of the favorite activities of our own time, and camping elegantly can't be beat. The
collision of rustic and elegant, when handsome linen is spread on the grass
and wicker hampers disgorge fancy edibles, affords us special pleasure—
and an entire palace for camping in, where rooms are gardens and gardens
are rooms, seems the ultimate luxury. The rooms and courts are still rich
with intricately patterned glazed tile, pierced-stucco decoration, and ceilings of even greater elaboration. Imagine even more patterns and colors in
the rugs and pillows thrown down for the picnic, plus braziers making
warm centers on a chilly night, and places to sit around splashing fountains on a warm summer day. The intricacy and surprises from pattern to
pattern or from courtyard to courtyard must have made for continuing
excitement, whether the inhabitant wandered or stayed put. In a camp-
ground without the usual trees, we find ourselves in a forest where the columns are trunks and the stucco capitals and the decoration beyond them
are like branches and leaves. The surfaces, of tile and stucco and wood,
make artificial foliage as rich and varied as that of plants in more familiar
gardens, as they catch the light of the sun and, even more wondrously,
catch the shimmering reflections from fountains and pools.

The opulent play of overlaid patterns loses none of its luster when we discern the almost Spartan rigor behind all this complexity: there is really very little water, for instance, and a careful placement of the nozzles makes the most of every drop. And the apparently limitless patterns are ingenious variations on very simple themes: the five thousand pieces of stucco in the Hall of the Two Sisters are of only eleven patterns, based on just four plan shapes. Beneath all the diversities of surface are just the seven possible frieze symmetries and the seventeen possible wallpaper symmetries. The compositional message of the Alhambra, surely, is that intricacy is more satisfying if built on order, even simplicity, and that simplicity's pleasures can comfortably include the dazzlingly intricate.

The Generalife

The Alhambra is patterned of sun and stucco and water. On the breezy slope of the mountains to the south, its symmetries were remade with more water, with shade, and with real green plants, whose foliage would aspirate during the long Andalusian summers to make hot days seem cooler and whose blossoms could make festive measurements of the seasons. It must have felt good, we suppose, to escape the enclosure of the Red Fort and rest sometimes in a cooler, more open, more natural place. In any case, the Jinnah al-'Arif (which can translate as "the Garden of the Architect" or "Noblest of Gardens") was begun before 1319 in a form typical of the Spanish version of the pattern garden. Hillsides were often available in Spain, and their views and breezes recommended them as garden sites. The gardens were formed by turning the slope into level strips, each with planting set against the hill, patterned parterres, walks, beds of green, and perhaps fountains and bosques, and an overlook on the downhill side.

Leafy patterns: the foliage of the Generalife

The architects of the Generalife played a series of variations on this basic garden theme. Entrance is from the nearest corner in the axonometric, along the slope between rows of cypress, or up the colonnaded ramp, through an arch, and up a flight of steps to the entrance courtyard, with its topiary arcade. Just beyond the entrance court is a thin, tall (three-story) building with some small and apparently casual openings. If you choose the middle one, you will find yourself in a loggia facing the largest of the Generalife's parterres, the *Patio de Acequia*. Ahead is a long trough of water into which thin jets arch from both sides. It is backed by thin, straight cypresses, which are in turn backed by luxuriant planting and a straight hedge. Beyond that, on the uphill side, is a walk and a high wall topped by the balustrade of the next garden. On the downhill side, there is again a walk and a shaded arcade whose line of arched openings looks out over a garden terrace, studded with fountains, to the Alhambra, the city beyond, and the vast plain stretching toward Jaen. At the end of the long panel of water opposite the entrance is another tall and narrow building, with a tower at the downhill corner. On this building's ground floor is an arcade. The loggia behind it has a projecting vantage point (on axis with the long pool), which allows a dramatic view over a small square garden wrapped with an arcade.

THE GENERALIFE
.
Overview
.
Buildings and terraces

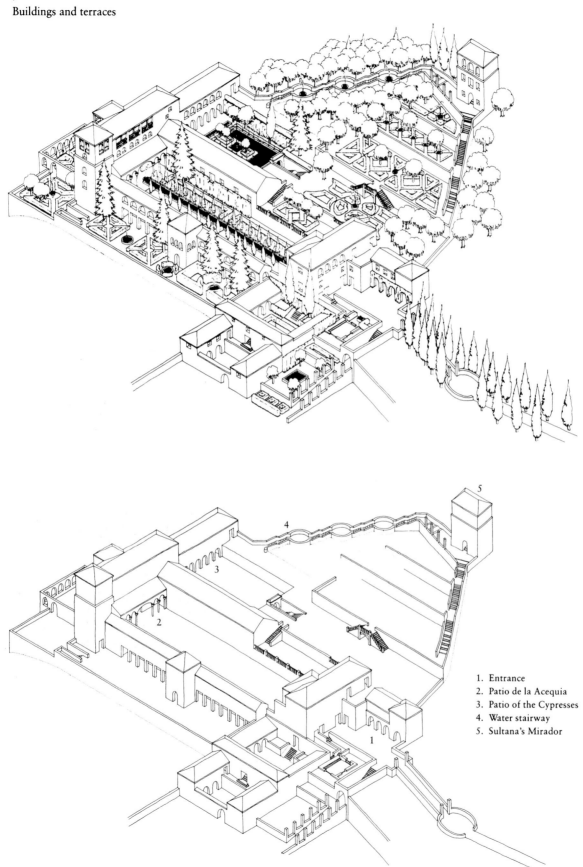

1. Entrance
2. Patio de la Acequia
3. Patio of the Cypresses
4. Water stairway
5. Sultana's Mirador

Water
·
Plantings

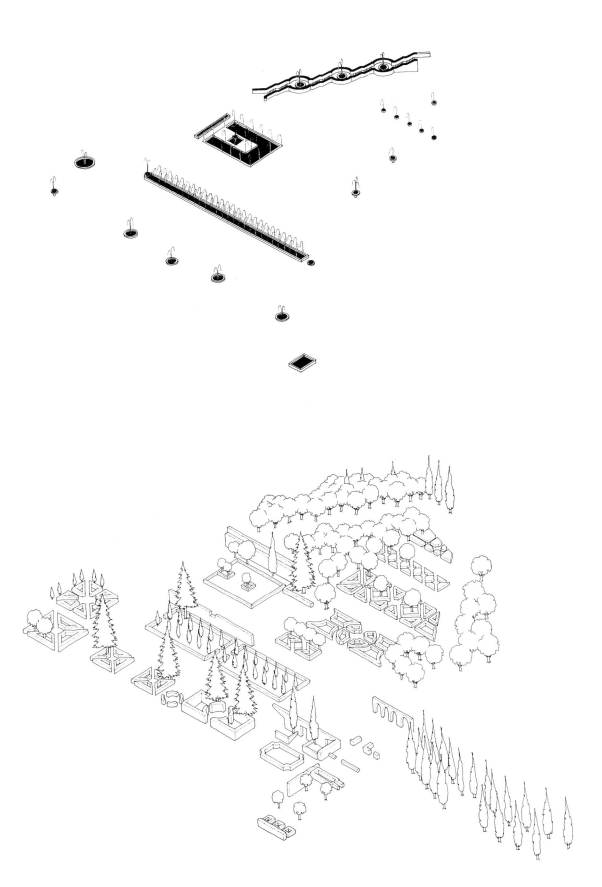

Patio of the Cypresses

Next to this low, sheltered garden is a square, open terrace with a fountain in the center. Up a flight, the terrace continues, with alternating diagonal walks in a square and tiny fountain plazas, to the group of buildings where we first entered the garden. The building with the loggia at the far end of the long pool casts a sheltering wing in front of the *Patio of the Cypresses,* which is also embraced by walls against the hill. Its designers made skilled use of very small changes in level to create a paradoxical place, a garden in full view that seems to be submerged in another world. A peninsula, inaccessible to humans because of the thick planting, emerges from a square pool with a fountain in it. Around it is a brick terrace, dry except for the mist from the jets, which surprises us by being just a few inches *below* the level of the surrounding pool, symbolically engulfed and remote, the brick terrace of a distant kingdom.

Above the Patio of the Cypresses are three more terraces bounded by a diagonal stair ascending toward *Sultana's Mirador.* The farther stair, in the axonometric, is particularly celebrated for its railings, whose tops are channels down which water courses, in splashing counterpoint to the jets in the center of three circular landings. The water channels are simple, without the refinements of surface that mark later Italian water gardens, where balustrades sport channels carved with shells, to curl and splash the water that runs in them. But in the dusty heat of an Andalusian summer, the stairway is a cool delight.

Vaux-le-Vicomte

The garden at Vaux-le-Vicomte, south of Paris, figures prominently in the history of empire, as it does in the history of gardens. Its message, in the former realm, is of vanity punished; Nicholas Fouquet, the treasurer to Louis XIV, secured the services of the young landscape architect André Le Nôtre to lay out a splendid garden. At its inauguration, Fouquet proudly invited his king, who sensed that too much French money had been lavished on the premises and ordered Fouquet imprisoned. He then hired Le Nôtre for a string of subsequent triumphs, including Versailles.

The château at Vaux-le-Vicomte

In the history of garden design, Vaux-le-Vicomte has a more central place. It marks a profound revolution in attitude, for here, for the first time, the pattern garden, previously cut off from a hostile world by a clear and definite edge, plunges through that edge and invades nature, while it eludes containment. At Vaux the canal is placed *across* the axis, so it vanishes out of the manicured garden into wild and uncontrolled nature, which had for so long seemed too hostile to penetrate but which seemed at last, in the confident seventeenth century, ready for human engagement.

The moated château at Vaux is squeezed into the far third of its rectangular island. A bridge leads to the spacious forecourt, which occupies the first two-thirds of the island. The forecourt seems generous, but the house's jumble of roofs pushing against its central dome speaks still of medieval jostling and crowding. On the mainland side of the bridge is a square court, quartered, with walks to the right and left leading to other courts flanked by pavilions strung together with colonnades. Opposite the bridge, just behind a wall from the square court, is a big roundish place into which a number of roads lead, in the "goose-foot" pattern characteristic of roads in French forests.

To the right and left of the château are patterned parterres. The one on the left, twice as long as it is wide, is laid out in two squares, each quartered diagonally by a pair of walks. There is a circle in the center of each square, and an almost circular spiral or shell at every corner, decoratively elaborated. To the right of the château a much narrower parterre, undivided, has planting beds at its edges to form three connecting panels of grass.

Most of the garden, however, lies beyond the château and slightly below it, past a transverse promenade. The building's domed front connects with this promenade—across a bridge over the moat, then down a stair. Subsequent flights step down to a fanciful split parterre (with a wide walk along the center) leading from the house to a circular fountain basin. Just past the fountain is a first cross canal, which doesn't extend past the patterned garden. Past it on the main axis lies a large, strikingly simple parterre, with a square basin of water on axis and a pair of elliptical basins flanking. Here the land begins to rise away from the house and to the left. Its slope is gentle, but it creates, on so large a site, a considerable difference in elevation. To the left of the square basin is a high square of lawn, a particularly attractive place flanked by rows of pleached trees, reached by a flight of stairs that climb along the wall supporting the raised plot.

Along the main axis past the square basin are enormously wide shallow steps, then a wall and statues, some water, then the breakthrough canal, extending out of sight (until the viewer arrives at its bank, whereupon its ends finally become visible). There is a view across the canal to long ramps, fountains, steps, basins, an arcaded grotto, and beyond that a dome of water balancing the dome of the château at the other end of the long axis. Trees extend the axis some more, then form a concentric set of spaces that receive the "goose feet" of roads radiating into the forest.

It is all vast, straight, linear, simple, formal, strong, and generous, a pattern that speaks of power, over nature and over men. It uses finite formal geometries to bring us to the brink of infinity. The strengths it hints at would be developed at Versailles, in gardens richer in detail and far vaster than these, but never clearer, nor more effective.

What was it like to inhabit such a place? There seem to be two opposite answers. The first, more respectable, is that inhabitation can include actions that are for show, that are mannered, formal, ritualistic. A formal setting, then, is appropriate for formal behavior—with, in the case of Vaux-le-Vicomte, the suggestion via the large canal that there is some escape from it (if not the exit that was arranged for poor M. Fouquet). A series of formal gestures in the landscape, then, support prescribed formal gestures among inhabitants in prescribed formal dress.

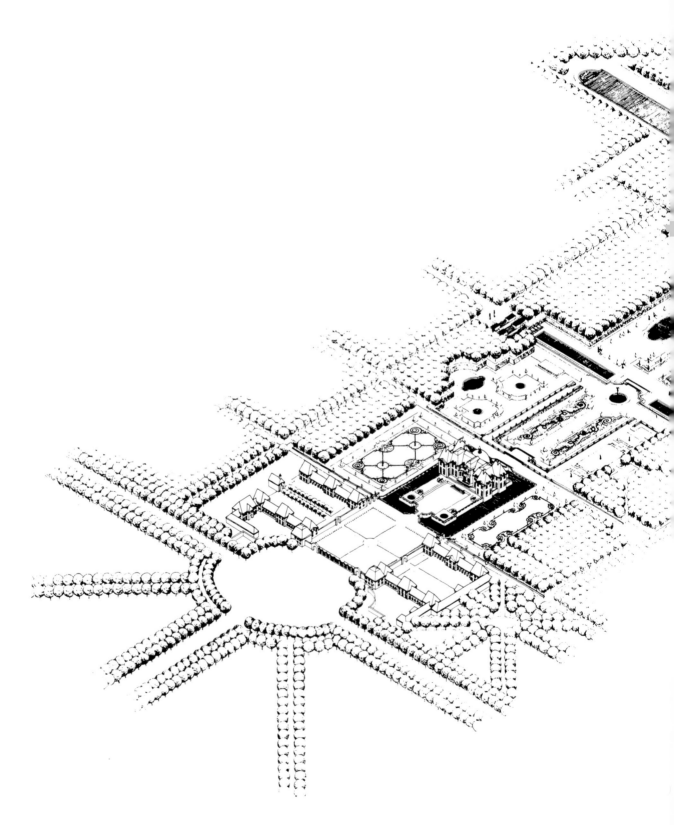

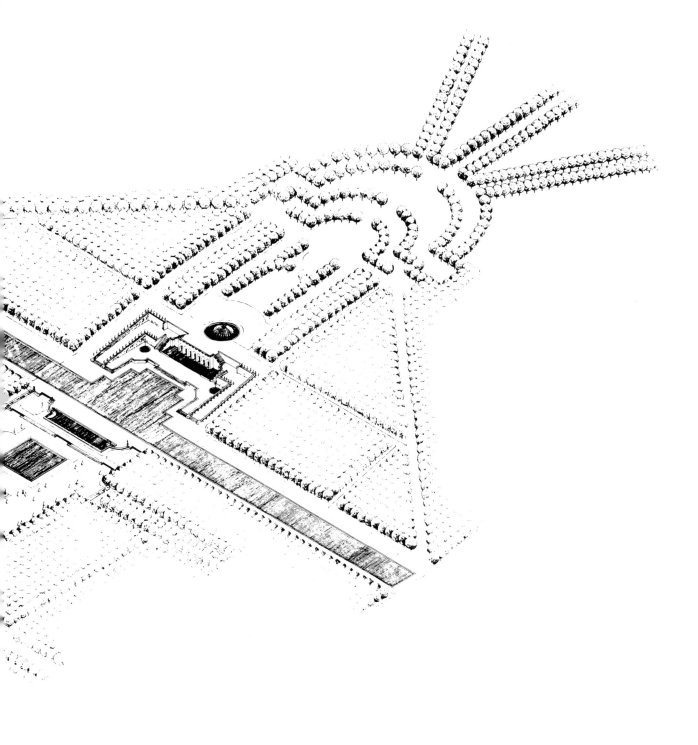

VAUX-LE-VICOMTE

·

Buildings and terraces

·

Water

·

Planting

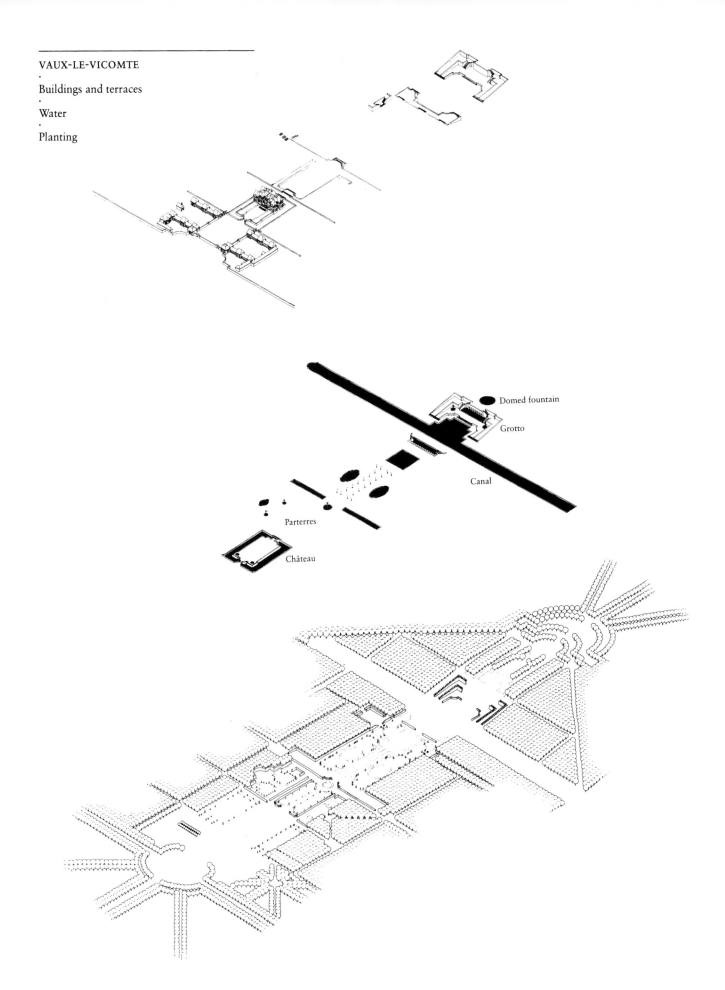

Domed fountain

Grotto

Canal

Parterres

Château

The opposite answer, one with even more interesting implications, has been suggested to us by the architect Jean-Paul Carlhian. He notes that, in the centuries of their origins, formal symmetrical spaces were inhabited in an altogether casual manner: objects on elaborate symmetrical mantel-pieces were never matched and symmetrical, furniture grouping was straightforwardly functional and ad hoc, not formal at all. The formal order of the architecture (and the garden), that is to say, freed the inhabitants from formal manners and left them ready to inhabit their symmetrical spaces as they chose.

Studley Royal

The Mughul and Moorish paradises we have explored form symmetrical patterns in the sunlight where the water sparkles, and Le Nôtre's gardens glorify the gilded reign of the Sun King, but Studley Royal is a northern garden, a place of greens and browns, misty distances, and the silver reflections of a pale sky in quiet water. It was laid out in a wooded valley near Ripon, in Yorkshire, by John Aislabie, a character out of the Brönte sisters' world. He had been Chancellor of the Exchequer (in the early eighteenth century) but was disgraced by the bursting of the South Sea bubble and imprisoned in the Tower of London for "infamous foolhardihood and corruption." He was not the first, nor would he be the last, to find solace in cultivating his garden.

Like Ryoan-ji and the Alhambra, Studley Royal contrasts the rough with the perfectly finished and craggy irregularity with meticulous symmetry. Ryoan-ji does this by arranging stones upon a perfect rectangle of smooth, white sand, and the Alhambra by jamming glittering, crystalline, rectangular courtyards in a rough, stony husk. Studley Royal does it by placing symmetrical patterns of water and shaven lawn among wild hills and shattered ruins.

The site is an L-shaped stretch of the valley of the tiny River Skell, where it narrows between steep hills. When in the valley you can't see what is around the corner, which allowed Aislabie to create a dramatic surprise. Studley Royal is, in fact, two gardens: the first along the upper stroke of the L, and the second along the lower. It is a green palindrome; you can follow it in either direction and it works.

At the lower end is a weir that creates a large, roughly circular lake. There is a path around the shore, and an obelisk with water jets once stood at the center. One side of the lake is formed by the high, straight stone wall of a second dam, which stretches across the mouth of the valley. In the center of the dam is a stepped, semicircular cascade, and square, pyramid-roofed "fishing lodges" with fine Palladian windows stand symmetrically on either shore. Apparently these were the work of Colen Campbell.

This geometry suggests a water axis leading back into the valley, but it is not possible to confirm this expectation immediately. The path to the fishing lodges and cascade enters from the east, runs straight along the top of the wall, and crosses to the western shore by stepping stones. When you reach the stepping stones, you indeed discover that a long, straight canal

The garden of Studley Royal

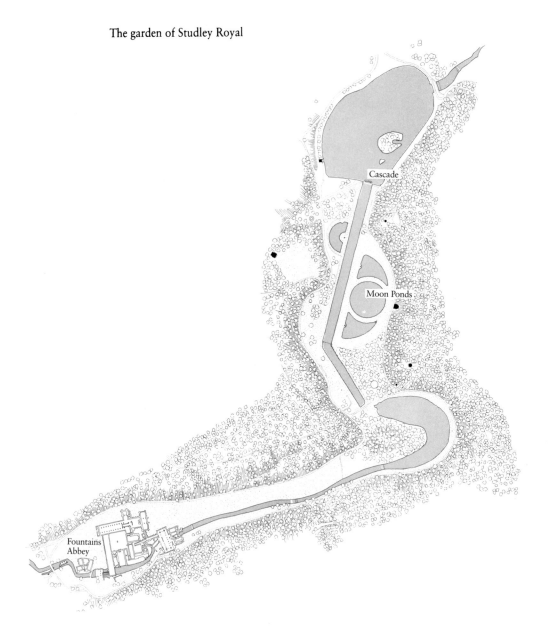

The beautiful: Moon Ponds and the
Temple of Fame at Studley Royal

The sublime: The River Skell flows
through the ruins of Fountains Abbey

forms a perpendicular to the path, leading you into the hidden heart of the garden: smooth planes of grass and water, composed in a symmetrical arrangement with Euclidean precision.

The canal bisects the valley floor and forms a chord to a circle of wooded hills. To one side is a round pond, with a statue marking the point where Aislabie placed his compasses to strike out the circle. A perpendicular to the canal has been constructed through this center; it forms an axis of symmetry for horn-shaped ponds on either side and terminates at the hillside with a Doric temple set back into the trees. Another perpendicular to the canal, farther back toward the weir, is the axis for concentric semicircles that enclose an annular pond and that have another statue at the centerpoint. The uphill end of the canal is terminated by a second weir with screens of trees on either side. This pattern of planes and parallels and perpendiculars, of arcs and axes, is called the *Moon Ponds*. There are dark, rugged crags all around, with places to look down on its shapes: a beautiful Palladian stone banqueting house by Colen Campbell, an open Doric rotunda called the Temple of Fame, and (once, but now gone) a Chinese temple.

Beyond the upstream cascade the canal strikes off at an obtuse angle into the trees, then (past yet another dam) broadens into a fat, sausage-shaped pond that sweeps around the corner and into the upper garden. This is later work, and was not completed until after the succession of Aislabie's son William to the estate.

This upper garden is simply a long, narrow valley, with the stream and a path hard by one edge. An enormous stretch of lawn, tree-covered slopes, and the medieval ruins of *Fountains Abbey* close the end. The roof is gone, Cistercian bees buzz through the now-empty windows, the waters of the Skell flow between the fallen stones, and the sun casts shadows of broken walls across the dewy grass.

One of us (innocent of the later history of this place) first came to the valley of the Skell to visit the famous ruins, then strolled down the river, through a little wood, to find what seemed a secret garden—a wonder of manicured perfection. Geometric diagrams appeared on the ground, signaling (as they did to the shipwrecked philosopher on the wild Rhodian shore) the presence of human intellect. Ruins were left behind; the unblemished symmetries of the white Doric temple glowed bravely against the hillside in the afternoon sunlight.

The other first came to explore the Moon Ponds, then walked upstream in the soft Yorkshire rain to find a place of fragments and elegy—recollections of the proud power of the monasteries, which came to such a catastrophic end with the Dissolution, of John Aislabie's own ruined hopes and the darkness of the Tower, and of lines from Gray and Wordsworth. The suggestion of lost symmetries may surpass present perfection.

4

OUR OWN PLACES

Somebody once suggested, T. S. Eliot recounts in his essay "Tradition and the Individual Talent," that our predecessors seem remote because we *know* so much more than they did. "Precisely," he replied, "and they are that which we know." Now that we have come to know something of the great garden makers and connoisseurs of the past and have seen something of their works, how can we, their successors, extend and renew the traditions of gardening on our own shrunken sites, with our own modest means?

We shall approach some possible answers to this question by first exploring the uses that Americans have made, over the last 350 years, of the older garden traditions that were carried to the New World. Then we shall interject a brief polemic about our own particular moment on the surface of this planet and the urgent suggestions we sense that it carries. Finally, we shall stage some engagements of site and memory and see what comes of them.

PARADISE REPLAYED

The Pilgrim Fathers had been struggling for just four years with the wild and recalcitrant North American continent when Francis Bacon wrote, in 1625, that "when Ages grow to Civility and Elegancie, Men come to Build Stately, sooner than to Garden Finely." The hardships and perils of the frontier (as well as the thrills and challenges) that were to shape the relations of Americans to their gardens for the ensuing centuries have seldom pressed them into full, great monuments of garden art like those of Europe and Asia that we have described, but often into edited replays of the highlights—condensations, extrapolations, fragments, and inversions of these works, suitable for a nation in motion.

There were a few important early exceptions to this rule—most notably the gardens of Middleton Place, in South Carolina. These were created for Henry Middleton by an English landscape gardener with a hundred slaves at his disposal. They have the full sweep and grandeur of their eighteenth-century European equivalents and bring to mind, in particular, the earthworks and ponds of their close contemporary Studley Royal. But, where fewer hands could be put to the task, more modest attempts were made to impose the garden forms of the old world on the soil of the new. Spanish settlers carried versions of the walled, geometric, formal garden to the dry

Southwest, and forms of the natural garden took root with the English in the damp Northeast. The ghosts of these early gardens can be found, still, among the gravestones of pioneers in New Mexico and New England.

At the pueblo of Ranchos de Taos, for example, the whitewashed adobe church (built around 1780) stands symmetrically within a rectangular garden enclosure scattered with crosses. A straight path to the front door, flanked by trees, divides the walled rectangle precisely in two. There is little water, so the garden is mostly a flat surface of gray-brown pebbles. But this is broken, at intervals, by miniature, adobe-bordered circular oases—small enough to be watered with a bucket carried from the well, and crammed with flowers. The concentrated brilliance of these blossoms shatters the parched simplicity of the gravel plane, just as a few bursts of exuberantly carved and painted ornament (skilled craftsmen were in as short supply as water for flowers) contrast with the white masses of the church walls.

The custom of the pueblos was to turn the backs of dwellings to the dry, dusty land and create a protected, central plaza. When the Spanish arrived, they brought with them the Mediterranean practice of claiming some private turf by surrounding it with a building or a wall. The Spanish missions, then, fused the two traditions by collecting dwelling spaces around a central courtyard—the place for a cool, shady garden with fountains and fruit trees and memories of monastery gardens left far behind in Europe. Later still, in Southern California, the builders of bungalow courts were shrewdly to recognize that the same pattern afforded, on modest suburban lots, the opportunity to fabricate hidden garden romances of palm fronds and banana leaves, white stucco and splashes of bougainvillea, and nostalgia for the colorful (though largely imagined) time of Helen Hunt Jackson's *Ramona*—the tear-stained but triumphant tale of a half-Indian, half-Scottish beauty and her ill-fated Indian lover Alessandro. "It was a picturesque life, with more of sentiment and gaiety in it, more that was truly dramatic, more romance, than will ever be seen again on those sunny shores," wrote Jackson as she set her scene. "The aroma of it all lingers there still; industries and inventions have not yet slain it."

From almost the beginning, though, the cooler, rainier parts of North America have bred an opposite tradition—that of the isolated, self-sufficient cottage, looking not inward to a protected courtyard, but outward to the surrounding wilderness, with a ring of open space, instead of

The church of Ranchos de Taos

an enclosing wall, as the device for establishing a property. Henry David Thoreau's cottage in the woods at Walden Pond, "a mile from any neighbor," serves as its purified exemplar.

If we were to choose a cool-climate New England romance to match *Ramona* teardrop for teardrop, it would have to be Nathaniel Hawthorne's *The House of the Seven Gables*. Ramona and Alessandro wandered from refuge to refuge in the wide, wild California landscape, but Hawthorne's chronicle of Phoebe and Clifford is set, claustrophobically, in "a rusty wooden house, with seven acutely peaked gables, facing toward various points of the compass, and a huge, clustered chimney in the midst." The warming chimney (not a shaded courtyard) is placed at the heart of the action, and Hawthorne presents the walls not as embracing and gathering arms, like those of a mission, but as a "human countenance, bearing the traces not merely of outward storm and sunshine, but expressive, also, of the long lapse of mortal life, and accompanying vicissitudes that have passed within."

Foundation planting yields the rose-covered cottage

Where early American detached houses were assembled into villages and towns, they formed dispersed patterns, very different from the condensed clusters of pueblo and mission dwellings. Each house stood alone in the center of its lot; the larger the dimension from the house to the street, and to the side and rear of the property, the greater the house's claim of importance. The purpose of surrounding planting was not so much to make an inhabitable garden as to adorn the house, even to camouflage it a little. From this derives the curious American institution of foundation planting, inserted to soften or even to mask an unsightly masonry foundation. The combination of overzealous planting and uncontrolled growth has caused many a house to be enveloped in its bushes and has given the institution a bad name, though the right combination of house and planting can produce, for instance, the rose-covered cottage that so delights us. By now these customs, firmly written into local law, have come to mean that a suburban house must be somewhere in the middle of its site, with the land left uncovered by it divided into an unenclosed front yard providing a foreground of lawn, trees, and shrubs visible from the street and to the neighbors; side yards separating the house from its neighbors; and a concealed backyard traditionally devoted to service and more recently to parking cars.

Along streets of detached houses it is frequently the greenery, rather than the architecture, that unifies the discrete pieces and provides a suitably formal public face. Just as the continuous facades and regular fenestration of the terraces in Bath and London weld relatively insignificant individual dwellings into the much more notable whole, the uninterrupted sweep of shaven lawns and the rhythm of the street trees—arching elms (until recently) in the Midwest or palms in Beverly Hills—often elevate an otherwise unremarkable suburban street to a surprising public grandeur.

Early New England towns established the custom (later take up as far afield as rural Texas) of giving important public structures more generous space, still, than the houses. A courthouse might sit in the center of a

The importance of a building is often signified by the green space left around it: Texas courthouses

Mount Auburn cemetery in the spring

block (the "courthouse square"), and a church might be surrounded by a green. The graveyards around more rural churches often remained unfenced and simply merged, gradually, into the surrounding woods and fields. Then the graveyard monuments themselves began to fade, like the Cheshire cat, into the foliage. This process began in 1825, at Mount Auburn near Boston, when Dr. William Bigelow (a botanist) began to plan a "rural" cemetery on a scale grand enough, and in a style sufficiently asepulchral, to qualify it as America's first green public park. It had undulating hills and a lake, like the parks of Capability Brown, and curving roadways named after American trees and shrubs. Uncomfortably explicit intimations of mortality were all but eradicated, though a faint Cheshire grin of death lingered: the clumps of trees shaded not flocks of sheep and herds of cows, but arrays of gravestones, and the temples were not follies but tombs. In our own century Dr. Hubert L. Eaton, the founder of Forest Lawn Cemetery, found a way to perfect the semblance of English pastoral paradise by setting the gravestones flush into the grassy slopes. (This had the additional advantage of allowing unobstructed power mowing.) But an occasional, sudden glint of polished tablets in the sunlight still flashes the message *Et in Arcadia ego.*

Andrew Jackson Downing, the first American landscape theorist of note, was much impressed by Mount Auburn and by other such "rural" cemeteries. He wrote, in the 1840s, that "the great attraction of these cemeteries is not in the fact that they are burial places . . . [but] in the natural beauty of the site, and in the tasteful and harmonious embellishment of those sites by art." For the brilliant half-century after, Frederick Law Olmsted and others created the grand gardens of democracy (for the taxpaying public, rather than for aristocratic patrons) on the Mount Auburn-minus-gravestones model: city parks like Central Park in New York, Fairmount Park in Philadelphia, and the Fenway in Boston; college campuses like that for Stanford University on the San Francisco peninsula; even garden subdivisions, like Roland Park in Baltimore.

The planners of America's great urban public gardens found their own solutions to the problem (which we have illustrated by the examples of Isfahan, Suzhou, and Beijing) of relating picturesque tangle to orderly geometry. Central Park is a gigantic rectangular outdoor room chopped out of the Manhattan grid. Within it a fragment of green nature, contrived according to the principles of Capability Brown as interpreted by his disciple Humphry Repton and reinterpreted by Olmsted and his partner Calvert Vaux, is framed like a picture. There are ingenious new arrangements to serve large groups of people: hills and tunnels separate vehicular traffic (carriage originally, automobiles since) from pedestrian and equestrian circulation. In Chicago a string of green parks forms the margin between the insistent Chicago grid and the meandering shore of Lake Michigan: there is a straight, urban edge belonging to the automobile, and a natural edge frequented by strollers, joggers, and cyclists. In Boston's Back Bay Commonwealth Avenue is a formal garden spine, much as the *chahar bagh* is to Isfahan. At one end is Boston Public Garden: a precisely edged green

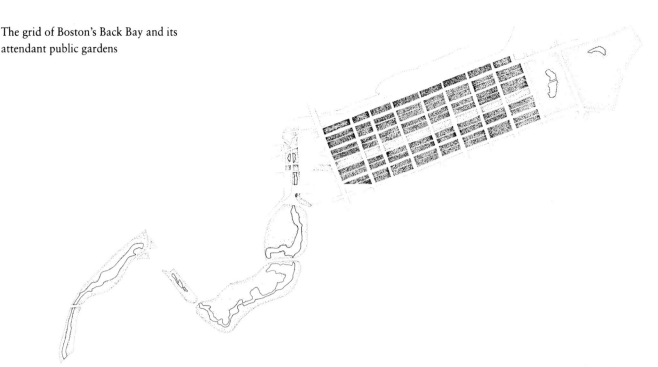

rectangle becoming, at the center, a picturesque lake with swan boats. At
the other end the Back Bay Fens straggle out across the street pattern like
the lake gardens across the grid of Beijing.

The residents of cities that have mushroomed in the twentieth century,
though, have shown less inclination to invest their resources in public
parks. Perhaps it can be argued that the loose texture of the cities of the
automobile age has allowed many people gardens of their own, so that
public green space has lost many of its more intimate functions. But it
does retain an important visual one—recalling the wilderness that was the
New World, as the spreading cities render it more and more remote.

Bigger Patterns

The orderly layout of the wilderness and the transformation of useless
lands into useful ones are two recurrent American themes that have paral-
leled, and often overshadowed, American gardening in its more traditional
senses.

In the century before the Pilgrim Fathers, even the mighty Babur could not
summon much running water into his gardens, so his Ram Bagh enclosed
just a few acres of ground. But in America the place of wells has been
taken by huge reservoirs, the canals have become aqueducts hundreds of
miles long, the *chadars* have become prodigious outflows (such as that at
Boulder Dam), and the patches of irrigated land have become whole agricultural valleys. Babur could survey his green paradise from a pavilion,
but these larger systems can only be appreciated from a transcontinen-
tal jet.

Sometimes the distribution of water yields symmetries perfect, grand, and
ruthless enough to amaze even the haughtiest of Mughuls. Vast green
circles (the bloated descendants of the flower circles at Ranchos de Taos)
are overlaid on prairies and valleys by irrigation pipes that revolve slowly

around water sources. They are the opposite of those contoured rice paddies that animate the hillsides of Asia in detailed and intricate response to the shapes of the hills, on which they lie very flat. The American circles can go uphill and down, making a pattern quite independent of the contours and insouciantly abandoning patches in the corners of square fields to unwatered desolation.

The mountains, too, can be machined into synthetic *shan shui*. In some of the rugged country behind Los Angeles, earth-moving machines have sliced the tops off hills to acquire dirt to mix with huge quantities of garbage to fill up a canyon. Constructed on the resulting spongy, more-or-less level surface is a golf course dotted with pipes to vent the explosive methane brewing underneath. At the rim of the now flat-topped hills, the still-solid earth supports a row of very expensive new condominiums, tightly packed side-by-side but open at their fronts to overlook the golf course floating on its cushion of sanitary landfill. It is a brand new and highly profitable artificially green landscape, which bears almost no relation to the shape or color of the chapparalled slopes that were there before.

Babur's compulsion to rule squares on a disorderly demesne has often been felt in America. The Mormon pioneers of Utah, for instance, were instructed by their prophets to lay out their towns in square ten-acre blocks. But it is the great grid conceived by Thomas Jefferson and laid down by the National Survey of 1785 that most insistently proclaims the dominance of man's geometry over nature's topography. This pattern of parallels and perpendiculars, made visible from the air by the long, straight lines of roads and the rectangular shapes of fields, extends over nearly three-quarters of the surface of the country. Some parts of it are as single-mindedly perfect as the grid of the Ram Bagh. The whole state of Indiana, for example, is laid out on a recursively subdivided checkerboard, which is varied only at those few places where collision with major natural features necessitates it. There is a grid of counties, within which are 36-square-mile townships, within which are 640-acre sections, within which, finally, are the basic 160-acre quarter-section farms. Exactly at the center of this Brobdingnagian *bagh*, where the emperor would have located himself (alive or dead), is the state capital of Indianapolis.

Swifter Pilgrimages

An important inheritance from our national pioneering past is an interest not so much in arrival as in movement. Many of the most vivid images we share are not of places but of routes—the Oregon Trail and the Sante Fe Trail, the Boston Post Road, getting your kicks on Route 66—and of events along the trail, like the Cumberland Gap and the Mississippi River. The market square (traditionally a center, and a destination) has become the commercial strip—stretching itself along the highway at the edge of town, with little attention to place or to arrival.

Daunting distances and the need for speed soon prompted Americans to mechanization of movement. Railways traversed the landscape, then highways, and eventually airline routes. We found our Amarnath in the Mat-

An enlargement of the *chahar bagh:* the state of Indiana

Mechanized pilgrimage to a cave in the mountains: Disneyland

Eden in the interchange: Los Angeles

The garden is completed with calligraphy

terhorn at Disneyland: a steel-framed, concrete-encased painted mountain containing a cave filled with madly whirling bobsleds, to which rapid pilgrimage is made by paying customers suspended aloft in motorized gondolas.

The emphasis on movement instead of on settling down diminishes, of course, the ease with which we can inhabit our outdoor spaces. The difficulty is compounded by their size: many American places seem too big (like the Grand Canyon) to encourage a sense of comfortable belonging and too far away from home, so Americans feel an urgent need to take mobile pavilions (Airstreams, Winnebagos) with them when they go.

As the automobile age dawned, the American crossroad became first the roundabout (or rotary, in Boston) then the freeway interchange—and some interchanges must be numbered among our most impressive national monuments. They open up, in the urban fabric, a new kind of situation for a garden. There is, for example, a four-level interchange just north of downtown Los Angeles that has become over the past four decades, as its vines and trees have grown, a high-speed subtropical paradise. You can sweep through it in your car, but you can never, never stay there—unless you happen to be one of the unfortunate hermits who sleep, unseen, in cardboard pavilions beneath the bushes.

Perhaps the most characteristically American garden form, though, is the extended, speeded-up stroll-garden for the automobile—the parkway or scenic highway. The Taconic Parkway in New York and the Merritt Parkway in Connecticut are renowned for their Burkean beauty; traffic is swiftly drawn over their smooth surfaces and around their gentle curves, with, of course, gradual ascents and declivities. The Northway out of Albany, the Blue Ridge Parkway in Virginia, and Route 1 along the California coast, in more dramatic territory, shade (within the constraints of highway engineering) into the sublime. In the more successful ones, woods, meadows, copses, hedgerows, streams, swamps, lakes, hills, and even the occasional great tree are big enough to be seen from the window of a speeding automobile and are arranged to make a coherent event out of the automobile's pilgrimages through them. Rest stops with parking lots take the place of garden seats, signs and labels are enlarged to billboard size, and there may even be statuary at automobile scale: in the Black Hills of South Dakota a scenic highway bores through ridges for repeated tunnel vistas of the four huge American presidential stone faces on Mount Rushmore, especially dramatic when they are lit at night.

Costlier Collections

Variety and contrast in the landscape are highly prized American virtues. Southern California, especially, is renowned for its jostling profusion of disparate natural settings. In the days before air travel made it commonplace, high drama was seen in the opportunity to take a cog railway up to a snowy mountain in the morning, to picnic at noon in an orange grove, then to spend the afternoon at the beach. The movie industry located in California, it is said, for the rich palette of available backgrounds. Visitors to California from wintry states have always been astonished, too, by lux-

A collection of graves finances a collection of picturesque scenes: Forest Lawn cemetery near Los Angeles

uriant blooms—roses and flowering vines of implausible dimensions—and have discovered establishments like Rogers Gardens (south of Los Angeles), where collections of dazzling flowering plants are arrayed for sale. In a curious inversion of a typical pilgrimage ritual, where the pilgrim brings an offering to the special place, Rogers Gardens encourages the pilgrim to take an offering away, and leave money.

One comfortable aspect of taking away an offering is that *buying* something is *doing* something, and it is probably accurate to note that Americans are happiest in their gardens and landscapes when they are doing something—barbecuing or swimming or drinking or answering the phone at poolside or driving a dunebuggy, speedboat, or golf ball. Golf courses are collections of nine or eighteen pieces which flourish in America, we suspect, because the rather elaborate rules for their layout provide a disciplined formal structure that ensures a certain amount of both order and variety, with an associated pilgrimage sequence and very precisely defined rituals to be performed at each stopping point. The smooth greens repeat rhythmically, interspersed with grassy fairways, rough meadows, sand traps, hills or woods, all arranged to keep the player (and often the viewer) surprised and beguiled.

Even the visible opportunity to do something is important to us; it matters less whether we actually do it. Mark Twain remarked that a golf course would be a very pleasant walk, if you didn't have to keep hitting a little white ball. It is a safe bet that our yards contain more swimming pools than swimmers, and if we could figure out how to transform our lawns into tennis courts without rendering them impassable, baselines and nets might fringe every street.

Collectors everywhere covet unique pieces, and irreplicable sports of nature are hard to beat. Chinese gardeners satisfied their lust for singularity with the most bizarrely formed rocks that they could procure, and British gardeners resolutely pursued the rarest and most exotic plants that the empire on which the sun never set could provide, but Americans opening up the West found themselves with the opportunity to acquire some much more sizable specimens—complete chunks of especially choice wilderness: Yosemite, Yellowstone, the Grand Canyon, Monument Valley, the Petrified Forest, the Painted Desert, the Tetons, the Everglades, and other prizes that were to become not an emperor's private collection but (in an era of more democratic temper and greater mobility than those presided over by Hadrian and Ch'ien Lung) the enormously popular attractions of the National Parks System. The pieces are carefully bounded, preserved, labeled, and presented as found objects in a continent-sized, automobile-traversed outdoor museum.

American collectors have often distinguished themselves by the costliness of their collections, and by figuring out particularly ingenious entrepreneurial strategies to pay for them. William Randolph Hearst (who collected treasures and fantasies in the rooms and terraces of San Simeon), J. Paul Getty (with his reconstructed Pompeiian villa/museum, art collection, and garden overlooking the shores at Malibu), and Henry E. Huntington (who made a collection of roses, another of camellias, and a stunning one of cacti around his mansion near Pasadena) did it the old-fashioned way: by amassing wealth first. The proprietors of Rogers Gardens sell the pieces and immediately replace them with more, and the National Parks Service sacrifices some of its trees to help support its collection of landscapes. Walt Disney kept the pieces, but charged admission to see them. Tax deductions make possible the collections of gentleman's farms, in the environs of Baltimore, for instance, where rolling fields and cows and hedgerows maintained by people in high tax brackets are encouraged for the visual pleasure they give the rest of us. The collections of meticulously constructed synthetic landscapes, reproduced statuary, and replicated buildings at Forest Lawn are financed by accumulating an ever-increasing collection of authentic human bones.

Simpler Settings

American attention to the landscape seems often to have focused on natural settings unchanged by the hand of man, big enough and empty enough of humankind to allow the viewer to imagine himself the first ever to contemplate their aboriginal virginity. The unique landscapes of the national parks have especially engaged the national imagination. They achieve what the artist seeks, beyond where most garden makers dare aspire: they are monumentally themselves, altogether unlike any place else on earth.

Perhaps an effect of this interest in unbeatable natural wonders combined with a recurrent strain of Emersonian Deism (which seems to insist that God dwells in trees), has been to push man-made settings out of the competition, to cause them to be very simple. A memorable example is the front lawn of the Breakers, the enormous Vanderbilt mansion in Newport, Rhode Island, built in 1895. It is a summer place by the seaside, but it is huge and formal. On the ocean side are a terrace, a few steps, and then an unbroken lawn to the edge of the cliff, where the ocean starts. Just a lawn.

An unbeatable natural wonder: playa and mountains in Death Valley

It is hard to imagine a European house of comparable magnificence that would not have sported a much more elaborate garden. Yet on that site the lawn is a splendor, suggesting in its simple sweep a dominion that extends across the Atlantic to Spain.

Two of America's most memorable settings never actually appeared outdoors, but remained within the covers of books: Edgar Allan Poe's Domain of Arnheim and Landor's Cottage. True to their American sources they are far from any city and described from the viewpoint of a traveler. The narrative of "The Domain of Arnheim" stops, in fact, just short of reaching the goal of a pilgrimage and concentrates on the progressive emergence of an eerily unnatural perfection. By the end of the journey there is not a pebble in the crystal-clear water whose shape is not perfect, nor a dead limb or fallen branch upon the unblemished mossy banks. It might have been the North American representative among our great gardens, but we did not trust ourselves to draw it; certainly it would have been a perfect garden for a country that adores youth and movement, and cannot face death.

EDENS TO ORDER

Making our own gardens is a pastime, a civility, a game, an obsession. But we cannot rely on a single comprehensive, authoritative set of rules (like, for example, those provided by *Sakuteiki*) to guide our actions. In an era like our own, with its dizzying intricacy of connections and its fast-forward pace, though our gardens may be simple and focused, any rules for them won't be, can't be, probably shouldn't be. The images we know about are legion, our memories seethe with overlapping complexities. We admire mobility and embrace the notion of the moveable feast, even as we yearn for roots and cherish a garden for the opportunity it gives us to put some down. We are touched by the spare purity of Ryoan-ji, yet are willingly seduced by the shamelessness of Isola Bella. Resonances appear with the other arts: winemaking with its inseparability from a particular place and climate, and its long view, or opera, with its entanglement of space and time and virtuosity (from coloratura to green thumb). We feel the painter's obsession with the integrity of the picture plane, then the pleasure (and need) of breaking it apart to experience objects from more than one side. We are delighted by structures that unfold sequentially in time, like those of music, but also take pleasure in those that present themselves simultaneously, in space. Our key word is *and*.

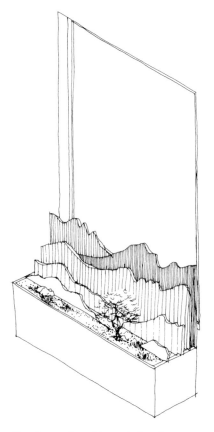

Paradise replayed in a window box

In some ages cosmic connections flourish (eat everything on your plate or, somehow, children will starve in Armenia or China), engendering an urgent need to replace *and* by *not*. Igor Stravinsky, earlier in this century, described in *The Poetics of Music* the drive to make art within the tightest possible limits; his contemporary Josef Albers stripped from his paintings everything except the interaction of color, so as to focus on that; meanwhile, the architect Ludwig Mies van der Rohe vigorously expunged from his buildings everything but the chastest gridded rectangularity. The underlying claim of such artistic fundamentalism is that there are absolutes to be sought and purified, but an age of diminished faith in absolutes is more likely to side with a claim that the images haunting our memories are inexhaustible. The great gardens of the past hold no essences that we can extract once and for all, but each of us may find myriad essentials in the land and the sun and the rain and our recollections. Our own readings of them will suggest new rules and new games. Poetry will lie at the edge, where conventions (rules hardened into stereotypes) are challenged and subverted.

So each of the gardens we have drawn and described provides a starting point for exploration by the imagination and holds within it the seeds of infinite newness. We have included in our selection a few landscapes untouched by the hand of man, where, magically, the elaborate chaos of nature falls into a memorable order. (The Hand of God may be suggested to people grateful that He has finally done something they can figure out.) But we have concentrated on ones arranged by men and women, out of the elements of nature (mountains and water in the East, with emphasis shifting to plants and even flowers in the West) and architectural inclusions or surrounds, that are generally called gardens. It would have been fun perhaps to build a grand synoptic system—to distill a set of rules from them, collapsing all the overlapping and conflicting principles that formed most of them, but it wouldn't have been fair: we have discovered too many ways to make a satisfying garden, too many ways to design a building, too many ways to construct a poem or a melody, to presume to select just one way to proceed.

The lessons that we can learn are all modally shaded, with mights and shoulds, maybes and maybe nots, and there is always another, perhaps contradictory or at least demurring, view to consider. Our situation is not, of course, unique: we were talking recently with an architect friend who is adept at the Japanese game of *Go*. Though it is an ancient and complex game, there are few rules for it. There exists, however, a vast and still-growing accumulation of hints and advice, dividing wise moves from unwise and assisting in the development of strategies, so as to make quick and wonderful extensions of one's experience. The gardens that we have examined illustrate particularly successful strategies—or fortunate ones, anyway. Each one has a point to make, each one takes hold of us, soothes us, then pricks a little astonishment, and wonder.

Speculation about the forms that our own gardens might take is not, then, an orderly, linear process of deriving specific consequences from established general rules. It is a colloquium of the clamorous voices of memory—urging and intimating, sometimes reaching satisfying agreements and sometimes staking out contradictions, catching allusions and sharing jokes, making asides and getting back to the point, sporting with irony and flirting with whimsy, and finally concluding, somehow, that some particular ideas are right for a particular site at a particular moment. Long ago the Greek author Lucian recorded imaginary colloquia between famous protagonists of differing views, and we shall illustrate this process in the same way. Lucian himself will be our guide. He will convene discussions about garden proposals for some typical American sites: a retiree's lot in the California desert, an urban backyard, a suburban front yard, and a side yard. Finally, he will take up the question of graveyards. Let us eavesdrop . . .

AMERIKANERGARTEN CHATS

Lucian records a colloquium

LUCIAN: Two thousand years ago I used to organize dialogues—of the gods, sometimes, and of the dead. Once I had a sale of creeds, where grumpy old Diogenes the Cynic (he said "my enemy is pleasure") went for three pence (serves him right) and Socrates couldn't keep his mind on the business at hand—kept running off after every boy that took his fancy. Naturally I couldn't shift any of the Epicureans—nobody could afford to support their expensive habits. I've had my imitators; Walter Savage Landor (who Nature loved, and after Nature, Art) tried his hand at *Imaginary Conversations of Literary Men and Statesmen*—not nearly as funny as mine—Edgar Allan Poe penned some colloquies, and Louis Sullivan imagined *Kindergarten Chats* (in Chicago, with excursions to the countryside, and a finale on the shores of Biloxi Bay) between an architecture student and a professor. But I'm afraid that my reputation has suffered since the Christians showed up, decided that they didn't like my attitude at all, and circulated the lie that I'd been torn to bits by dogs.

After an extended sabbatical, I'm back. For your amusement and instruction I've assembled great garden makers of the past to offer their advice on how *you* might make your own gardens. (I'm hoping to get this on public television.) Here come my first protagonists now.

Courtyards

PROFESSOR S: Let us pause at this oasis in the desert. Let us rest awhile beneath its cool and satisfying calm and drink a little at this wayside spring . . .

LUCIAN: Where exactly are we?

PROFESSOR S: We're in Palm Springs, California, where I intend to while away my sunset years beside the pool. (Far better, this, than a lonely hotel room in Chicago.) I shall build myself a house, with a garden, as I once did near Biloxi. You have assembled some eminent advisors to discuss the garden design, I believe.

LUCIAN: Yes, I've summoned the shade of Alexander Pope (who was always generous with his epistolary admonitions, invited or not), and the Emperor Babur (renowned for his skill in making gardens in hot climates). Joining the group, as well, are the British architect Owen Jones, who made a careful study of the courtyards of the Alhambra (and who shares with you, Professor, a particular interest in ornament), the author Washington Irving, and the celebrated Italian Carlo Fontana. Mr. Pope, how should we begin?

ALEXANDER POPE: I'd begin, if I were you, by adopting a rather less flippant tone. As for this garden, I'd suggest we commence by consulting the Genius of the Place.

LUCIAN: I thought you might say that, so I've asked him to join us. He's driving up right now.

GENIUS: Just a minute while I shake the sand out of my shoes! Palm Springs, as you can see, is remarkably hot and dry, though it gets cool in the evenings. It began as a patch of desert, but now there's water (piped in) for gardens. All around are new subdivisions for vacation and retirement houses. Nice to see you, Babur! It seems that all the moguls have places here!

BABUR: Yes, but what a dump! It reminds me of Agra, when I got there after the Battle of Panipat; it's charmless and disorderly, there's too much sand, it's too damned hot, of genius and conversation there are none ("Have a nice day" passes as a witty remark here), there are no elephants, no iced mangoes, the people aren't good looking, I don't think much of the colleges . . .

PROFESSOR S: Do stop whining, Babur; just have another margarita and mellow out! Have you any constructive suggestions?

BABUR: You might begin by making an enclosed, protected place. Capture some space with a wall; fill it with shady greenery and the sound of water. Create some clarity and symmetry where you can—in your own little corner of a most unsatisfactory world. (I suppose it's out of the question just to conquer this whole town and clean it up properly?)

GENIUS: Ah, memories! The old Spanish missions introduced courtyard gardens to this corner of the world. An arcaded court could evoke romantic characters of that era: Ramona and Alessandro, Zorro . . .

WASHINGTON IRVING: Yes, but it won't work at all if you just make a sealed-up, air-conditioned house, without intimate connection to the outdoors. And applying a few trendy motifs to the facades certainly won't save it; you'll just get what the architect Charles Correa (one of your compatriots, Emperor) has called a "tattooed box." Gardens are to be *inhabited*, not just looked at through a window. I want to be able to loiter through the chambers (as I did at the Alhambra), hearing the murmur of the fountains and the songs of birds, inhaling the odor of the rose and feeling the influence of the balmy climate, fancying myself in the paradise of Mahomet—accompanied by bright-eyed houris . . .

OWEN JONES: Your cheesy orientalism is quite unsound, Washington, but you're right about the lessons of the Alhambra. Look at my measured drawings to see exactly *how* it works. Notice how the Cuarto Dorado, though small and simple, is enlivened by water. The Court of the Lions is much fancier, with rooms on all sides connected by cross axes of water. If you want to fit in a pool big enough for swimming, you should see how it's done in the Court of the Myrtles. Something like that could cost you big bucks, though.

CARLO FONTANA: You two gotta be kidding! You want that it should look like a Taco Bell? And as for the Alhambra, it's all *too* rectangular and two-dimensional, with those tacky patterns everywhere you look. No, what I'd suggest is this. Even though the site is flat, you should build up some steps and terraces—just enough to let the foliage seem to hang above the water. Since I doubt that your budget will really extend to something on the scale of the Court of the Myrtles, you might also think about some tricks of false perspective, and using cutout walls like stage sets. Talking of tricks, a few water surprises wouldn't hurt either . . .

BABUR: Don't get carried away! I don't know about the rest of you, but I certainly don't think it's funny to get peed on by a marble cupid. If one of my gardeners tried that I'd cut off his insolent head!

PROFESSOR S: Times have changed, Babur; calm down! Look, I've been making some sketches based on all your suggestions, and it's becoming a pretty good scheme. The garden is a thirty foot square, with arcaded passages on two sides, from which you look into it. My proposal is to make a walled inner space (itself about twelve feet square) at the center. I see this as a kind of magic secret garden, which can enlarge the psychic dimension of your space even while it is actually using up the central part of your nine hundred square feet.

CARLO FONTANA: Yes, but how? What makes the illusion work?

PROFESSOR S: I don't have a lot of room so I've exploited the evocative power of glimpses and fragments. Wherever you look from within the house, or along the arcades, the peek through the openings of the secret garden reveals only a little and intimates that much more may lie beyond. I'm counting on sound, too—on the splash of water where it drops into the sunken pool beyond the central square—to suggest something not yet seen. The pool is to soak in; it lets you do anything you could in a larger pool, except swim laps, and because it's sunken, it adds, I think, a poetic dimension of mystery—the image of Debussy's Engulfed Cathedral, or the Lost Atlantis.

BABUR: I see the order of a square within a square, and the slightly skewed symmetries (appropriate, I suppose, for an age that prefers reflective irony to straightforward assertion), but I'm curious about your planting plan. These squares would seem stiff and barren without the refreshment of scent and shade and color.

PROFESSOR S: Against the two outer edges of the court I've shown tropical looking plantings: banana palms, which grow very fast and come back after a freeze, and Carolina jasmine, which is hearty through cold spells. I've shown bougainvillea, which blossoms in many colors of red and orange, evergreen ivy, and trumpet vine or bignonia, on the pergola adjoining the house. The foliage along the outer wall will reflect in the ripples on the pool, which should be attractive, and we'll choose the vines for the color of their blossoms. That should be riotous and very tropical. I must be sure, too, to have plants with berries to attract the songbirds.

OWEN JONES: I like the frieze of ornament, made with tiles, on top of the walls enclosing the secret garden . . .

WASHINGTON IRVING: And I can imagine the romance of shady vines and palms, the fragrance of jasmine, the cool of the pool and the splash of the fountain, the warmth of the walls in the desert evening, chatter and laughter drifting up to the stars . . .

A courtyard garden in
Palm Springs

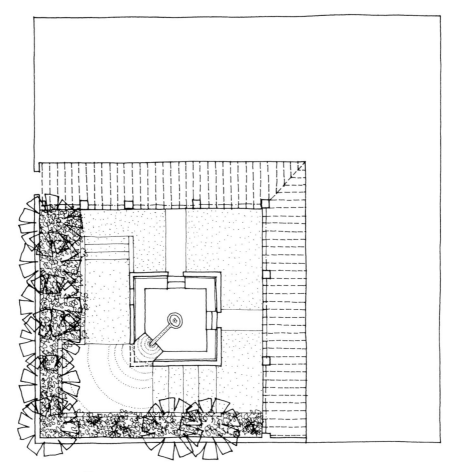

Plan

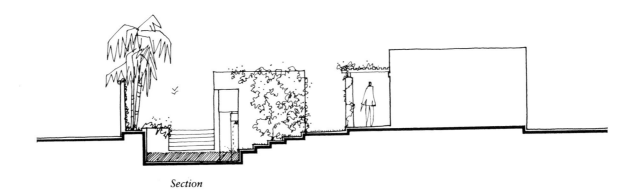

Section

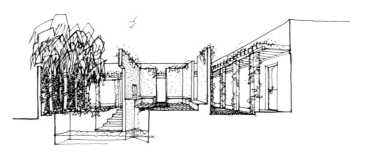

Sectional Perspective

Front Yards

LUCIAN: Welcome to Chicago—or, more precisely, Oak Park, Illinois—a pleasant and rather expensive suburb. We've been asked by an ex-student of Professor S to advise on new landscaping for the front yard of his parents' home here. I've called in Mr. Capability Brown, who pulled off such a triumph in front of Blenheim Palace, and the well-known British architect Sir Edwin Lutyens, who has come with his friend Miss Gertrude Jekyll. To represent other viewpoints, we have the renowned Prince Genji, all the way from Kyoto, and from Sydney (out on parole, I believe) the colonial architect Mr. Francis Greenway. But who's this?

FRANK LLOYD WRIGHT: Hi! I'm the Genius of Oak Park, and an old friend of Professor S. You look like you need some consultation.

CAPABILITY BROWN: Indeed we do! I left my horse at home, so I haven't been able to survey the capabilities of this place. What's it like? (Looks a bit flat to me.)

FRANK LLOYD WRIGHT: In his autobiography the old Professor called early Chicago "The Garden City." He spoke of the great lake and the prairie and the wonderful horizon. And here's what he said of the suburbs:

Around this city, in ever-extending areas, in fancied semi-circles, lay a beauteous prairie, born companion to the lake; while within this prairie, at distances of some seven to twelve miles from the center of the Garden City, were dotted villages, forming also an open-spaced semi-circle, for each village nestled in the spacious prairie, and within its own companionable tree growth. To the north and west of the city there grew in abundance lofty elms and oaks.

The Chicago grid has seeped into those spaces between the villages now, but we still have the lake and the sky, and memories of a tree-strewn prairie.

FRANCIS GREENWAY: All these suburban houses sit in the middle of their own little patches of gridded prairie. What is the *use* of these grassy front yards? When I design a building (in the Georgian style that I learned in England, before my trouble with the law and transportation to Australia), I'm careful to present a continuous, formal face to the street and to follow conventions of propriety that serve (like manners and codes of dress) to give form to public life. How do you do that with just a lawn?

The Royal Crescent at Bath presents a continuous formal face to the street

FRANK LLOYD WRIGHT: In this great democracy, with its wide-open spaces, we have established our own conventions; the size of a building's setback from the street often signifies its importance, so a generous front lawn has become an indispensable part of everybody's image of the comfortable suburban house. It's correct to have living room windows facing the street across the lawn, but not bathroom or kitchen windows. The distance from the sidewalk usually provides sufficient privacy for the living room, and if that's not enough we use draperies.

STUDENT: But I still can't see how to begin designing a garden here. What are the elements of a front yard, and the rules for their composition?

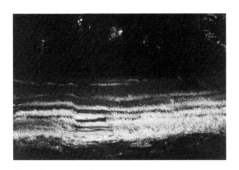

A path across a lawn

FRANK LLOYD WRIGHT: They're almost as well-defined as those of the traditional Japanese garden. The lawn (like the guardian stone) is essential and forms the starting point for the whole composition—though the limits of the convention may sometimes be stretched to allow variants such as ice-plant or ivy or even paving. Sometimes there will be a picket fence or low wall at the front, with higher fences running back along the sides. Alternatively, there are no front fences, so that the lawns along a street form a single, uninterrupted sweep of grand dimensions—playing much the same unifying role as the continuous facades of Georgian terraces. Regularly spaced trees may reinforce the lines of the street and shade the sidewalk: maples, perhaps, in the East and Midwest, palms in California and Florida, and occasionally surprises such as jacarandas, pepper trees, coral trees, or eucalyptus. Traditionally, there is a path across the lawn from the front gate to the front door. With the automobile has come, as well, the driveway, and sometimes the carport.

PRINCE GENJI: I'm Genji the Resplendent, and I've been called "The greatest seducer ever to have astounded Asia." The secret of my success was to make gardens for all my ladies. Perhaps an example of my style would be useful here. What do you think of this sketch featuring foundation planting around the front door?

MISS GERTRUDE JEKYLL: I think it reveals your well-known obsession with pubic hair! Stop posturing like a broken-down Marlboro cowboy! Next you'll be telling me that the function of the front yard is to provide a place for the husband to mow the lawn and wash the car while the little wife is inside cooking dinner.

CAPABILITY BROWN: You have a point, Miss Jekyll. Let's carefully avoid elements with infelicitous connotations. I think the pieces that I habitually deploy are innocent enough, but I just can't see how to fit them into this shrunken space. There's not much room for cows, and I really can't see a lake between the mailbox and the carport. Perhaps you could get a bulldozer in, and a few truckloads of dirt, and shape that little rise into a more plausible hill. You can buy decent-sized trees from nurseries now (you couldn't in my day), so you can make some belts of greenery to conceal the fences and a nice clump on top of the hill to make it seem bigger. Plant some lawn (right up to the walls), take the path around in an *S,* and there you have it: instant England.

PRINCE GENJI: *Very* expensive, Brown-San, with all that earth movement! And I really *don't* think there's room. Your style won't work for anything that you can't ride a horse in!

FRANCIS GREENWAY: I think my Pommy pal is onto something, though. Since I had to leave England for England's good I *do* like the idea of recreating the mother country wherever you want it. (Forgery has it uses.) Do you see any way to make his ideas a bit more workable, Prince Genji?

PRINCE GENJI: I do agree with my honorable colleague that it's a good move to conceal the boundaries and to shape the earth to suggest a larger landscape, but at this scale you *have* to use some tricks of compression. You'll find them all described in the *Sakuteiki* and dozens of more recent

Precarious stepping stones
approach the Old Shoin at
Katsura

books. You could, for instance, make the path out of precarious little stepping stones, so that it expands the space by making it *seem* a long way to
the front door. That will make the visitor look down, too, so you could
make a delicate surface—not just grass, but stones and sand and moss and
perhaps some tiny flowers. The hill is okay, I suppose, but it will just become an insipid berm unless you very carefully set up a layering of foreground, middle ground, and background to create some recession, and
control the grain of stones and foliage to produce the illusion of greater
distances.

STUDENT: What about the lake? Can we fit that in?

PRINCE GENJI: You don't have to be as *literal* as Brown-San seems to
think. You can *imply* a lake, if you want it, with some raked sand and
rocks to suggest the shore. A spray of blossom can suggest a waterfall.
Other stones, carefully placed, can make you think of the force of
a stream or waterfall pushing against them, though there isn't really
any water.

FRANCIS GREENWAY: Be careful! False pretenses can get you into trouble!
Perhaps it would be better to explore the possibilities of a more formal,
Georgian treatment.

SIR EDWIN LUTYENS: That's the first sensible suggestion I've heard—and
from a colonial, too! (In my opinion, no decent architectural idea ever
originated east of Suez, and I've always detested Brown's limp green
salads.)

STUDENT: You seem very sure of yourself, Sir Edwin. Perhaps you can tell
us how *you* would do it.

SIR EDWIN LUTYENS: It's simple! *A garden should have one clear, central
idea.* Concentrate on one thing, or a few things, that you really want. This
does not mean that you are doomed to diminishment or dilution. For
some useful American examples you should look at the altogether satisfying residential gardens of Thomas Church in California. They usually got
their power, and made their point, by concentrating on *one* fine old tree or
remarkably shaped swimming pool or striking hedge.

STUDENT: What would you use as the focus for this garden?

SIR EDWIN LUTYENS: Some formal architectural elements, of course. The
garden should face the street with proper, symmetrical decorum; after all,
even you Americans wouldn't appear in public in your underwear. I would
use walls and steps and terraces, and approach the front door through a
sequence of formal enclosures.

MISS GERTRUDE JEKYLL: That's where I come in! You must choose a color
scheme for each of those enclosures and carefully furnish it with flowers as
you might furnish a front parlor. Make arrangements of dense, brilliant
herbaceous borders.

FRANK LLOYD WRIGHT: That connects with our Midwestern traditions.
The Professor had poignant memories of old Chicago's gardens flowering
in season:

In winter was the old time animation with heavy, lasting snows. . . . And then again came equinoctial spring; crocuses appeared; trees, each after its kind, put forth furtive leaves; for "April Showers" all too often were but chilling northeast rains. Indeed there was no Spring—rather a wave-motion of subsiding winter and progressing summer. But in June the Garden City had come again into its own. From a distance one saw many a steeple, rising from the green, as landwards, and in the distances the gray bulk of grain elevators.

MISS GERTRUDE JEKYLL: You can select the flowers to transform the garden enclosures with the seasons, too. Perhaps you should look at some of the projects I did with Sir Edwin, or at Major Johnston's work at Hidcote, or at Miss Sackville-West's at Sissinghurst.

STUDENT: With all due respect, Sir Edwin and Miss Jekyll, a full-dress formal garden is a bit much for a modest house on a quiet suburban street. (My parents don't have twelve servants to run the house, as you did, Sir Edwin.) And since they don't have squads of gardeners, either, an ambitious flower garden is probably out of the question. But your insistence on one clear, central idea does make eminent sense, especially since I have so little space at my disposal. Look, I've sketched a scheme that makes a single fine tree the centerpiece. Plum might be nice, to celebrate the rhythm of the Chicago seasons—in spring clouds of white blossoms drift down to the grassy bank; leafy greenery shades the path to the front door in summer; a patch of brilliant color erupts in fall; and in winter bare branches over windblown snow allow sunlight to stream in through the bedroom windows.

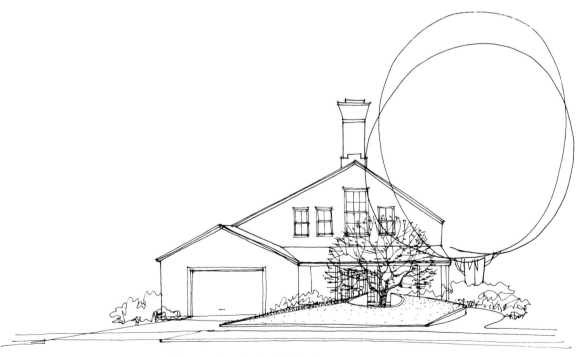

A front yard garden in Oak Park

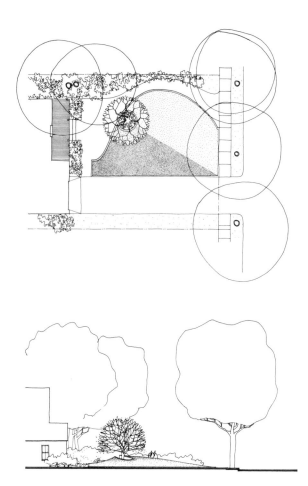

Plan and section of the front yard garden

Notice how I've used a sinuous S-curve to approach the front door, Mr. Brown. From the street side I create the illusion of a miniature grassy natural landscape, which should please you and Prince Genji; but for Sir Edwin and Miss Jekyll I've also been able to make a more formal, paved entrance court with walls, beds of flowers, and symmetrical steps.

PRINCE GENJI: I think we're finished. Shall we share a cab to the airport, Lady of the Herbaceous Borders?

Backyards

LUCIAN: Our conference on backyards takes place in New York, where my friend Mr. H owns a three-story row house on a lot seventeen feet wide. The street is to its south. Behind the house is a space seventeen by thirty-four feet, with a large, not especially attractive highrise lying beyond that. Mr. H wants to design a garden. To advise him I have once again called on Alexander Pope, the British rhymer of couplets and friend of (some) gardens; the Chinese emperor Ch'ien Lung (whose garden at the Yuan Ming Yuan you all know); the Persian poet Omar Khayyam, accompanied as usual by Mr. Edward FitzGerald; and the early-twentieth-century writer Edith Wharton, who penned some interesting descriptions of Italian gardens, particularly Isola Bella. Pope, I thought, might be expected to espouse a pilgrimage garden, Ch'ien Lung a collection, Omar Khayyam a pattern, and Edith Wharton might favor establishing a setting. I know! I know, Mr. Pope, we'll consult . . .

A garden statue of King Kong

EDITH WHARTON: Eek! It's a gorilla!

KING KONG: Yes, large as life! Since my well-publicized downfall I've served as honorary Genius of the Place around here. You should commence, I think, by considering the special character of a backyard. Where the front yard presents a public face to the street, the back is private, sheltered, suitable for objects and acts not meant to be shown off. In Australian towns, Mr. Greenway tells me, it is acceptable to have chickens, even goats, in the backyard, but not in front (though in the front yard sheep, which enjoy extraordinary national prestige, have sometimes been tethered as resident lawn mowers). In earlier American usage, backyards were for utilitarian purposes, from hanging out the laundry to growing vegetables, but by the 1930s expectations had changed and the shelter magazines were pointedly urging that the major living rooms face the serenity and privacy of the backyard, leaving kitchen, service, and garage to face the dust and public tumult of the street. The problem became one of making the backyard your own, inhabiting it, figuring out what to do there. Swimming pools were a popular addition, less, it might appear, for their own sake than because they offered the dwellers an excuse to take off most of their clothes, which turns out to be a powerful way of taking possession of a place.

MR. H: Thank you for your erudite analysis, Mr. K. And thank you all for coming. I've been working on a scheme for this garden for hours. I thought it would be attractive to have a garden structure at the end of the yard, in the sun (for part of the year, anyway) to make the garden feel complete and private, and to be more interesting than the big building beyond, but everything I've drawn so far is static, symmetrical, and dull.

ALEXANDER POPE: You bet! It's the old boring bit of "Each alley has a brother, and half the platform just reflects the other." It's neither beautiful nor even efficient, much less sublime. I'd recommend Mr. Hogarth's "line of beauty" as a compositional device to lead the eye more gracefully to the far end of the garden.

CH'IEN LUNG: "Line of beauty" indeed. The limp curve of humanism leads you nowhere. Poetry will come when the places evoke names. Or maybe it would be a good idea (since you don't seem to have an idea) to make some names and let them evoke a place. I like "Pinnacle of Diligent Appreciation," though you might prefer "Mirror of Heaven," which might suggest a structure that reflects the sun into the garden. Or, you might make here a miniature of the Empire State Building and establish a *mise-en-scène* for its most interesting inhabitant, our distinguished colleague, Mr. K. "Kong's Kottage" the sign might say, or "King You Top This?"

EDITH WHARTON: Oh, shut up, Ch'ien Lung! This is all much too flat-footed. This garden is (and in the tiny space has to be) a *setting*, a place that can be seen and visited in the mind, serene and evocative, dreamy and above all beautiful. It doesn't need any of your invocations. I favor a garden structure covered with vines, perhaps hanging in the air for conjectural inhabitation.

EDWARD FITZGERALD: Omar says he has the opposite sense; a garden is a place to be, to sit with your beloved. He thinks you have to *be* there, not just in the reflection of the place. A stairway to an inhabitable shrine, and sun, and wine.

ALEXANDER POPE: In this tiny space, you may be right (though I doubt it), but I'd like you not to forget the possibility, even here, of making a pilgrimage place. I have some friends in Palo Alto who have just commissioned, in their somewhat larger backyard, such a place, where the pavilion to rest in seems miles away. The design ignores the line of beauty, and is therefore a bit jerky, but it has the right impulses. Let's ask the architects to explain it to us.

CHARLES W. MOORE: Good grief! How did I end up here? I'm supposed to be on the red-eye to Los Angeles. Well, since you ask, the rear yard of the recently remodeled Pirofski house on a fifty-foot lot in Palo Alto, California, has a surprising bonus: an extra rectangle of space 35 by 50 feet at the left rear, already walled in by the neighbors. It made an admirable change, Mr. Turnbull and I thought, to devise a species of maze with more than the usual reward at the end: a walled secret garden, at the end of a long path, with a pavilion and an orchard and a fountain. (Look at Mr. Turnbull's drawing.)

The view from the glassy living room at the rear of the house will be a rather simple and symmetrical one, a pattern backed by a wall, at the very rear of the yard, with a piece of sculpture on the wall lighted from under the water, in which it reflects in the daytime. Pittosporum lines the view.

Garden for the Pirofski house, Palo Alto

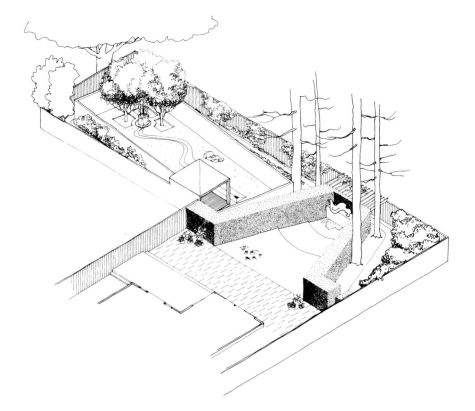

Toward the far end of the space, the trees close in on the waterway to make the sculpture seem farther away.

Only after the pilgrim passes through the narrow slot at the waterway can he discover a path to the left, which takes him along a narrowing walk toward rhododendron at the end. (The narrowing forces the perspective to increase the apparent distance.)

KING KONG: What's the finale? (I like happy endings.)

CHARLES W. MOORE: At the rhododendron a left turn discloses another narrowing walk with an acacia at the end, where yet another left turn reveals a third narrowing walk, with a pavilion near the end of it. From the pavilion opens up the secret garden, its plastered walls colored a soft salmon with some mauve in it, like the walls of an ancient Chinese temple garden. Flowering plum (*prunus bleriana*) trees add to the picture with leaves of purple or, in February, blossoms of palest pink. And the scene is completed by a small fountain, with the cool sound of water splashing. We considered the pleasures of a fountain at the end of the first long axis, visible from the house, but decided that restraint (still water, reflective sculpture) would enhance the surprising drama of moving water at the end of the trail.

KING KONG: Nice scheme, Charles. But I must say that I'm getting quite sick and tired of these fashionable Derrida-da games. You should ask your coauthor to take you out of the text and put you back on the plane where you belong.

WILLIAM J. MITCHELL: Let's go, before the monkey gets mad!

ALEXANDER POPE: Now that we're rid of those two, let's get back to our business. What have you made of our advice, Mr. H?

MR. H: I think you're saying that it could be better, in a seventeen-foot dimension, not to seek symmetry or a closed form, but rather to suggest, with fragments and miniatures of really grandiose gestures, the presence of a structure much larger. Here's my scheme. It's a garden house, not all that different from those at the Yuan Ming Yuan; you must propose a name for it, Ch'ien Lung. It is unsymmetrical, as you have suggested, open both on the side toward the house and on the side away from the house. It is small scale, for this tiny yard. But it is complex, so I've kept the garden in front of it very simple, just some paving stones laid on the diagonal, to suggest some generous preexisting arrangements lost in the mists of time. There's a sundial in front—a rhetorical flourish, to heighten the sense of sunniness. And in its heart there is a fireplace, for warmth on crisp autumn days. The chimney also becomes an eyrie, a miniature place surmounting a fragment.

EDWARD FITZGERALD: Paradise enow!

Side Yards

LUCIAN: Our next Platonic interlocutor, Mr. J, is interested in buying a house in Houston, Texas, in a sizable development where he has a choice among gardens, all the same size (16 by 72 feet) facing each of the cardi-

A backyard garden in New York City

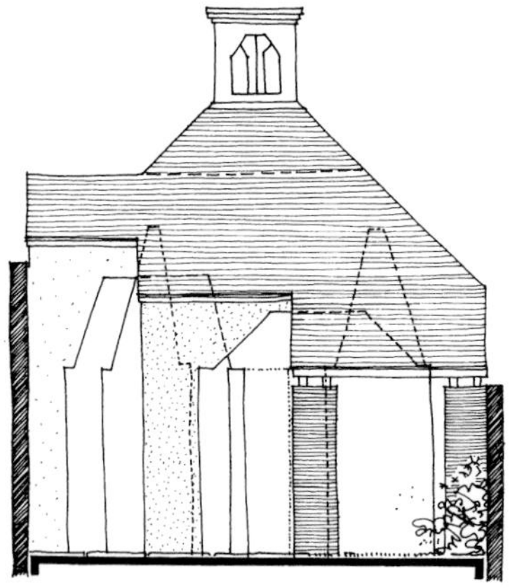

Section of the pavilion

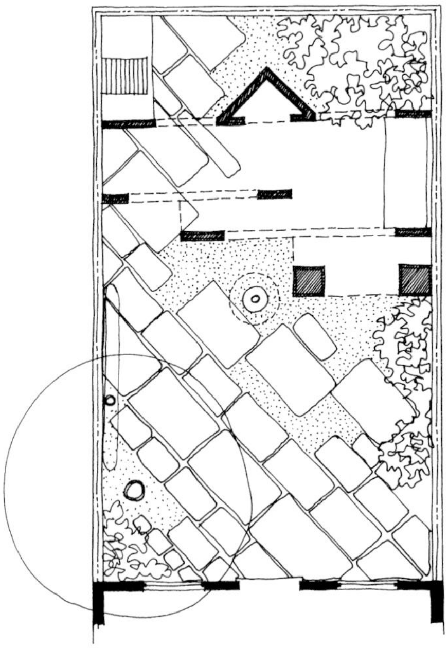

Plan

Perspective

nal points. He seeks help with the choice and with the design of the garden for the site selected. He asked for a colloquium. I invited Francis Bacon, whose essay "Of Gardens" established his credentials; Vita Sackville-West, whose gardening columns in the *Observer* established hers; Capability Brown (making a return appearance, by popular demand); Prince Toshihito, on the strength of his successes at his Katsura Imperial Villa; and Walt Disney, whose accomplishments at Disneyland qualify him. Good afternoon, Mr. J. Where's the Genius of the Place?

MR. J: We rarely see him in Houston now; he's always stuck in traffic on the freeway. I encountered him briefly, the other day, and he gave me diagrams of the sun angles and the prevailing breezes on the four potential sites. But he had to drive off somewhere before he could tell me the criteria for selecting one.

FRANCIS BACON: Maybe the authors can help. Have you seen them recently, Lucian?

LUCIAN: Not since King Kong chased them out of the text. I think we're on our own from now on.

FRANCIS BACON: Well, let's first collect all the relevant facts. Empirical science shall be our guide! I notice, to begin with, that these sites are neither at the front nor at the back, but *alongside* houses. What are the *purposes* of side yards? What do you Americans *do* with them, anyway?

WALT DISNEY: In the small Midwestern towns that I remember from my childhood, the houses sit in the middle of generous lots, with plenty of room at the side for trees to grow and children to play. But in more urban settings (especially where the houses are built of masonry or otherwise fireproofed) side yards are often squeezed out of existence. Even wooden houses are often placed so close together that the side yards shrivel into passageways, three or four or five feet on each side of the house, with windows uncomfortably opening onto them and, just beyond, to the house next door. But sometimes, with careful attention to the planning, with codes that allow houses to be located directly on the lot line on one side, the land between two houses can go to one of them, for a narrow but pleasant garden that can bring light and a sense of space into the center of the house.

PRINCE TOSHIHITO: In Japanese towns and cities this has, for centuries, been a traditional solution; long narrow town houses of one or two stories face, on one side, through sliding paper *shoji,* a garden backed by the wooden wall of the next house. The garden may be no more than three or four feet wide, but it is scaled and carefully shaped so as to suggest a miniature world and to give a sense of openness, air, and distant places. In the long and very narrow spaces, linear designs sometimes unfold, meant to be considered sequentially, like a book.

WALT DISNEY: Charleston, South Carolina (with a climate much like that of Houston) is, I think, the only American city where a house type that makes use of side yards is much employed. It is called the "single house" and is composed of a string of rooms perpendicular to the street, usually two or three stories high, all of them facing onto a multistoried porch called a "verandah" or a "piazza," beyond which lies a side yard of whatever width the lot affords. The house generally abuts the street, with windows in the front rooms and an elaborated front door set into the end of the piazza. At the street edge of the side yard might be a wall pierced by a carriage entrance, now used for cars. Charleston is a very old city densely packed onto the peninsula, where, as they say locally, "the Ashley and the Cooper Rivers meet to form the Atlantic Ocean." The climate for much of the year is hot and extremely humid, and the circulation of air without too much loss of privacy has been critical. The single house is an admirably effective form for achieving airiness and privacy and density and even a place to put the cars. The houses are usually fairly big, meant for large or extended families, but the gardens are often small and challenging.

FRANCIS BACON: It sounds as if a single house might make sense here, but you will need a *theme* for the garden. Perhaps you could have gardens for all the months of the year in which things of beauty may be in season. You're going to want winter sunlight to have the garden grow in Houston's cold months. If I were you, I'd pick the site where the sun comes from the street, so you can see the sunshine on the plants as you look into the garden. In a garden so long and narrow, you'll have to decide whether you want a single long vista, modified in some way, perhaps by walls, or planting flanking a central opening, or whether you want to divide the garden into outdoor rooms. I rather favor the outdoor rooms, myself.

VITA SACKVILLE-WEST: So do I. They present you with a fine chance to make spaces where all the blooms are one color or all happen at once, in seasonal rotation. Your garden is small, but it should be big enough for that. The important thing is to go *with* the climate, not against it. You might think of one of the rooms as lush and close in the summer, with banana palms that would die back with the first killing freeze and leave you with a sunny, empty terrace, where the sun could reflect from light bright walls in the winter. Some Carolina jessamine would stay green but fairly flat against the wall. You might try pergolas covered with wisteria, for summer shade and for winter sun when the vine has lost its leaves. You can get it to blossom white or blue, of course.

CAPABILITY BROWN: All these little rooms filled with flowers give me the creeps. I would propose making the space very simple—all grass—with clumps of shrubs and trees to flank the long view. Clarify! I'd like to propose some water, but I'm afraid you just don't have the room. But what you *might* do—and I think there is just room—is to grade the far end up so that the wall to the neighbors doesn't show and the garden seems to go over the hill into the infinite. (It's a pity you don't have room for some decorative cows; I'm told there are plenty of them in Texas.)

PRINCE TOSHIHITO: That applies the principle of "borrowed scenery" in an appropriately Texan manner; you borrow not an object or image, but just the sense of space from your neighbor. I think it's a wonderful idea, but your own space is so small that it seems a bit strained, not natural. It would be more appropriate, I think, to apply the Japanese maxim that says to make the near come forward and the far go back. If you made a simple garden of sand and moss, and maybe stones, that diminished in scale back away from the house, I believe you could achieve an illusion of great size in your small space. You should have asked Francesco Borromini to this conference. I see him often in the hereafter and like him a lot, though he is sometimes irascible. Do you know his Palazzo Spada, in Rome, where he manipulates perspective to make a little statue very close to you look larger and very far away? Westerner that you are, Mr. J, you might prefer that technique to our Japanese ones. You could even slope it up to get Brown-San's infinite vista. But I must say that leaves me uneasy, it's the opposite of *shibui,* so hopelessly artificial. (Though so is Nikko, and I love it.)

WALT DISNEY: You guys keep talking about distance, and just *looking* at something. I'm certainly happy to mess the scale around to have this dinky little garden look bigger, but I want to know what you *do* there. If it were mine, I'd install my electric train. I understand you have one, too, Mr. J.

MR. J: Choo Choo Shibui, Walt.

A miniature train at Disneyland

PRINCE TOSHIHITO: I like the idea of mechanized miniatures! Perhaps we should make a collection of toy robots—the kind that transform themselves into spaceships and automobiles and other improbable things. One of them might personify the Genius of the Place, like Venus in that beautiful Vale at Rousham. Or we might arrange them in tableaux, like those wonderful ones at the Tiger Balm Gardens in Singapore. They could be electrically driven and computer controlled . . .

WALT DISNEY: Let's talk technology, Prince T!

VITA SACKVILLE-WEST: Oh, come off it, you two! You should make a *plant* collection, of course, and spend your time and ingenuity cultivating the exotic specimens. And don't forget, however you do this narrow side yard, the views of it from inside are going to be very important. You should look at some paintings of windows with views: Matisse, Dufy, and others.

MR. J: How about this layout? A diagonal stepped path cuts across the space, connecting two decks with garden furniture. The one at the far uphill end is actually a miniature, but the forced perspective created by the convergence of the path makes it seem to be on a distant hilltop. If you stroll up there (looking, to your companions at the lower end, increasingly like our New York colleague King Kong), you will find the surprise of a tiny, terraced stone and sand garden. Perhaps you can work out the details for me, Prince Toshihito? And Miss Sackville-West, I'll need your horticultural assistance, to help me plan a gradient of colors and textures from the lower to the upper end. Jessamine clings to the walls . . .

PRINCE TOSHIHITO:

Perspective and sky;
    Miniature is raised to clouds.
Deception of eye!

A side yard garden in Houston

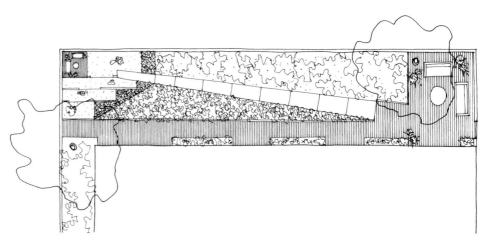

Plan

Elevation

Perspective

234 · *Our Own Places*

LUCIAN: With typical irresponsibility the authors have simply disappeared, leaving the characters in charge of the book. I suppose it's up to me to bring it to a fitting close. Let's conclude with a discussion on the banks of the River Styx, where I'll see you all, sooner or later. The last time I put on a conference here, one of my guests found the skull of Helen of Troy and asked "Is this the face that launched a thousand ships?"—or words to that effect; my imitators have been stealing that line (and usually getting it wrong) for centuries. Philip of Macedon endlessly berated that juvenile delinquent son of his. And old Diogenes cast his usual gloomy pall over the proceedings.

Charon the Ferryman keeps bringing them in. This time I think I'll just wait on the dock and see who shows up. Here's a particularly cadaverous looking specimen now.

EDGAR ALLAN POE: I couldn't keep up with the literary fashions any more, so I left. (Am I deconstructing or decomposing?) Thank Heaven, anyway, that the fever called "Living" is conquered at last! Perhaps I'll catch up with Annabel Lee here; I haven't seen her since she got herself chilled and killed, and caused me to put in all those hours in her sepulcher there by the sea. I'd like to find Helen, too, for an update on the glory that was Greece and the grandeur that was Rome. Where do they stash the skull these days, Lucian?

LUCIAN: Beats me. Lets ask yonder old lady—the one with the walking stick, and the *very* determined look.

MARGARET MEAD: Forget it, Mr. Poe. My extensive fieldwork here has convinced me that one skull looks very much like another (except for King Kong's, of course). But I'd be glad to enlighten you both on the fundamentals of funerary landscaping.

LUCIAN: We're all ears.

MARGARET MEAD: The Balinese (of whom I once made a detailed study) believe that the forces of life and vitality flow down from the great mountain at the center of their island world, while the forces of death and decay flow up from the sea. Everything in their culture is oriented to the coordinates of life and earth, defined by the center and the shore. There is, of course, a special place for the temple of death on the downhill side of every village, where the magnificent cremations take place. That mountain is the essential thing. You *must* have a cosmic mountain . . .

LUCIAN: Sorry to interrupt, Miss Mead, but here comes Walt Disney (late of Anaheim, California), accompanied by Emperor Akbar, from Sikandra. Let's ask them what they think.

WALT DISNEY: Thanks for the ride, Charon. (I'm thinking of putting one of these ferries into Adventureland.) Jeepers! This place is even spookier than my Haunted House.

Hello, Miss Mead. I think you're right about cosmic mountains. I located one prominently in the center of my Magic Kingdom. (It doesn't erupt, like Gunung Agung, but that could be arranged, perhaps as part of the Main Street Electric Parade.) And, there's a sea of cars all around, to which, of course, we turn our backs. I'm not sure about cremations, though; snap freezing (like a package of peas) is much neater and cleaner. (Incidentally, Mr. Poe, your friend Annabel Lee's big mistake was to get chilled *before* she died.)

MARGARET MEAD: Freezing instead of cremating! Your kingdom has evolved some remarkable customs, Mr. Disney. It might be interesting to study teenagers coming of age there. And now I see why that skull I found the other day, with its cute little nose and round black ears, was so cold. I had to microwave it before it could talk—and even then it sounded like some sort of rodent.

AKBAR: Just wait till you defrost the duck! I must say, though, that I've always greatly admired my friend Walt's work. His Magic Kingdom is arranged very much like my mausoleum, with a great monument at the center of a pleasure ground and a wall all around. But he missed a profitable opportunity; he should have placed his sepulcher in that Matterhorn. Then he could have had the bobsleds going past—a kind of high-speed Lenin's Tomb.

MARGARET MEAD: Stop trying to pull my leg, Akbar! I can tell when I'm talking to an unreliable informant.

LUCIAN: Charon is just back from one of his regular cemetery shuttles to Forest Lawn, California, to pick up a few Immortals (the dead kind). Among them is its founder, Dr. Hubert L. Eaton. He looks quite agitated.

DR. HUBERT L. EATON: Has anybody here had the misfortune to bump into a cheap journalist by the name of Evelyn Waugh? I have a score to settle with him!

LUCIAN: You'll have plenty of time for that, Hubert. Meanwhile, you might tell us what you think of Akbar's notions.

DR. HUBERT L. EATON: Well, I certainly like the idea of burial in a pleasure ground, but I prefer quite a different style—the natural but carefully perfected English park, rather than the symmetrical *chahar bagh*. Since Mount Auburn, that's been the American way.

EDGAR ALLAN POE: My friend Mr. Ellison (who made the Domain of Arnheim) would be glad to hear that, Hubert. It was he who suggested that the apparent imperfections of untouched natural landscape were "prognostic of death." God had intended earthly immortality for man, but man blew it, so he's mortal, and he can't see the true perfection of God's wild nature. You have to clean it up a bit, make it seem prettier, if you want to suggest the blissful estate of eternal life.

DR. HUBERT L. EATON: I've done just that—smoothed the stony Californian hillsides and replaced the chapparal with verdant, shady lawns. Not an errant leaf, no mussed blade of grass.

AKBAR: But how do you water it all? Southern California must be almost as dry as Sikandra.

DR. HUBERT L. EATON: I use an extensive network of underground pipes, with closely spaced pop-up sprinklers. (Even my severest critics agree that there is genuine poetry in a hillside field of spray glowing against the foliage in the low evening light.) This allows me to have uniformly lush green grass wherever I want it. Another innovation of mine is to set the headstones flush into the ground, so that it's even more like a park (they didn't think of that at Mount Auburn), and of course that makes power mowing much easier because you can just run right over them.

EDGAR ALLAN POE: Very ingenious. But what happens if somebody is accidentally buried alive? (You may remember my tale "The Fall of the House of Usher.") I'd suggest some precautionary mechanism—perhaps a Jack-in-the-Box spring to pop up any live ones.

AKBAR: Lawn mowers, sprinklers, and spring-loaded sepulchers—American technology is the envy of the rest of the world. Speaking of which, allow me to introduce two newly arrived colleagues-in-empire, Hadrian and Ch'ien Lung.

DR. HUBERT L. EATON: Pleased to meet you in this time of need.

HADRIAN: Your green hills remind me of the Vale of Tempe, Hubert. Do you collect world-famous scenes, as I did in the graveyard of my travels at Tivoli?

DR. HUBERT L. EATON: You bet! I've got Annie Laurie's Wee Kirk o' the Heather from Scotland, and the English village church that was the subject of Gray's "Elegy." And, Ch'ien Lung, you'll probably approve of the way that I've chosen names for each part. There's Comfort, Harmony, Affection, Mercy, Brotherly Love, Tranquility, and, of course, Immortality. Some of the names are topographic: Sunrise Slope, Cathedral Slope, Inspiration Slope, Resurrection Slope, Benediction Slope, and Vale of Memory. Walt would like Vesperland, Borderland, Slumberland, and Lullabyland for kids, with a nice poem about "a mother's hope"—don't neglect any segment of the market.

CH'IEN LUNG: You should have some paintings made.

DR. HUBERT L. EATON: I've done that, too.

WALT DISNEY: Perhaps you should add a Tomorrowland.

DR. HUBERT L. EATON: Not a bad idea! Oh, and then there's Babyland . . .

PROFESSOR S: Hello everybody, Charon just ferried me in from Graceland, where I'm buried myself and where I built some pretty good tombs . . . for my client Martin Ryerson and for Carrie Eliza Getty. Tombs should have massive, stony serenity, allusions to the everlasting . . .

MARGUERITE YOURCENAR: Bonjour, mes amis! Sorry to be late, but I just got written into this distinguished literary gathering when it was in galleys. Hadrian! I'm so glad to meet you finally. And Hubert L. Eaton! See my decorations, Hubert: I really *am* an Immortal (the French kind). You have the right idea, Professor S. As I grew very old I had a headstone made for myself—complete with date of death, though I left the last two digits blank, to be filled in at the appropriate moment.

DR. HUBERT L. EATON: You're both dead wrong! The public doesn't want to have its nose rubbed in mortality. My "Builder's Creed" says it all:

The cemeteries of today are wrong, because they depict an end, not a beginning. They have consequently become unsightly stoneyards full of inartistic symbols and depressing customs. . . . Forest Lawn shall become a place where lovers new and old shall love to stroll and watch the sunset's glow. . . . A place that shall be protected by an immense Endowment Care Fund, the principal of which can never be expended—only the income therefrom used to care for and perpetuate this garden of Memory.
This is the Builder's dream; this is the Builder's Creed.

HADRIAN: *Mater tua,* Hubert! That's sentimental drivel! *I* built a reproduction of *Hell* in my villa, and composed frivolous verses about my approaching end. Then, like the clear-sighted Socrates, I died with my eyes open (the eagle waiting). As always, I wanted to see exactly where I was going.

LUCIAN: Your valor is legendary, Hadrian, but your judgment is bizarre. Most of the rest of us need some support when Charon loads us aboard. Oh, good! Here comes Rainer Maria Rilke. He got some very extensive messages from the other side of the Styx, which he wrote down as they came, in the *Duino Elegies* and *The Sonnets to Orpheus*. I was so impressed that I sent another message, asking him for a landscape design for this part of the valley of the Styx. Hello, Rainer, did you bring the scheme?

RAINER MARIA RILKE: Yes, but this place is far tackier than I had supposed. Nonetheless, I am excited by the scheme. I hadn't expected to come across the shade of Dr. Hubert L. Eaton here (How do you do, Hubert?), but I expect he can find some posthumous profit in this. How do *you* do, Walt? I'm sorry not to have worked out the cryogenic dimensions, but I'm sure that if you can get them perfected on this side they can be worked in.

Here is the graveyard scheme; through the entrance gate a curving asphalt driveway, Styx Drive, divides our world from Hades. One side of the drive is where burial occurs, to seem to hold our loved ones with us. I'm proud of the burial arrangements; gentle but grand steps, apparently of a generous former time, are partly submerged under the drifting hills of times since. Burial is under the steps, with monuments in the risers—much more dignified, I think, than flat markers that you mow over. It's a sunny pretty place, a pleasant realm for the departed.

The other side of Styx Drive, of course, represents Hades. Charon's boat is moored there, and a road leads back into the shade of the trees. Do you know my poem "Orpheus. Eurydice. Hermes"? I think it is appropriate here to envision Orpheus, his lyre grown into his side, so ardent have been his outpourings of grief over the death of his young wife Eurydice. He has arranged her release, and she is following him out of Hades on condition that he not look back. But she has come upon a new virginity in Hades, so that even the gentle touch of her guide, the slim young Hermes, is unwelcome to her. Orpheus, of course, does look back, to the despair of

A graveyard

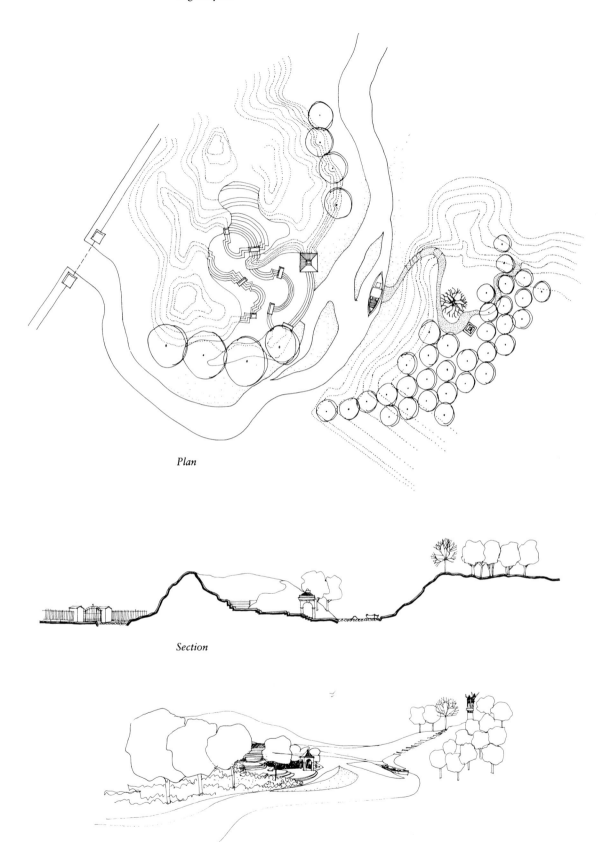

Plan

Section

Perspective along Styx Drive

Hermes, but Eurydice's only reply is "What?" as her serenity takes root and she turns into a tree. Here is the tree on the bank, where Orpheus would last have seen her, with a statue of Hermes nearby. Behind are the shady groves of a classical Hades, sunless but full of peace.

LUCIAN: Look! Charon is coming with the last load of the day. There's just one passenger, a bearded old gentleman with a kind and dreamy look. Welcome.

EDWARD FITZGERALD: Greetings Lucian, Herr Rilke, Mr. Poe. I see the distant figures of Virgil and Alexander Pope . . . and could that be, in the mists, my old friend Omar? One by one we poets forsake the gardens of the living for this garden of the dead. May I offer my Epicurean eclogue?

Ah, Moon of my Delight who know'st no wane,
   The Moon of Heav'n is rising once again:
How oft hereafter rising shall she look
   Through this same Garden after me—in vain!

Sunset and moonrise, Death Valley

BIBLIOGRAPHY

We have included in this bibliography the works that were most useful to us as sources and that provide good starting points for further study of the places we have discussed. Some of the entries are scholarly histories and monographs, some are more popular works, some are guides and travel books, and a few are particularly relevant works of fiction. Following a short list of general historical and theoretical works, the arrangement is by country or region.

GENERAL HISTORY AND THEORY

Benoist-Mechin, *L'Homme et ses Jardins,* Albin Michel, Paris, 1975.

Berrall, Julia, *The Garden, An Illustrated History,* Penguin Books, New York, 1978.

Clifford, Derek, *A History of Garden Design,* Praeger, New York, 1966.

Gothein, Marie Luise, *A History of Garden Art from the Earliest Times to the Present Day* (2 volumes), E. P. Dutton, New York, 1928.

Huxley, Anthony, *An Illustrated History of Gardening,* Paddington Press, New York, 1978.

Hyams, Edward, *A History of Gardens and Gardening,* Praeger, New York, 1971.

Jellicoe, Geoffrey and Susan, *The Landscape of Man,* Thames and Hudson, London, 1975.

Macaulay, Rose, *The Pleasure of Ruins,* Thames and Hudson, New York, 1984.

Newton, Norman T., *Design on the Land: Development of Landscape Architecture,* Belknap Press of Harvard University, Cambridge, Mass., 1973.

Norberg-Schultz, Christian, *Genius Loci: Towards a Phenomenology of Architecture,* Rizzoli, New York, 1980.

Prest, John, *The Garden of Eden: The Botanic Garden and the Re-Creation of Paradise,* Yale University Press, New Haven, 1981.

Thacker, Christopher, *The History of Gardens,* Croom Helm, London, 1979.

AUSTRALIA

Bligh, Beatrice, *Cherish The Earth, The Story of Gardening in Australia,* Ure Smith, Sydney, 1975.

Chatwin, Bruce, *The Songlines,* Elizabeth Sifton Books/Viking, New York, 1987.

Clark, C. M. H., *A History of Australia,* Vol. 1: *From the Earliest Times to the Age of Macquarie,* Melbourne University Press, Melbourne, 1962.

Crittenden, Victor, *The Front Garden,* Mulini Press, Canberra, 1979.

Cuffley, Peter, *Cottage Gardens in Australia,* The Five Mile Press, Melbourne, 1983.

Gilbert, Lionel, *The Royal Botanic Gardens, Sydney,* Oxford University Press, Melbourne, 1986.

Hughes, Robert, *The Fatal Shore,* Alfred A. Knopf, New York, 1987.

Layton, Robert, *Uluru,* Australian Institute of Aboriginal Studies, Canberra, 1986.

Mountford, Charles P., *Brown Men and Red Sand,* Angus and Robertson, Sydney, 1948.

Pescott, R. T. M., *The Royal Botanical Gardens Melbourne,* Oxford University Press, Melbourne, 1982.

Smith, Bernard, *European Vision and the South Pacific,* Clarendon Press, Oxford, 1960.

BALI

Blackwood, Robert, *Beautiful Bali,* A. H. and A. W. Reed, Sydney, 1980.

Covarrubius, Miguel, *Island of Bali,* Oxford University Press, Selangor, Malaysia, 1972.

Daniel, Ana, *Bali, Behind the Mask,* Alfred A. Knopf, New York, 1981.

Fox, David J. Stuart, *Once a Century: Pura Besakih and the Eka Dasa Rudra Festival,* Penerbit Citra Indonesia, Jakarta, 1982.

Moerdowo, R., *Ceremonies in Bali,* Bhratara Publishers, Jakarta, 1973.

Moojen, P. A. J., *Kunst op Bali,* Adi Poestaka, The Hague, 1926.

Ramseyer, Urs, *The Art and Culture of Bali,* Oxford University Press, Oxford, 1977.

CHINA

Beijing Summer Palace Administration Office, *Summer Palace,* Zhaohua Publishing House, Beijing, 1981.

Blaser, Werner, *Chinese Pavilion Architecture,* Architectural Book Publishing Company, New York, 1974.

Boyd, Andrew, *Chinese Architecture,* Tiranti, London, 1952.

Cao Xuequin, *The Story of the Stone,* translated by David Hawkes, Indiana University Press, Bloomington, 1979.

Chen Congzhou, *On Chinese Gardens,* Tongji University Press, Shanghai, 1984.

Chinese Academy of Architecture, *Ancient Chinese Architecture,* China Building Industry Press, Beijing, and Joint Publishing Company, Hong Kong, 1982.

Danby, Hope, *The Garden of Perfect Brightness,* Williams and Norgate, London, 1950.

Eitel, E. J., *Feng Shui,* Trubner, 1873.

Keswick, Maggie, *The Chinese Garden,* Rizzoli, New York, 1978.

Lip, Evelyn, *Chinese Geomancy,* Times Books International, Singapore, 1979.

Liu Junwen, *Beijing: China's Ancient and Modern Capital,* Foreign Languages Press, Beijing, 1982.

Malone, Carroll Brown, *History of the Peking Summer Palaces Under the Ch'ing Dynasty,* Illinois Studies in the Social Sciences, Vol. XIX, Nos. 1–2, The University of Illinois, Urbana, Illinois, 1934.

Morris, Edwin, T., *The Gardens of China,* Scribner's, New York, 1983.

Nanking Polytechnic Institute Department of Architecture, *Soochow Gardens,* China Building Industry Press, Beijing, 1979.

Qian Yun, *Classical Chinese Gardens,* China Building Industry Press, Beijing, and Joint Publishing Company, Hong Kong, 1982.

Seth, Vikram, *The Humble Administrator's Garden,* Carcanet, Manchester, 1985.

Siren, Osvald, *Gardens of China,* The Ronald Press Company, New York, 1949.

Skinner, Stephen, *The Living Earth Manual of Feng-Shui,* Graham Brash, Singapore, 1983.

Yang Hongxun, *The Classical Gardens of China,* Van Nostrand Reinhold, New York, 1982.

Zhong Junhua, *Sights and Scenes of Suzhou,* Zhaohua Publishing House, Beijing, 1983.

ENGLAND

Anthony, John, *The Gardens of Britain,* Vol. 6: *The East Midlands,* B. T. Batsford Ltd., London, 1979.

Bisgrove, Richard, *The Gardens of Britain,* Vol. 3: *Berkshire, Oxfordshire, Buckinghamshire, Bedfordshire and Hertfordshire.* B. T. Batsford Ltd., London, 1978.

Blunt, Wilfrid, *In for a Penny: A Prospect of Kew Gardens,* Hamish Hamilton, London, 1978.

Brown, Jane, *Gardens of a Golden Afternoon,* Van Nostrand Reinhold, New York, 1982.

Brown, Jane. *Vita's Other World: A Gardening Biography of V. Sackville-West,* Viking, New York, 1985.

Clark, H. F., *The English Landscape Garden,* Pleiadies Books, London, 1948.

Girouard, Mark, *Life in the English Country House,* Yale University Press, New Haven, 1978.

Hadfield, Miles, *A History of British Gardening* (third edition), J. Murray, London, 1979.

Hadfield, Miles, *The English Landscape Garden,* Shire Publications Ltd., Aylesbury, 1977.

Harvey, John, *Mediaeval Gardens,* Timber Press, Oregon, 1981.

Hunt, John Dixon, and Peter Willis, *The Genius of the Place, The English Landscape Garden 1620–1820,* Harper and Row, New York, 1975.

Hussey, Christopher, *English Gardens and Landscapes 1700–1750,* Funk & Wagnalls, New York, 1967.

Hussey, Christopher, *The Gardens of England and Wales,* Country Life, London, 1933.

Hussey, Christopher, *The Picturesque.* Archon Books, Hamdon, Conn., 1967.

Hyams, Edward, *The English Garden,* Harry N. Abrams, Inc., New York, n.d.

Hyams, Edward, and Edwin Smith, *The English Garden,* Thames and Hudson, London, 1964.

Jekyll, Gertrude, *Colour Schemes for the Flower Garden,* Antique Collectors' Club, Woodbridge, Suffolk, England, 1982.

Jourdain, Margaret, *The Works of William Kent,* Country Life, London, 1948.

Lemmon, Kenneth, *The Gardens of Britain,* Vol. 5: *Yorkshire and Humberside,* B. T. Batsford, Ltd., London, 1978.

Manwaring, Elizabeth Wheeler, *Italian Landscape in Eighteenth Century England,* Frank Cass & Co., Ltd., London, 1965.

Nicolson, Philippa, *V. Sackville-West's Garden Book,* Atheneum, New York, 1979.

Paterson, Allen, *The Gardens of Britain,* Vol. 2: *Dorset, Hampshire and the Isle of Wight,* B. T. Batsford, Ltd., London, 1978.

Scott-James, Anne, *Sissinghurst: The Making of a Garden,* Michael Joseph, London, 1975.

Strong, Roy, *The Renaissance Garden in England,* Thames and Hudson, London, 1979.

Stroud, Dorothy, *Capability Brown,* Faber & Faber, London, 1975.

Synge, Patrick M., *The Gardens of Britain,* Vol. 1: *Devon and Cornwall,* B. T. Batsford, Ltd., London, 1977.

Thomas, Graham Stuart, *Gardens of the National Trust,* The National Trust/ Weidenfeld and Nicholson, Norwich, 1979.

Watkin, David, *The English Vision,* Harper and Row, New York, 1982.

Weaver, Lawrence, *Houses and Gardens by E. L. Lutyens,* Antique Collectors' Club: Woodbridge, Suffolk, England, 1981.

Woodbridge, Kenneth, *Landscape and Antiquity: Aspects of English Culture at Stourhead 1718–1838,* Clarendon Press, London, 1970.

Wright, Tom, *The Gardens of Britain,* Vol. 4: *Kent, East & West Sussex and Surrey,* B. T. Batsford, Ltd., London, 1978.

FRANCE

Adams, William Howard, *The French Garden 1500–1800,* George Braziller, New York, 1979.

Caisse Nationale des Monuments Historiques et des Sites, *Jardins en France 1760– 1820,* Paris, 1977.

de Ganay, Ernest, *Les Jardins de France,* Editions d'Histoire et d'Art, Paris, 1949.

Hazlehust, F. Hamilton, *Gardens of Illusion: The Genius of André Le Nôtre,* Vanderbilt University Press, Nashville, 1980.

MacDougall, E. B., and F. H. Hazlehurst (eds.), *The French Formal Garden,* Dumbarton Oaks Colloquium on the History of Landscape Architecture III, Harvard University Press, Cambridge, Mass., 1974.

Wiebenson, Dora, *The Picturesque Garden in France,* Princeton University Press, Princeton, 1978.

INDIA

Beveridge, Annette S. (translator), *The Babur-Nama in English,* Luzac and Co., London, 1922.

Correa, Charles, *Charles Correa,* Concept Media, Singapore, 1984.

Crowe, Sylvia, Sheila Haywood, Susan Jellicoe, and Gordon Patterson, *The Gardens of Mughul India,* Thames and Hudson, London, 1972.

Gothein, Marie Luise, *Indische Gärten,* Drei Masken Verlag, Munich, 1926.

Irving, Robert Grant, *Indian Summer, Lutyens, Baker, and Imperial Delhi,* Yale University Press, New Haven and London, 1981.

Kak, Ram Chandra, *Ancient Monuments of Kashmir,* The India Society, London, 1933.

Marg 26 (December 1972). Special issue on Mughul gardens.

Michell, George, *The Hindu Temple,* Paul Elek, London, 1977.

Moynihan, Elizabeth B., *Paradise as a Garden in Persia and Mughal India,* George Braziller, New York, 1979.

Naipaul, V. S., "Pilgrimage," in *An Area of Darkness*, Penguin, Harmondsworth, 1968.

Nath, R., *Some Aspects of Mughal Architecture*, Abhinav Publications, New Delhi, 1976.

Sanwal, B. D., *Agra and its Monuments*, Orient Longmans, New Delhi, 1968.

Villiers-Stuart, Constance M., *Gardens of the Great Mughuls*, A. and C. Black, London, 1913.

ITALY

Boissier, Gaston, *Rome and Pompeii* (trans. D. Havelock Fisher), Unwin, London, 1905.

Clark, Eleanor, *Rome and a Villa*, Doubleday, New York, 1950.

Coffin, David R. (ed.), *The Italian Garden*, First Dumbarton Oaks Colloquium on the History of Landscape Architecture, Harvard University Press, Cambridge, Mass., 1972.

Comito, Terry, *The Idea of the Garden in the Renaissance*, The Harvester Press, New Brunswick, NJ, 1978.

Masson, Georgina, *Italian Gardens*, Thames and Hudson, London, 1961.

Shepherd, J. C., and G. A. Jellicoe, *Italian Gardens of the Renaissance*, Scribners, New York, 1925 (reprinted by Tiranti, London, 1966).

Wharton, Edith, *Italian Villas and their Gardens*, Da Capo, New York, 1976.

Wölfflin, Heinrich, "The Villa and the Garden," in *Renaissance and Baroque* (translated by Kathrin Simon), Cornell University Press, Ithaca, New York, 1966.

Yourcenar, Marguerite, *Memoirs of Hadrian*, Farrar, Straus and Young, New York, 1954.

JAPAN

Bring, Mitchell, and Josse Wayembergh, *Japanese Gardens*, McGraw Hill, New York, 1981.

Harada, Jiro, *The Gardens of Japan*, A. and C. Boni, New York, 1982.

Hayakawa, Masao, *The Garden Art of Japan*, Weatherill, New York, 1973.

Horiguchi, Sutemi, *Tradition of Japanese Garden*, East West Center Press, Honolulu, 1963.

Ito, Teiji, *The Japanese Garden: An Approach to Nature*, Yale University Press, New Haven, 1972.

Kuck, Loraine, *The World of the Japanese Garden*, Weatherill, New York and Tokyo, 1980.

Murasaki Shikibu, *The Tale of Genji* (trans. Edward G. Seidensticker), Knopf, New York, 1982.

Newson, Samuel, *A Thousand Years of Japanese Gardens* (third edition), Tokyo News Service, Tokyo, 1957.

Ota, Hirotaro (ed.), *Japanese Architecture and Gardens*, The Society for International Cultural Relations, Tokyo, 1966.

Shimoyama, Shigemaru (trans.), *Sakuteiki: The Book of Garden*, Town and City Planners, Inc., Tokyo, 1975.

Treib, Marc, and Ron Herman, *A Guide to the Gardens of Kyoto*, Shufunotomo, Tokyo, 1980.

Yoshida, Tetsuro, *Gardens of Japan*, Praeger, New York, 1957.

LADAKH

Cunningham, Alexander, *Ladakh: Physical, Statistical and Historical,* London, 1854.

Franke, A. H., *Antiquities of Indian Tibet* (2 volumes), Calcutta, 1914 and 1926.

Harvey, Andrew, *A Journey in Ladakh,* Houghton Mifflin, Boston, 1983.

Snellgrove, David L., and Tadeusz Skorupski, *The Cultural Heritage of Ladakh,* Aris and Phillips, Warminster, England, 1977.

Tucci, Giuseppe, *Transhimalaya,* Nagel, Geneva, 1973.

Tucci, Giuseppe, *The Religions of Tibet,* University of California Press, Berkeley, 1980.

PERSIA

Brookes, John, *Gardens of Paradise: The History and Design of the Great Islamic Gardens,* New Amsterdam Books, New York, 1987.

Byron, Robert, *The Road to Oxiana,* Jonathan Cape, London, 1937.

Gaube, Heinz, *Iranian Cities,* New York University Press, New York, 1979.

Lehrman, Jonas, *Earthly Paradise: Garden and Courtyard in Islam,* University of California Press, Berkeley, 1980.

MacDougall, Elisabeth B., and Richard Ettinghausen (eds.), *The Islamic Garden,* Dumbarton Oaks Colloquium on the History of Landscape Architecture, Harvard University Press, Cambridge, Mass., 1976.

Michel, George (ed.), *Architecture of the Islamic World,* William Morrow, New York, 1978.

Pope, Arthur Upham (ed.), *A Survey of Persian Art* (6 volumes), Oxford University Press, London, 1938–39.

Pope, Arthur Upham, *Persian Architecture,* George Braziller, New York, 1965.

Pope, Arthur Upham, *Introducing Persian Architecture,* Soroush Press, Tehran, 1976.

Sackville-West, V., "The Persian Garden," in A. J. Arberry (ed.), *Legacy of Persia,* Clarendon Press, Oxford, 1952.

Wilber, Donald, *Persian Gardens and Pavilions,* Charles E. Tuttle, Rutland, Vermont, 1962.

SPAIN

Dickie, James, "The Hispano-Arab Garden, its Philosophy and Function," *Bulletin of the School of Oriental and African Studies,* XXXI (1968).

Goury, and Owen Jones, *Plans, Elevations, Sections and Details of the Alhambra* (2 volumes), London, 1842–45.

Grabar, Oleg, *The Alhambra,* Harvard University Press, Cambridge, Mass., 1978.

Irving, Washington, *The Alhambra,* Putnam, New York, 1851.

Villiers-Stuart, Constance M., *Spanish Gardens: Their History, Types and Features,* Batsford, London, 1936.

UNITED STATES

Banham, Reyner, *Scenes in America Deserta,* Thames and Hudson, London, 1982.

Church, Thomas D., *Gardens are for People* (second edition), McGraw-Hill, New York, 1983.

Jackson, J. B., *American Space: The Centennial Years, 1865–1876*, Norton, New York, 1972.

Jackson, J. B., *Landscapes,* edited by Ervin H. Zube, University of Massachusetts Press, Amherst, 1970.

Jackson, J. B., *The Necessity for Ruins,* The University of Massachusetts Press, Amherst, 1980.

Van Dyke, John C., *The Desert,* Scribner, New York, 1901. (Reprint by Peregrine Smith, Salt Lake City, 1980.)

Waugh, Evelyn, *The Loved One,* Little Brown, Boston, 1948.

INDEX

First MIT Press paperback edition, 1993

This book was set in Sabon by Graphic Composition, Inc. and printed and bound in the United States of America.

Library of Congress Cataloging-in-Publication Data

Moore, Charles Willard, 1925–
   The poetics of gardens / Charles W. Moore, William J. Mitchell, William Turnbull, Jr.
      p.   cm.
   Bibliography: p.
   Includes index.
   ISBN 978-0-262-13231-2 (hc. : alk. paper)—978-0-262-63153-2 (pb. : alk. paper)
   1. Gardens—Design.   2. Landscape architecture.   I. Mitchell, William J.   II. Turnbull,
William.   III. Title.
SB472.M64   1988   712—dc19   88-2079   CIP

10 9